VOLUME FOUR

ALIGNING
WITH THE
APOSTOLIC

AN ANTHOLOGY OF APOSTLESHIP

APOSTLES AND APOSTOLIC MOVEMENT
IN THE SEVEN MOUNTAINS OF CULTURE

DR. BRUCE COOK
GENERAL EDITOR

Copyright © 2012 VentureAdvisers.com, Inc. d.b.a. Kingdom House Publishing

First Printing May 2013

ALIGNING WITH THE APOSTOLIC: VOLUME FOUR

Printed in the USA

ISBN: 978-1-939944-03-0

Library of Congress Control Number: 2013905712

Cover Design: Wendy K. Walters with James L. Nesbit

Interior Formatting: Wendy K. Walters

Published By KINGDOM HOUSE PUBLISHING | LAKEBAY, WASHINGTON, USA

To contact the Publisher or General Editor, call 253-858-8929 or text 512-845-3070, or email kingdomhousepublishing@gmail.com, or Skype: wbcook1, or visit:

www.KingdomHouse.net | www.KEYSnetwork.org
www.GloryRealm.net | www.VentureAdvisers.com

DEDICATION

TO THE CHIEF APOSTLE: JESUS, THE ONLY-BEGOTTEN SON OF GOD

(John 3:16-18, John 14:6, Rom. 8:32,
Rom. 10:9-13, 1 John 4:9-15)

*"Therefore, holy brothers, who share in the heavenly calling,
fix your thoughts on Jesus, the apostle and high
priest whom we confess."*
(Heb. 3:1, NIV)

AND TO THE NEXT GENERATION OF APOSTLES –

We Invite You to Stand Upon Our Shoulders

CONTRIBUTING AUTHORS

In Alphabetical Order

LaRue Adkinson

John Anderson, M.B.A.

David Andrade, Ph.D.

Doug Atha, D.S.L.

Ted Baehr, J.D., Hh.D.

Gary Beaton, B.A.

Ken Beaudry

Sharon Billins, B.S., Hh.D.

Laurie Boyd

Gordon Bradshaw, Ph.D., D.D.

Kari Browning

John Burpee, D.Min.

Philip Byler, D.R.E.

Duncan Campbell

Al Caperna, B.S.B.A.

Nick Castellano, Ph.D.

Bob Cathers, Hh.D.

Bruce Cook, Ph.D., Th.D.

Paul Cuny, B.A.

Tony Dale, M.D.

Stan DeKoven, Ph.D., D.Min.

Henry Falany

Tommi Femrite, D.P.M.

Charlie Fisher

Daniel Geraci

Berin Gilfillan, D.Min.

A.L. ("Papa") Gill, Ph.D.

Curtis Gillespie, B.S.B.A.

Max Greiner Jr., B.E.D.

Jon Grieser

Fernando Guillen, M.B.A.

Tim Hamon, Ph.D.

Mark Henderson

Robert Henderson, Hh.D.

Ray Hughes, D.D.

Kent Humphreys, B.A.

Christopher James

Stan Jeffery, M.B.A., D.Tech.

Bill Johnson, Hh.D.

Wende Jones, B.S.B.A.

Rick Joyner, Th.D.

Mark Kauffman, Ph.D.

Stephanie Klinzing

Erik Kudlis, Ph.D.

Candace Long, M.B.A.

Lee Ann Marino, Ph.D., D.D.

Joseph Mattera, D.Min.

Michelle Morrison, J.D.

CONTRIBUTING AUTHORS CONTINUED

John Muratori, D.C.L.

James Nesbit

Alice Patterson

Mark Pfeifer, B.A.

Lloyd Phillips, B.A.

Cal Pierce, B.S.B.A.

Walt Pilcher, M.B.A.

Paula Price, D.Min., Ph.D.

Gayle Rogers, Ph.D.

Morris Ruddick, B.S., M.S.

Michael Scantlebury, D.D.

Axel Sippach, Hh.D.

Kluane Spake, D.Min.

Tim Taylor, B.S.B.A.

Lorne Tebbutt

Ed Turose, B.S.B.A.

Larry Tyler, M.B.A.

Joseph Umidi, D.Min.

Thomas Webb, B.A., B.Th.

Arleen Westerhof, Ph.D.

Dick Westerhof, M.Eng.

Carl White Jr., D.D.

Dennis Wiedrick, B.A.

In addition to the General Editor, this multi-volume anthology was contributed to by 70 authors—almost all apostles and a few apostolic leaders; these are 70 spiritual elders in the body of Christ. Their contribution adds a depth of experience and authority to this historic work.

SPECIAL ENDORSEMENTS

The truth of apostolic ministry has been increasing over the last two decades. When I first began to study the subject of apostles, there was very little information available and very little encouragement to pursue apostolic ministry. This has changed because of many who have written new material on the role of apostles in today's church. I have learned much concerning apostolic ministry, but I believe there is still much to learn. I could not imagine having this much information when I began my ministry over 30 years ago. Many are now embracing it because of a greater understanding through preaching, teaching and writing.

Aligning With the Apostolic is much more exhaustive than previous books on apostolic ministry. The next generation of ministers will have a greater revelation of this important ministry because of the contributions of these authors. I highly recommend these volumes, and believe they will contribute to the increasing knowledge of the importance of apostles and apostolic ministries.

Dr. Bruce Cook has done an excellent job in gathering many of the greatest apostolic voices of our day, and I believe it will cause many in the church to have a new level of faith and boldness to advance the kingdom of God in generations to come. Get ready to move ahead with revelation and understanding to see breakthroughs in society. God is able to do exceedingly, abundantly above all we can ask or think. Congratulations, Dr. Cook, and may your labor be rewarded by seeing many apostles released in the years to come.

John Eckhardt

Founder & Presiding Apostle, Impact Network | Overseer, Crusaders Churches
www.impactnetwork.net | www.johneckhardtministries.com

A fresh wind will blow across the globe when Dr. Bruce Cook's book series, *Aligning With The Apostolic,* is released. This anthology will establish an alignment of present truths integrated by 70 authors from various regions who know as well as comprehend the Word of the Lord, the direction for the Kingdom, and the encroachment upon the Seven Mountains in God's schematic for the 21st century.

Even as Jesus drew a line in the sand to identify and dismiss religious spirits during His earthly ministry (John 8), so has Apostle Dr. Bruce Cook drawn a line here to give voice to the proper role of apostles in the 21st century, to provide a platform for many new apostolic voices to be heard, and to explain how apostles must align themselves in order to align the Body of Christ...moving forward."

Apostle Elizabeth Hairston, B.A., M.F.A.,
M.Div., D.Min., D.B.S., Ph.D.

Founding Apostle: The Apostolic-Prophetic Connection, Inc., Women With A
Call International, Inc., City of Excellence Miracle Center International, Inc.
Author, Apostolic Intervention | www.tapcglobal.org

Note: Dr. Hairston was the first female apostle ordained by Dr. Bill Hamon in 1997. Dr. Hairston has established apostolic works since 1973 with branches of ministries in Europe, Asia, West Africa, East Africa, India, Japan, the Caribbean Islands and the United States.

ADDITIONAL MATERIALS

VOLUME FOUR
ALIGNING WITH THE APOSTOLIC:
AN ANTHOLOGY OF APOSTLESHIP

This five-volume anthology represents an extensive body of work covering a wide range of topics discussing apostles and the apostolic. In order to keep the length of the volumes manageable, the General Editor has chosen to keep certain elements exclusive to Volume One. Each of these elements are an important part of the anthology as a whole, and reading them will provide you with a richer experience. We invite you to reference these materials in Volume One.

AVAILABLE IN VOLUME ONE:

"Whether generals or patriarchs, *nepios, teknion, paidios,* or *pater,* apostles are ambassadors of the Kingdom, duly appointed and commissioned to carry out the duties of their office. They need the strength of their weaponry, and they need to be able to use it effectively in times of warfare and in times of peace, with righteousness, peace, and joy in the Holy Spirit being the operable status of Kingdom relationships."

Dr. Bruce Cook
General Editor of *Aligning With the Apostolic, An Anthology of Apostleship*

CONTENTS

SECTION IX—APOSTOLIC CREATIVITY & INNOVATION

FOREWORD BY
JOHNNY ENLOW

When my friend Bruce Cook asked me to look at this sizable apostolic anthology, I was initially reluctant to even want to be a part of a topic that can be so polarizing in the Body of Christ. I personally have seen more counterfeit apostles than real apostles. I have seen more 'apostolic' pride than apostolic humility. I have seen more apostolic smoke than apostolic fire. I have watched entire network streams seemingly swept out to sea by the apostolic 'title' waves.

I have also seen amazing men and women of God who are apostles get no recognition as such, and I have watched men and women carry the titles while having no evidence of an apostolic grace. Yet, here I am honored to write a Foreword endorsing what I think is an unprecedented compilation of apostolic writings. In the following paragraphs I would like to share why I believe this book to be an important foundation for all future discussions on the apostolic.

In Revelation 2:2, the church at Ephesus is praised for *"you have tried those who say they are apostles and are not, and have found them to be liars."* This one line provides us with amazing insights that could be missed by the common observer. Before I address that matter, it should be pointed out that in the subsequent verses, this very church of Ephesus is rebuked for having left its "first love." The church is then urged to repent or its "candlestick" would be removed. The sad end reality is that this church who did become experts at exposing false apostles succumbed to lovelessness, and their candlestick was removed.

This becomes, I think, a warning to those who would be zealous to attack the apostolic. In fact, if you purchased this book with the pointed purpose of "exposing false apostles," I invite you to please consider the starting place of your heart and to make sure you don't become an Ephesian. The apostolic when properly functioning is all about the exponential and intentional release of God's love into the peoples and structures of our society. To attack its proper function is ultimately to attack the advancement of love.

Back to the quote, *"you have tried those who say they are apostles and are not, and have found them to be liars."* Several applicable thoughts jump out at us from that statement. First, we have to deduce that there were similar arguments even in "New Testament times" as to this entire topic of apostles. They had those who claimed they were apostles and were not. You didn't become an apostle through a clear chain of command or ordination. It seems to reveal that the establishing of apostles was a bit more murky of a process than what we would be comfortable with. They apparently developed a test for apostolic authenticity but we are not told here nor anywhere the precise nature of that test. We can surmise from Paul's writings that apostolic legitimacy was tied in to "apostolic humility," "apostolic signs and wonders," and "apostolic works." One can only wonder though where the line of "not enough humility" is and when you have descended below it so far that you are no longer an apostle.

Then the test of "signs and wonders" could be troubling and inexact. Is a healing enough of a sign and wonder? What if it wasn't an instant healing? Or does it need to be a sign that extends beyond healings—since healings are for all believers. What kind of sign is valid enough? Does a rainbow at a prayer gathering seal the deal or do we need a strategic earthquake? Then on the matter of having an apostolic work—how does that get qualified? Can three pastors ask you to be their covering and zap you are now an apostle? Truly troubling that you couldn't just go through Paul's School of the Apostles and suddenly you were legit.

Where am I going with all of this? I believe that scripture itself invites us to be not overly legalistic about that which is called apostle or apostolic. I believe there is room for discussion and room for apostolic descriptions and manifestations that fit the day, so to speak. I love that Peter Wagner has been instrumental in bringing the topic to the table and been willing to be "extra-biblical" as to apostolic definitions—in the light of the scriptures seemingly excessive silence on key matters of apostolic authenticity and implementation.

If a church in Ephesus can be praised, by the Lord, for a healthy discussion and test on what true apostles should look like—then I think an apostolic anthology such as this can serve a vital purpose even for future generations. This work includes scores of slants and perspectives on apostles and the apostolic and I believe it begins to serve as an apostolic symphony of truth and foundation for advancement with that which is undeniably a Biblical priority. 1 Corinthians 12:28 says that He has set apostles FIRST in the church, with the word "first" being PROTON, meaning "firstly in time, place, order or importance." It is an unshakeable reality for all who consider themselves lovers of the scriptures that apostles must be brought to this place of PROTON in the Body of Christ. Yes, we have made mistakes in doing so, but so did they in the idealized New Testament times.

An apostolically-led church will change the culture. A pastorally-led church will navel-gaze its way into irrelevance. To be apostolically driven is to be thermostatic. To be pastorally driven is to be thermometric. One imposes, through love, vision and service, *"on earth as it is in heaven."* The other reflects that which is around it, and tries to hang on and survive.

You tell me in what direction we need to go. If I were to boil down the apostolic to two words it would be KINGDOM THERMOSTAT. If your thermostat is really significant then you are no longer only apostolic but an apostle. However, if you really need that title upgrade you may fail the "apostolic humility" test. So, just be who you are and ultimately heaven records the truth. Kingdom advancement is accelerated when apostles are properly recognized here on earth, but recognition must come from without anyway, so you just be the biggest kingdom thermostat you can. His Love needs to be personalized and institutionalized in government, arts and entertainment, media, education, the economy, family as well as in church.

I applaud this monumental effort by Bruce Cook and I believe that it will ultimately greatly assist in the proper restoration of apostles and the apostolic. What marks this work above other pioneering apostolic books I have read, is that it so validates apostles and the apostolic—outside the Religion mountain where the church is.

Since apostles' assignments have specifically to do with inculcating with another culture and DNA, how could that even be possible only in church settings? Being 'salt' and 'light' are cultural descriptives of the assignment we have been given by the Lord Himself. The society we do not effectively influence will in fact "trample" us as He stated. Bad times are not a sign Jesus is about to come to rapture us. Bad times are a sign that God's people have not been apostolic. May this book serve as a clarion call for the church to be apostolic in a real way that extends beyond titles. May this book be used by God to strategically and practically advance His people into a truly new apostolic reformation.

Johnny Enlow
Author/Speaker
7 Mountain Prophecy
7 Mountain Mantle
Rainbow of God: The Seven Colors of Love

FOREWORD BY
RICH MARSHALL

"What is all this talk about the apostolic?" "Is this just another trend, a fad that will soon pass out of sight?" "Are there still apostles today?"

Questions, questions, questions! It seems like I hear them all the time. The good news is this—whether you are one who is asking these questions or even doubts the validity of the apostolic, or one who endeavors to answer those questions, Bruce Cook's new *Aligning with the Apostolic* series is just what you need. This is a thorough, practical, well thought out series, from a variety of viewpoints as 70 authors have contributed. I first met Dr. Cook at a marketplace ministry conference in Texas and have developed a deep appreciation for his scholarly and yet practical approach to this subject. He is both a practitioner and a student of the modern apostolic movement. And when I say modern, I really mean that which is founded solidly upon scripture and is still very relevant today.

Personally, I had to fight my own theological understanding to come to the point where I could embrace the powerful move of the Lord today with His current anointed apostles. This was just not acceptable to my conservative background, and I found it to be equally hard to accept for some of my very charismatic friends. I listened, I studied, I watched, and my mind began to grasp in a very preliminary way what Dr. Cook is presenting here. As I began to teach, particularly to those involved in some sort of business enterprise, the Lord took me further as He showed me how this could, and should, function within the Kingdom.

As I now read *Aligning with the Apostolic*, I am thrilled that this gift will be available to all who follow. I am not sorry for the path that brought me here today, but I can see how much faster and therefore how much more effective I might have been with these books in hand.

I don't know what will touch your heart; it could be the practical or even testimonial style of some of the authors; it might be the deep theological understanding that comes to you; maybe it will be a resource for teaching and ultimately for living in God's powerful anointing. For me, Bruce had me at the definitions. He calls it the Glossary and there are over 80 of them. Just reading these definitions moved me and had me shouting (quietly and in my heart, of course) HALLELUJAH!

And now I say, as this powerful weapon is released for the Body of Christ and for the advance of His Kingdom: may you be blessed as you read, may God add His favor to all that He calls for you to do and be for Him, and may the Kingdom advance as you in turn release your ministry weapon with apostolic power.*

*APOSTOLIC POWER...that which occurs when God's anointed men and women function with His authority in the Kingdom realm (definition #82).

Rich Marshall
God@Work Volumes I and II

SECTION VII:

APOSTOLIC FATHERS & MOTHERS

CHAPTER FORTY-TWO

APOSTOLIC BIRTHING

SHARON BILLINS

In ancient Egypt, midwives were found in temples, and midwifery was considered only suitable for god-fearing women. Midwifery was also associated with the care and service to poor women. The early midwives were strong and had a deeply-held conviction for assisting women and caring for them and their families after the babies were born. Midwives were celebrated and highly respected because they supported the women during the pregnancy, the birthing process and after the delivery of the child.

The Greek word *Maieutics* pertains to midwifery. It is a method based on the idea that the truth is latent in the mind of every human being due to innate reason but has to be "given birth" by answering intelligently-proposed questions or problems. Therefore, *Maieutics* invites the individual to discover truth that is latent in a person. Jer. 29:11 says, "'I know the thoughts I have towards you,' saith the Lord, "thoughts of peace, and not of evil, to give you an expected end.'" Therein lies the entrance of the Apostolic Midwife.

The Apostolic Midwife has been assigned and sent by God to help in the birthing process of that expected end. There are countless numbers of men and women whose identity in Christ have not been yet identified, nor whose divine purpose has been birthed out. In this season, God is raising up and equipping Apostolic Midwives to assist Him in the birthing forth of divine purposes upon this earth. Jer. 1:5 says, *"I formed you in the belly. I knew you; and before you camest forth out of the womb I sanctified you, and I ordained you a prophet unto the nations."* God has already known us before we came to this earth. He has breathed into each one of us a seed of righteousness, a seed of faith and a seed of purpose. We go through a divine process of being pregnant with purpose and need the assistance of the Apostolic Midwife (birthing coach) to help us in birthing forth our divine purpose on earth.

The Apostolic Midwife is the designated birthing coach in an individual's life. They have been given an apostolic mandate by God to spiritually discern the abilities, talents and skills of an individual.

THE ROLES OF AN APOSTOLIC MIDWIFE

The Apostolic Midwife is not a gender-specific role. In both modern and ancient times the majority of midwives were female. But, in this season, God has called forth men and women in the church and the marketplace to assume their positions as apostolic midwives. Eph. 4:11-12 says, *"And he gave some, apostles, and some, prophets; and some, evangelists; and some, pastors and teachers; For the perfecting of the saints for the work of ministry, for the edifying of the body of Christ."* Following are some of the primary roles and functions of an Apostolic Midwife:

- The Apostolic Midwife must recognize and identify the individuals that will be mentored, counseled, taught, trained and coached by them through the birthing process.

I Kings 19:19 says: *"So he departed thence, and found Elisha the son of Shaphat, who was plowing with twelve yoke of oxen before him, and he with the twelfth; and Elijah passed by him, and cast his mantle on him."* God will assist us in this process to find those sons and daughters who need our mantle in order to complete the birthing process. They will come from all walks of life to receive the guidance, encouragement and comfort that will enable them to give birth to the destiny that is locked up in their spiritual wombs.

- The Apostolic Midwife must establish a personal relationship with the son or daughter who is pregnant with purpose. This may include daily, weekly, monthly consultation, praying together and discipling via teaching and training. Matt. 28:19 says, *"Go ye and make disciples of many nations... We must incorporate the greatest commission as we help in birthing out purpose."*

- The Apostolic Midwife and the son or daughter must work collaboratively together to establish a short-term and long-term plan based upon their dreams, hopes, prophecies, aspirations, talents, giftings, skills and abilities. Hab. 2:2-3 says, *"And the Lord answered me, and said, 'Write the vision, and make it plain upon tables, that he may run that reads it. For the vision is yet for an appointed time, but at the end it shall speak, and not lie; though it tarry, wait for it; because it will surely come, it will not tarry.'"* It does not matter what your age is nor how long your dream has been lying in a dormant stage. What does matter is that God has foreseen and planned that Kairos moment (the perfect time) whereby He has already commanded the Angel of the Lord to come to you in the form of an Apostolic Midwife to trouble the water that you have been in. The Apostolic midwife is appropriately able to activate the gift within you and unlock the keys of your destiny.

- The Apostolic Midwife must speak to the son or daughter and prophesy with words of encouragement, comfort and edification throughout the process of them being pregnant, birthing out and even after the delivery. Many times the process of carrying spiritual babies is harder than the delivery, especially during labor when the pain is the most intense. 1 Cor. 14:4 says, *"But he that prophesieth speaketh unto men to edification, and exhortation, and comfort."*

The tasks and the assignments always become more difficult as the time of delivery nears. Ex. 5:1-23 says, *"Pharaoh commanded the taskmasters to work the Israelites harder than they had ever worked before."* This was the enemy trying to frustrate them and make them give up the idea of being delivered out of Egypt. But thank God for Moses, who was the Apostolic Midwife commissioned by God to deliver the people of God out of Egypt. Moses became the birthing coach for destiny and purpose for the life of a whole nation. We, too, must have that perseverance, zeal, and enthusiasm in advancing the kingdom of God by assisting in the divine birthing process of individuals and nations.

- The Apostolic Midwife's role is to encourage the son or daughter to 'Let Go and Let God.' Childbirth requires a surrender to nature's course. When the baby's ready to come down that canal, it is ready and you must submit to the fact that the power or force behind this baby being birthed is far greater than anything you can do humanly possible to stop it. 1 John 4:4 says, *"Greater is he that is in you, than he that is in the world."* James 4:7 says to surrender unto God.

In order for the seed of greatness to be birthed in each of us, we must allow ourselves to totally surrender to the will of the Father. Some deliveries are very quick and relatively painless, and other deliveries or births are longer and more painful and difficult (hard labor or complications). We must let go of everything and everyone that is not a part of the birthing process. This season of letting go is very painful to many, because we have held on so long to things that please the lust of the flesh, lust of the eye and the pride of life. But the mandate of God on your life requires you to release the garments of old, the old wineskins and replace them with the new garments that the Lord wants to bless you with.

- The Apostolic Midwife must be bold and daring. The Apostolic Midwife dares to go where no one else has the guts to go. They forge paths that many will not take on due to the risks involved. These risks include being criticized, being ridiculed, being ostracized, and being killed. But, there were many matriarchs and patriarchs in the Bible who were willing to take the risk in order for God's kingdom to come forth. Esther was willing to risk her life to save a nation as she went before the king. Her assignment was to save a nation and birth out that nation's purpose. Ruth came into agreement with her mother-in-law Naomi and together they walked into her divine inheritance with Boaz, which was part of the lineage of Jesus Christ.

We all have an assignment to fulfill which includes birthing out our own purpose in addition to helping to assist in the birthing out of purpose for others in the body of Christ and the marketplace. Sometimes the one that God chooses for you to assist in the birthing process, is not the one that everyone feels you should help. 1 Sam. 16:7,13 says, *"But the Lord said to Samuel, 'look not on his countenance, or on the height of his stature; because I have refused him; for the Lord seeth not as man seeth; for man looketh on the outward appearance, but the Lord looketh on the heart.' Then Samuel took the horn of oil, and, anointed him in the midst of his brethren; and the spirit of the Lord came upon David from that day forward. So Samuel rose up, and went to Ramah."* Apostolic midwives see in others what most people can't see.

- Apostolic Midwives are God's partners in creation. Their sole assignment is to fulfill the coaching and bringing forth or birthing out of individual and corporate Kingdom purposes on earth. We are called to the task of slicing the enemy's efforts to attempt to abort the destinies of God-ordained individuals and nations. 1 Cor. 3:9 says, *"For we are labourers together with God; you are God's husbandry, you are God's building."*

- Apostolic Midwives stand to receive a supernatural blessing from God for their obedience in fulfilling their assignments. Ex. 1:20-21 says, *"God bestowed goodness upon the midwives and the people multiplied and became very strong. It was because the midwives feared God, that He made houses for them."* The NIV translation says: *"And because the midwives feared God, he gave them families of their own."* Prov. 28:20 notes, *"A faithful man shall abound with blessings..."*

Apostolic Midwives come in all shapes and sizes from every walk of life. Ananias was the midwife that God used to birth Saul into the kingdom. Some people, like Joseph, only have the Holy Spirit as their midwife. We may even consider that Pharaoh's butler/wine steward helped birth Joseph's destiny after two years of silence and being pregnant in the Spirit, or that Pharaoh's wife helped birth Joseph's destiny by her false accusation and false charges to get him into prison. Even our accusers can sometimes be our midwives. The Lord can use other means to birth our destiny as well. God used a whale to be Jonah's midwife, and a lost donkey to be Saul's midwife to bring him to Samuel, and a ridden donkey to be Balaam's midwife to warn him of the angel in the road with a drawn sword. Too bad Balaam had a miscarriage (of justice and obedience), and did not heed the word of the Lord or the warning from the angel of God. It ultimately cost him his life and he died by the sword. Let us all be open minded to the leading and guiding of the Holy Spirit in our lives to become apostolic midwives in this season.

THE MANTLE OF SHIPHRAH AND PUAH

In the book of Exodus, we are introduced to two faithful and righteous women of God. They were assigned as midwives to the Hebrew women. Their names are written as *Shiphrah* and *Puah*. The Israelites were living in a time of great oppression. Pharaoh's astrologers had predicted that a male would rise up among the Hebrews and overtake Pharaoh's throne. In an attempt to destroy the destiny of one male child, Pharaoh ordered the Hebrew men into backbreaking slave labor. But, when the Hebrew people continued to multiply, Pharaoh was driven by evil and commanded the two midwives to kill all newborn Hebrew boys.

Isa. 59:19 says, *"When the enemy comes in like a flood, the Spirit of the Lord will lift up a standard against him."* The Lord had another plan. What the enemy means for our evil, God turns it around for our good. Ex. 1:17 says that the midwives, however, feared God, so they did not do as the king of Egypt had spoken to them, but instead, they enabled the boys to live.

In the Hebrew, *Shiphrah* comes from mishaperect, which means *"to beautify, to swaddle and clean, to improve the quality and to make something better."* (Strong's)

In the Hebrew, *Puah* means *"cry, groan, and a particular gift of speech."* (Strong's)

Shiprah and Puah were on a very high spiritual level. Isa. 60:1 says to *"Arise, shine, for thy light is come, and the glory of the Lord is risen upon you."* Ex. 24:1 states, *"And the Lord said to Moses, 'Come up unto the Lord...'"*

Apostolic midwives must arise out of darkness, obscurity and complacency and go up to a higher place in God to receive revelation, instruction and direction to implement the birthing of purpose for individuals in the church and the marketplace. We must come up higher in our prayer, in our fasting, in our giving, in our walk of holiness and in every area of our life pertaining to Christ. Isa. 58:14 says that if we delight ourselves in the Lord, he will cause us to ride upon the high places of the earth.

The Mantle of Shiphrah and Puah contains the following:

1. You will possess a boldness like the lion of Judah to stand against the wiles of the enemies. Prov. 28:1 says, *"The wicked flee when no man pursueth; but the righteous are bold as a lion."* Shiprah and Puah boldly refused to participate with Pharoah. They told him yes, but their hearts were far from him. There are times in our lives that the only way we can outwit the devil, is not to let the right hand know what the left hand is doing. Everyone cannot be made aware of your plans to outwit the devil.

2. Your mind will be renewed daily to receive a download from Heaven of battle-ready strategies in how to overcome the enemy and resist the devil. This mantle causes you to think in God's terms. Shiphrah and Puah had an INNATE ability given to them by

God to overcome their situation. This mantle gives you a mindset to outwit the devil every time he tries to come against you and the kingdom of God. Rom. 12:2 says, *"And be not conformed to this world; but be ye transformed by the renewing of your mind, that ye may prove what is that good, and acceptable, and perfect, will of God."*

3. You will possess a working knowledge of your heavenly assignment on this earth. You will be loyal to the voice of God in the church and in the marketplace in executing the safe delivery of purpose of all who come into your path. John 15:16 says, *"You have not chosen me, but I have chosen you, and ordained you, that you should go and bring forth fruit, and that your fruit should remain: that whatsoever you shall ask of the Father in my name, he may give it you."* 2 Pet. 1:10 says, *"Wherefore the rather, brethren, give diligence to make your calling and election sure: for if you do these things, you shall never fall."*

4. You will be imparted with a wisdom that allows you to discern methods and ways to improve and to make better every person that has been assigned to you. Prov. 4:5 says, *"Get wisdom, get understanding: forget it not; neither decline from the words of my mouth."*

5. Your voice will be anointed with a sound from heaven that enables you to speak forth the destiny of your assignment. When you speak to your son or daughter, their baby will leap in their spiritual womb. This is the Puah portion of the mantle. In the process of giving birth, the anointed sound in your voice shall speak into their ears which they will receive and the baby will be activated and prepare

to come forth. Luke 1:41-42 records, *"And it came to pass that, when Elisabeth heard the salutation of Mary, the babe leaped in her womb; and Elisabeth was filled with the Holy Ghost. And she spake out with a loud voice, and said, 'Blessed art thou among women, and blessed is the fruit of thy womb.'"*

6. You will become a warring ambassador to fight for God's will and not fight against it. Matt. 11:12 states, *"And from the days of John the Baptist until now the kingdom of heaven suffers violence, and the violent take it by force."* Ps. 18:34 adds, *"He teacheth my hands to war, so that a bow of steel is broken by my arms."*

7. This mantle causes the blessings of God to overtake you. Deut. 28:2 says, *"And all these blessings shall come on thee, and overtake thee, if thou shalt hearken unto the voice of the Lord thy God."* Ex. 1:20-21 adds, *"God bestowed goodness upon the midwives, and the people multiplied and became very strong. It was because the midwives feared God, that He made houses for them."*

I must pause and chuckle at this point to coin the infamous words from the movie *BeBe Kids*—"We don't die. We multiply!"

Now back to our story! In the Jewish teachings, the "houses" that God made for Shiphrah and Puah were in fact dynasties born through them. In the history of the Torah, it is said that Shiphrah was a psuedonym for Jochebed, and Puah was another name for Miriam. Jochebed was blessed to give birth not only to her daughter Miriam, but also to Moses and Aaron. Through Jochebed (Shiphrah), a nation of priests was born, and Miriam (Puah) was blessed to mother the Royal dynasty, the "House of David."

IMPARTATION OF THE SHIPHRAH AND THE PUAH MANTLE

Thank you Heavenly Father for the mantle of Shiphrah and Puah. I impart this mantle upon you now. I decree and declare that you shall execute the assignment of an Apostolic Midwife. I decree and declare that you shall go forth and birth out the purposes of sons and daughters in the church and the marketplace and the Kingdom, in Jesus' name I pray. Amen.

THE CHARGE

Arise and go forth, Mighty Apostolic Midwives. Assume your positions at the birthing stools in the church and in the marketplace. The "babies" (purpose) are waiting for you. Hurry, someone boil some water, get the scissors, get some towels, get some sheets! There is a mighty Apostolic birthing that is getting ready to be released upon the earth, in Jesus' name! Amen.

Author's Note: This chapter is excerpted from a forthcoming book entitled *The Spiritual Birthing Coach.*

ABOUT THE AUTHOR

Apostle Sharon Billins is the CEO and Founder of Palm Tree International Ministries, Inc., which serves as the spiritual covering for many churches and ministries. She is the Senior Pastor of The Remnant Church of Columbus, Ga. and The Remnant Church of Tallahassee, Fla. Apostle Billins is the President and Founder of The SAMUEL School of the Prophets. She holds a B.S. degree in Chemistry from Florida State University. She has two children, Tiffany Nicole who is a graduate of Columbus State University and is employed as a Counselor for The University of Phoenix and Norris Billins Jr. who is a student at Albany State University.

Reverend Billins worked as a Chemical Engineer for 10 years and has taught in the Public School System. She has over 27 years experience in management, supervision and training. She is a past business owner, having been the CEO of Diversified Training Systems. She has worked as a Consultant/ Instructor for the Georgia Department of Technical and Adult Education and the Pastoral Institute Business Resource Center. She also served as a Hospital Chaplain at St. Francis Hospital and is a graduate of the Clinical Pastoral Education Unit at St. Francis Hospital. She is also a graduate of the Pastoral Care Specialist Program at the Turner Clergy Center of the Pastoral Institute. Reverend Billins served as the first female President of the Muscogee County Clergy Association. She also served as the Chairperson of the Columbus Prison Task Force.

She is an outstanding speaker and energetic professional who is committed to service. She has hosted numerous conferences and workshops and has presented at many local events. Reverend Billins is active in community affairs and has sat on the Board of Directors and Governing Councils for many community organizations. She received an Honorary Doctorate in Divinity in 2012 for her humanitarian work from Kingdom Bible Institute, San Bernardino, Calif. To learn more or to contact her, visit her website at www. sharon-billins.org.

CHAPTER FORTY-THREE

FATHERS AND SONS

DR. MARK KAUFFMAN

In this present season God is administrating His Kingdom through a wineskin called Fathers and Sons. In ages gone by this has been God's order for fulfilling his purposes trans-generationally. It is God's pattern for building His Holy Nation in the earth. Presently the church is in transition. We are moving from the Church Age into the Apostolic Father-Son Kingdom Age. Apostolic Fathers are emerging in this hour to put vision in the sons of God to transform the planet and not leave it. In the previous season we experienced many inaccurate models of fatherhood. We will always experience the natural before the spiritual. There are many examples of false fathers in scripture and those false fathering spirits still roam the earth today.

- **Saul** is a false father who will try to kill every emerging David.

- **Laban** is a false father who will keep you in the house so he can take advantage of your favor.

- **Moab** is a false father who will sacrifice his own son to keep his own ministry.

- **Pharaoh** is a false father who wants everyone to worship him.

- **Herod** is a false father who will kill every new anointing in the house.

But, just because there are false fathers does not mean there are not true fathers. A true father comes in a spirit to cover while a false father comes in a controlling spirit. As a spiritual father myself, I often tell my sons that I am more under you than I am over you in God. The apostle Paul told the church at Ephesus in Eph. 2:20 that we *"are built upon the foundation of the apostles and prophets, Jesus Christ himself being the chief corner stone"* (KJV). As foundational ministry, the apostles and prophets stand under sons, lifting them up into Christ and into their destiny.

David is a true example of a father who covers his sons. Four hundred orphan-spirited men left Saul's table and fled into the wilderness in pursuit of David's fathering spirit. When they got to the cave of Adullum they were in debt, distressed, and discontented; this was a direct result of the lack of fathering they found in the Sauline order. At Saul's table their weaknesses were exposed but at David's table all of their handicaps, weaknesses and insecurities were covered by this true father who released their innate potential to become mighty men of valor.

Spiritual fathers must teach their sons to accurately carry the presence of God. During Saul's reign the Ark of the Covenant was kept in the home of one of the Levitical priests named Abinidab. Abinidab's name means father but it is very evident that in the 25 years of having the presence of God in his house, he did not teach his sons how to properly handle the presence of God. I am sure you are familiar with the story of how David fetched the ark to bring it to Mt. Zion and how they placed it on a cart that was led by an ox. This inaccurate method led to the death of Abinidab's son Uzzah after he mishandled the ark. David then went and sought the due order on how to carry the ark and instructed the priesthood that it was to be carried upon the shoulders.

After finding the due order, David's priesthood carried the Ark of the Covenant up to Mt Zion. Zion in the Hebrew means dry, parched, market. The heart of every father is to teach his sons how to carry the presence of God out into the world. The time has come for fathers to raise up sons so they can carry the presence and purpose of God into the dry, parched places of today's marketplace.

RESTORATION OF THE SPIRIT OF ELIJAH

In recent years Mal. 4:5-6, the closing verses of the Old Testament, has become a catalytic message for the father-son order. The prophet Malachi released the prophetic message that God would restore the spirit and power of Elijah in the earth through apostolic fathers. This prophecy came 400 years prior to the birth of Christ. What I find amazing is there was silence for 400 years until there was a voice crying in the wilderness through John the Baptist. I believe the reason for the silence was this: why should God speak His purposes in the earth and bless a man if he were to die and not leave that legacy to the next generation?

God is trans-generational. He always spoke of himself as the God of Abraham, Isaac, and Jacob and until there was a man who came in the spirit of Elijah the heavens remained closed. It is evident that during those 400 years the spirit of Elijah was no longer present in the earth. God's presence, power, provision, peace, protection, praise and prosperity were held back until this father-son order was restored.

Jesus, who represents sonship, at the age of 30, comes to the Jordan where he meets John the Baptist, who represents the restoration of spiritual fatherhood. After John the Baptist immersed Jesus in the waters of Baptism the heavens reopened, and after 400 years the order was right before God and a fresh anointing came and rested upon the pattern Son. For the first time in 400 years the heavenly father spoke, saying, *"Thou art my beloved son and in thee I am well pleased."* Through this father and son order the blessings were released and Jesus was sent forth as a son to fulfill his destiny in the earth. After this divine encounter Jesus was launched into his 3 ½ year campaign of ministry and miracles.

This model, when accurately restored, will release unprecedented miracles, signs and wonders in the earth. *"Behold, I and the children whom the LORD hath given me are for signs and for wonders in Israel from the LORD of hosts, which dwelleth in mount Zion"* (Isa. 8:18, KJV). When the father-son order is restored God visits the earth by pouring out His glory in unlimited fashion.

DIVINE ORDER IS REQUIRED

Presently the church is craving the miracles we have heard about from past movements. In order to see the restoration of the miraculous, God's divine order must be established. *"And God hath set some in the church, first apostles, secondarily prophets, thirdly teachers, after that miracles, then gifts of healings, helps, governments, diversities of tongues"* (1 Cor. 12:28, KJV).

Here the apostle Paul sets the divine stage for unprecedented miracles and healings in and through the body of Christ. God sets the order in the church: first Apostles, secondarily prophets, thirdly teachers, and "after that" order is established miracles will come. If we desire the "after that" we must first align ourselves with what comes before that. Once we have aligned ourselves with this apostolic order, it will release the miracles God has prepared for us in heavenly places. *"But as it is written, Eye hath not seen, nor ear heard, neither have entered into the heart of man, the things which God hath prepared for them that love him"* (1 Cor. 2:9, KJV). It is in this divine order of father-son ministry that God channels the blessings that have been prepared for us from the foundation of the world into our lives.

The call of God in this present hour is for the church to upgrade by finding the father assigned to their life. Like Jesus who left Galilee (the circle) and went to the Jordan (the descender), we must also leave our Galilee—the place where religion takes us in circles. The time has come to break away and find our John the Baptist at the Jordan where we can humble ourselves and submit to true spiritual authority. Every man and woman of God who wants to fulfill their destiny must find a spiritual father who will baptize and immerse them in the water of God's present truth so they can proceed to their destiny and live under an open heaven.

Remember—only after Jesus submitted to this divine order did the heavens open unto Him. This realm was open for Jesus during his entire three-and a-half-year ministry. It is within this open heaven that Father God takes the limitations off of the miracles we need. In an open heaven, God's treasury and armory will be open unto you. When His treasury is open, the resources you need to fulfill your destiny will come looking for you. *"The LORD shall open unto thee his good treasure, the heaven to give the rain unto thy land in his season, and to bless all the work of thine hand: and thou shalt lend unto many nations, and thou shalt not borrow"* (Deut. 28:12, KJV). Jesus is the accurate pattern and if you follow the pattern son you will get the same results.

In our day the prophets are declaring what is available in the open heavens but it will take the apostolic fathers to release what is in the heavens to the sons. Presently the Lord is releasing the anointing of the Sons of Issachar. *"And of the children of Issachar, which were men that had understanding of the times, to know what Israel ought to do; the heads of them were two hundred; and all their brethren were at their commandment"* (1 Chron. 12:32, KJV). The understanding of the times is the prophetic anointing and knowing what Israel shall do is the apostolic anointing. The prophets declare what is in the heavens and apostolic fathers release it to the sons.

God has never relinquished the original purpose and intent of mankind—to have Spirit-filled sons who forcefully advance and execute His Kingdom plan on the planet. The sons of God will overturn the curse Adam placed on God's creation. What a powerful end-time ministry spiritual fathers have to employ, rise up, equip and send sons into all creation with transforming power.

While visiting Zacchaeus' house, Jesus declared the Son of Man's mission statement: *"For the Son of man is come to seek and to save that which was lost"* (Luke 19:10, KJV). As a young boy, my pastor preached a partial truth from this passage. He would say: "The son of man is come to seek and save them that were lost." That is an accurate statement but there is a further revelation. Many quote "them" that were lost instead of "that which" was lost. "That which" covers so much more than "them." What was lost in Adam was recovered by Christ and will be completely restored in the father-son order. Adam lost his inheritance by losing his position of sonship and by moving back to our position as sons we will recover our inheritance. As fathers turn to sons and sons turn to their fathers, this scripture will be fulfilled in our day. We are on a journey together back to the garden and into our inheritance.

CYCLE OF RESTORATION

"And the seventh angel sounded; and there were great voices in heaven, saying, the kingdoms of this world are become the kingdoms of our Lord, and of his Christ; and he shall reign forever and ever"
(Rev. 11:15, KJV)

As we recover our inheritance in Christ, we will also see the recovery of the earth and Christ's Kingdom established therein. We are told there was one river that went out of Eden that became four heads. This is a headship principle for the cycle of restoration. The book of Genesis is a book of our forefathers and a book of beginnings. We came out of the fathers and to return to our inheritance we must go back through the fathers. These four rivers represent the four fathers of Genesis: Abraham, Isaac, Jacob and Joseph.

- Abraham represents Promises

- Isaac represents Provision

- Jacob represents Process

- Joseph represents Power

It is through these covenant relationships that we enter this sphere. The promises of God are released in sons, the provision of God is released to sons to fulfill their destiny, the process of God is released so Christ is formed in the sons and the power of God is released through the sons to influence their sphere and subdue all their enemies.

As a result of these father-son relationships, Father God is building a family. The Hebrew root meaning of family is "father's house." God started with a family in Genesis and in the end times He will restore His apostolic family back in the earth. Only in this divine order will the rain of God's presence fall. *"And it shall come to pass, that every one that is left of all the nations which came against Jerusalem shall even go up from year to year to worship the King, the LORD of hosts, and to keep the feast of tabernacles. And it shall be, that whoso will not come up of all the families of the earth unto Jerusalem to worship the King, the LORD of hosts, even upon them shall be no rain. And if the family of Egypt go not up, and come not, that have no rain; there shall be the plague, wherewith the LORD will smite the heathen that come not up to keep the feast of tabernacles"* (Zech. 14:16-18, KJV).

God will restore His apostolic family back in the earth.

During the Feast of Tabernacles the Lord required the families of the earth to come up and worship Him. In our first encounter with the Lord we experienced the Feast of Passover which was with Jesus our personal Savior. Then as we followed on to know the Lord, we experienced the Feast of Pentecost, which was a personal encounter with the Holy Ghost. Both of those divine encounters were personal experiences that have led us to this day.

The next Feast on God's agenda is Tabernacles. It is here we encounter the Father as His sons. This is the place of corporate anointing where we go beyond personal experiences to encounter God corporately. The rain of His presence will only fall upon worshipping families. We are promised He shall come to us as the rain. He is the rain and as He pours out His spirit on this father-son order, His provision, favor, power and supernatural manifestations will be a result of His coming to us.

This father-son paradigm will restore the family of God back into the earth, releasing days of heaven upon the earth. Every true apostle has a strong sense for family. The true heart of apostles is to build God's family in the planet. Without this apostolic order, there is no visitation of the Lord on the land. As this apostolic family is restored in the earth, it becomes the channel to release the desire of heaven upon the earth, whereby the Lord will visit the land again and heal the nations. In this new day Jesus will have a bride, the Holy Ghost will have a temple and the Father will have a family.

DIVINE ORDER

The true biblical definition of an apostolic father is one who guides, governs and guards. The father brings proper order, discipline and direction to the family unit. The father imparts and releases signature gifts and strengths in the sons. *"For I long to see you, that I may impart unto you some spiritual gift, to the end ye may be established"* (Rom. 1:11, KJV). The apostolic travail is to see the anointing formed in every son. *"My little children, of whom I travail in birth again until Christ be formed in you"* (Gal. 4:19, KJV). Building Christ in the body is true apostolic travail!

True spiritual fathers will lead their sons to a place of circumcision. When a father cuts a son dealing with his flesh, this is where many sons quit and abort the purpose of God for their life. For true covenant to be made, blood must flow. Fathers deal with attitudes, hidden sins, and character flaws. Every father carries a two-edged sword. One side reveals hidden potential and the other reveals hidden sins. Both sides are necessary in the circumcision of a son.

You will never fulfill destiny or reproduce anything until you have been cut by a father. As a spiritual father I have seen that there are three ways to respond to spiritual circumcision. A father can take the knife to his son, a son can bring the knife to the father, or a son can run from the knife. I have seen many who have fled from the process, aborting the purposes of God in their life. Many of these sons have remained sore and bitter as a result of a spiritual father dealing with hidden sins and flaws within their life.

Let me admonish you to bring the knife to your spiritual father, allowing him to cut away every fleshly trapping that would hinder you from fulfilling your destiny. Remember the children of Israel could not pass over into their Promise Land until Joshua took a sharp knife circumcising them at the hill of foreskins. There they dwelt in the camp until they were completely whole. When a man or woman has been circumcised by a father, hell cannot touch them or hurt them and then and only then are they prepared to enter the Promise Land of inheritance.

Many today are spiritually dead and trying to serve apart from spiritual covering. *"And Nadab and Abihu, the sons of Aaron, took either of them his censer, and put fire therein, and put incense thereon, and offered strange fire before the LORD, which he commanded them not. And there went out fire from the LORD, and devoured them, and they died before the LORD. Then Moses said unto Aaron, 'This is it that the LORD spake, saying, I will be sanctified in them that come nigh me, and before all the people I will be glorified.' And Aaron held his peace"*

(Lev. 10:1-3, KJV). Nadab and Abihu broke the divine order of God by ministering independently of their father Aaron. Nadab and Abihu had fire but it was strange fire.

Strange fire occurs when men and women rise up to minister without being sent by fathering ministries. I am amazed at the lack of discernment within the body of Christ to discern the difference between strange fire and heaven's fire. Strange fire fills our churches today. Presently there are many church-goers that in their ministry, messages, marriages, business and lives are trying to serve independently from spiritual fathers. Father God is raising up apostles and apostolic centers whereby through father -son relationship, heaven's true fire may be released in the earth. Only sons can be trusted with the tools of true ministry. A new day has dawned; we can no longer build with gifts—we must build with sons!

SUCCESSORS

Abraham, who raised up sons as successors, is a beautiful model of this father-son paradigm. Success without successors is failure in disguise. *"And when Abram heard that his brother was taken captive, he armed his trained servants, born in his own house, three hundred and eighteen, and pursued them unto Dan. And he divided himself against them, he and his servants, by night, and smote them, and pursued them unto Hobah, which is on the left hand of Damascus"* (Gen. 14:14-15, KJV). Herein lies the secret of Abraham's success:

- His sons were equipped

- His sons were trained

- His sons served in the house

- His sons received the covenant blessings of the house

- His sons ran with him

- His sons stood with him in night seasons

- His sons received the inheritance

The greatest move of God will come to those who see beyond their day into the next generation. Why should Father God anoint us to do great things if our anointing and gift die with us? Exponential anointing is only created in father-son relationships. We are to give our inheritance away while we are alive and not upon our death.

When a father dies he is to leave this world empty, giving all his love, wisdom, wealth, revelation and life away just like Paul the Apostle, who at the end of his life said, *"I have been poured out like a drink offering."* Elijah was a man who died empty while leading his spiritual son Elisha to his destiny. He left him with all that he had, thus creating exponentially a double portion anointing. We live in exciting times when the spirit of Elijah is standing up in fathers who are leading sons to the point of their destiny and empowering them to fulfill heaven's purpose and intent for their life!

ABOUT THE AUTHOR

Being passionately involved in both business and ministry, Dr. Mark Kauffman possesses a unique ability to equip and train marketplace ministers to link the idea of prosperity to a God-given plan that will advance the Kingdom of God. His heart is to see the body demonstrate the nature and ministry of the Lord Jesus Christ, thus fulfilling their destiny.

He is the founder and overseeing apostle of Jubilee Ministries International, located in New Castle, Penn. Since 1981 he has successfully owned and operated Butz Flowers Gifts and Home Décor, the second oldest florist in the United States and ranked in the top 100 of 30,000 florists nationwide. He is also the Chief Executive officer of Global Investments Gold and Mining Company as well as the Chief Executive Officer of Global Impact Mega Corporation, which was established as a Community Development Financial Institution to develop entrepreneurs in the local church, as well as train and empower young entrepreneurs to start businesses that will impact the community.

Dr. Kauffman also oversees Kingdom Regency Alliance Network which includes 100 pastors, churches and orphanages in the nation of India. He serves as the international editor of the *Vachanachoshanam Newspaper*, which spreads the message of the Kingdom throughout India, Asia and the Middle East.

For 24 years Mark has been happily married to Pastor Jill Kauffman, who works tirelessly alongside him to see the Kingdom of God advanced. They have three sons –

Anthony, Ryan and Christian Mark—and a granddaughter, Alexandra Irene. For more information or to contact him, visit www.KingdomRegencyAlliance.org.

CHAPTER FORTY-FOUR

DOES YOUR APOSTOLIC FATHER CALL YOU A SON?

CURTIS GILLESPIE

"And lo a voice from heaven, saying,
this is my beloved Son, in whom I am well pleased."
(Matt. 3:17, KJV)

"And Simon Peter answered and said,
Thou art the Christ, the Son of the living God."
(Matt. 16:16, KJV)

No relationship can properly define what it means to be in alignment with the Apostolic, other than the relationship between a father and a Son. For there can be no true alignment unless these two personalities are on the same page. There are numerous examples in the Bible that suggest to us that tragedy, turmoil, and sometimes death itself were from the result of a father and a son not being properly aligned or on the same page. It is important that we as the Body of Christ understand the dynamics of the relationship that existed between God the Father and his Son the Christ.

The Bible says in the gospel of John, and the *"Word was made flesh, and dwelt among us, (and we beheld his glory, the glory as of the only begotten of the Father,) full of grace and truth"* (John 1:14,

KJV). *"No man hath seen God at any time; the only begotten Son, which is in the bosom of the Father, he hath declared him"* (John 1:18, KJV). This position and title has been given to Jesus and to him alone; not even Adam himself could ever lay hold of such a claim as the only begotten of the Father.

The Greek word for begotten is *monogenēs* which is made up of two Greek words of *monos* which means: alone and only, and the word *ginomai* which means: to cause to be ("gen"-rate), to become (come into being). This suggests to us that it was the Father's plan all along for Jesus to come, for according to Rom. 5:14, Adam was made in the figure of him who was to come. The word figure in the Greek is *typos* which means: to be a pattern, form, fashion or a model, so Jesus as the only begotten Son of God was the pattern or form that the Father used when creating man, for he says to the Son, *"Let us make man in our own image and likeness"* (Gen. 1:26, KJV). This is good news for the Body of Christ, and for those of us who would suggest that we go back to the relationship that God had with Adam, that relationship ended without Adam ever becoming a son of the Most High God.

By not partaking of the tree of life, Adam never possessed the Life of God or the DNA of God, and so it is written, *"The first man Adam, was made a living soul; the last Adam was made a quickening spirit. Howbeit that was not first which is spiritual, but that which is natural; and afterward that which is spiritual. The first man is of the earth, earthy: the second man is the Lord from heaven"* (1 Cor. 15:45-47, KJV). This particular passage of scripture suggests to us that the first Adam was indeed soulish, and did not carry the DNA (life) of God, in the order of creation.

In the book of Genesis, we find out that everything reproduces after its own kind. The ability to reproduce was given to Adam by God himself, for he told Adam or man

"…..*be fruitful….and replenish the earth….*" (Gen. 1:27-28). So, it was Adam's assignment to be fruitful or *para* as it is called in Hebrew, which means: to cause to make fruitful, to grow, and to increase. Adam also had the duty to replenish the earth or what the Hebrews call *mâlê* which means: to fill or to make full. The plan was for Adam to eat of the tree of life, which was the life and DNA of God: this in turn would enable him now to become a Son of God, and by distributing the life and DNA of God to his offspring, he would then be reproducing more Sons of God, thus causing the earth to be replenish or filled up with more of his kind. Once Adam had sinned and lost his ability not to reproduce, but his ability to distribute the life of God, the Bible says that after the fall of man that Adam ("…..*begat a son in his own likeness, after his own image…*" Gen. 5:3).

As we can see, there was nothing spiritual or heavenly about Adam; he does not have the ability to affect the spiritual dimension because he is soulish. But, the last Adam and the second man being Jesus, is from heaven and was made a quickening spirit or *zōopoieō* in the Greek text which means: to revitalize, make alive, give life, quicken. So, the last Adam was not only from heaven, but he also was a life-giving spirit, finally! God now has someone in the earth-realm that not only has his life and DNA but has the ability to distribute his life and DNA to others, and that someone is none other than the only begotten of the Father. Jesus himself was generated or brought into being by the Father, so by possessing that same life force, he could impart it according to scriptures ("*To as many as received him, to them gave he power (ability) to become (come into being) the sons of God*" (John 1:12).

The Bible says in John 1:18 that Jesus was in the bosom or in the pocket of the Father, as the only begotten of God and he was the closest to Father, and by being that close, he understood what the Father's plans were and He properly aligned himself with those plans. As apostolic sons, we must also understand that we are birthed out of our Father's bosom or pocket, and just like Christ, we must know our Father's plans and desires for the sole purpose of giving ourselves up for the fulfillment of those plans. *"For Jesus said wherefore when he cometh into the world, he saith, 'Sacrifice and offering thou wouldest not, but a body hast thou prepared me: In burnt offerings and sacrifices for sin thou hast had no pleasure.' Then said 'I, Lo, I come (in the volume of the book it is written of me,) to do thy will, O God'"* (Heb. 10:5-8, KJV).

So, as true apostolic sons, we come in the volume of our Father's book with a desire to do our Father's will, as Jesus who is our supreme example did unto our heavenly Father. For as apostolic sons, we must possess the life and the spirit of our fathers, and then just as Christ did, we must distribute that life among the tribe to which we belong. The failure with Adam lies in this, and we as sons of our Apostolic Fathers must also understand this as well. Everything must be sustained or held together by the same life or spirit that created it (see Col. 1:17); in other words, we must not reinvent the wheel, and find ourselves giving birth to things that are after our own image and likeness, and not after the image and likeness of our spiritual fathers.

BUILDERS OF THE FAMILY NAME

"For unto us a child is born, unto us a son is given: and the government shall be upon his shoulder: and his name shall be called Wonderful, Counsellor, The mighty God, The everlasting Father, The Prince of Peace"
(Isa. 9:6, KJV).

No one enters the earth realm like the first Adam did as a full-grown adult; now everyone follows the same pattern that was established by the last Adam, Jesus, who was according to Isa. 9:6 born a child or a *yeled* in Hebrew which means: something born or offspring. As we stated earlier, Jesus was begotten of God, whereas Adam was created by God, so herein lies the difference between real sons and false sons. Real sons are born of their fathers, and are offspring, whereas false sons are self-made and are created by individuals who have not been properly fathered themselves. The relationship that exists between the father and sons must have its origin or beginning in the spirit; it must be one of birthing and not of creating, where the son is born out of the bosom of the father. The child is born, but the son is given, so by taking a look at Jesus, who was indeed born as a child, but was given to us as a son, we can see this.

The relationship between the father and sons must have its origin or beginning in the spirit.

After Jesus was baptized the Bible says, *"And lo a voice from heaven, saying, this is my beloved Son, in whom I am well pleased"* (Matt. 3:17, KJV). This was the Father affirming that Jesus was indeed his Son; we as sons must understand that the affirmation of sonship comes from our Apostolic Fathers, and not from us or other people. Now the Hebrew word for son is *ben*, which comes from the root word *bānâ* that means: to build or a son as a builder of the family name. So, it is the son who is the builder or who bears the responsibility of expanding the family name, and not the child. The problem is that there is a real shortage of Apostolic Fathers that exist. The apostle Paul says that *"For though ye have ten thousand instructors in Christ, yet have ye not many fathers: for in Christ*

Jesus I have begotten you through the gospel. Wherefore I beseech you, be ye followers of me" (1 Cor. 4:15-16, KJV).

Instructors do not have the ability to beget or to bring forth or even to procreate. That ability alone is given to the fathers. You have more instructors than fathers, and they are placing the responsibility of building on the shoulders of children, and not on the shoulders of sons. Everyone is a child of God, but not everyone is a son of God. Now what is it that the son is carrying upon his shoulder? It is the Government of God, or the Government of the apostolic father of that particular tribe or house that we as apostolic sons are in alignment with.

So then, we as sons carry the government or mantle of our fathers upon our shoulders for the sole purpose of building and expanding the family name and business. The father is the planner, and the son is the heir, but the father having conceived the plan, now the son proceeds to create or to build according to that plan.

CASE STUDY

"Now it came to pass, as David sat in his house, that David said to Nathan the prophet, Lo, I dwell in an house of cedars, but the ark of the covenant of the LORD remaineth under curtains. Then Nathan said unto David, Do all that is in thine heart; for God is with thee. And it came to pass the same night, that the word of God came to Nathan, saying, Go and tell David my servant, Thus saith the LORD, Thou shalt not build me an house to dwell in: For I have not dwelt in an house since the day that I brought up Israel unto this day; but have gone from tent to tent, and from one tabernacle to another. Wheresoever I have walked with all Israel, spake I a word to any of the judges of Israel, whom I commanded to feed my people, saying, Why have ye not built me an house of

cedars? Now therefore thus shalt thou say unto my servant David, Thus saith the LORD of hosts, I took thee from the sheepcote, even from following the sheep, that thou shouldest be ruler over my people Israel: And I have been with thee whithersoever thou hast walked, and have cut off all thine enemies from before thee, and have made thee a name like the name of the great men that are in the earth.

"Also I will ordain a place for my people Israel, and will plant them, and they shall dwell in their place, and shall be moved no more; neither shall the children of wickedness waste them any more, as at the beginning, And since the time that I commanded judges to be over my people Israel. Moreover I will subdue all thine enemies. Furthermore I tell thee that the LORD will build thee an house. And it shall come to pass, when thy days be expired that thou must go to be with thy fathers, that I will raise up thy seed after thee, which shall be of thy sons; and I will establish his kingdom. He shall build me an house, and I will stablish his throne for ever. will be his father, and he shall be my son: and I will not take my mercy away from him, as I took it from him that was before thee: But I will settle him in mine house and in my kingdom for ever: and his throne shall be established for evermore. According to all these words, and according to all this vision, so did Nathan speak unto David" (1 Chron. 17:1-15, KJV).

Now David had a desire to build God a house because the Ark of the Covenant remained under a curtain. So he expressed his plans to Nathan, who was the prophet at the time, and after hearing David's plan, Nathan said, "Surely do all that is in thine heart." Well, Nathan went away and the Lord told him that David was not the one He had chosen to build him a house, but it would be his seed or his son that builds him a house. Now you can see that although David was not allowed to build God a house, nevertheless, as a father, he still gave birth or was the originator of the plan.

The story unfolds in 1 Chron. 22:5 as the Bible says that David began to make preparations for the building of the house of God. The text says that David prepared abundantly before his death. Apostolic fathers must also understand that there are many assignments that they themselves will start but will not necessarily finish. This is why succession is on the heart and mind of God and this is why David understood succession.

Another example is how God gave Hezekiah a 15-year extension to get his house in order because Hezekiah did not have a son to carry out or to finish what he himself could not finish. During that time, two sons were born to Hezekiah. The story continues with David now giving instructions to his son Solomon in regards to him building the Lord's house. Included in those instructions were the promises of David's God whom he would introduce to his son Solomon. In order to have proper alignment in the apostolic, the God of the fathers must be known or revealed to the sons. David had prepared everything for Solomon, just like when Adam arrived on earth, God prepared everything. All Adam had to do was to manage it and expand it.

So, the Kingdom of David was upon the shoulders of his son Solomon, who then bore the responsibility of continuing to build the family name along with expanding the Kingdom of his father. In that same spirit, let us now as true sons of God and of our Apostolic fathers, lay hold of their Mantles, embrace their Governments, and let us align ourselves with their causes and their assignments. Let us in accordance with Luke 16:12 be faithful as we build another man's house. Let there be a cry that comes from our spirits like our Lord, saying, "nevertheless not my will but thine will be done" for the sole purpose of Rev. 11:15 ".......*The kingdoms of this world are become the kingdoms of our Lord, and of his Christ; and he shall reign for ever and ever.*"

ABOUT THE AUTHOR

Apostle Curtis Gillespie is part of the Global Effect Movers and Shakers (G.E.M.S.) Network, a Kingdom consortium of ministry, marketplace and municipal members led by Governing Apostle Dr. Gordon E. Bradshaw. He has a bachelor's degree in Business Management and Administration, and is currently the Commander of the SCOPE Vision Group (Strategic Company of Prophetic Engineers), which offers prophetic consultation to business leaders within the Marketplace. Apostle Gillespie also serves as Dean of the Apostolic Continuity Training School, and resides with his family in Michigan City, Ind. To learn more or contact him, visit www.scopevision.org or www.gemsnetwork.org or email scopevisiongroup@gmail.com.

CHAPTER FORTY-FIVE

SPIRITUAL FATHERS AND SONS IN THE MARKETPLACE

DR. A.L. ("PAPA") GILL

With the restoration of apostolic ministry to the church today, there has been a turning of the hearts of the fathers to the children, and the hearts of the children to their fathers (Mal. 4:6). Apostles function primarily as spiritual fathers in the body of Christ and as this is happening there has been more and more emphasis on marketplace ministry.

As apostolic ministries have been expanding from the pulpit back into the marketplace, it is important to look first at Jesus as our example. In Hebrews we read, *"Therefore, holy brethren, partakers of the heavenly calling, consider the Apostle and High Priest of our confession, Christ Jesus, who was faithful to Him who appointed Him, as Moses also was faithful in all His house"* (Heb. 3:1-2).

As we study the Gospels from this fresh perception, we find the ministry of Jesus, the Apostle and High Priest of our confession, took place mainly in the marketplace. He taught from homes, boats, streets, fields, villages, mountains, and sometimes, in places of worship. As we study the book of Acts, we find that the ministry of Peter and Paul who were apostles, was again, mainly in the marketplace. In the ministry of Paul, we see a father-son relationship between himself and others he was mentoring, especially between himself and Timothy.

The Greek word for "apostle" was *apostolos,* meaning one sent forth. Today, many leaders are being sent forth into the professional, business, entertainment, and financial worlds. They are being sent from the pew to the marketplace. They are being sent forth to take the Seven Mountains of Influence in our culture today.

The word *apostolos* was used in the classical Greek world to refer to an emissary or ambassador. It was used in referring to a fleet of ships that was sent out with the purpose of establishing a new colony. It was used in referring to the Admiral who led or commissioned the fleet, and it was used to refer to the new colony that had been established. The word *apostolos* in its usage implied a faithful relationship to the ones by whom they were sent, and a faithfulness to the commission and purpose for which they were sent.

In recent years, what is often referred to as "five-fold ministries" are being restored to many local churches. Many of these churches are now functioning according to God's purpose. In addition to corporate worship, they have become equipping, training, discipling, sending out missionaries, and being church-planting centers.

The apostle Paul wrote, *"When He ascended on high, He led captivity captive, and gave gifts to men. ...And He Himself gave some to be apostles, some prophets, some evangelists, and some pastors and teachers, for the equipping of the saints for the work of ministry, for the edifying of the body of Christ, till we all come to the unity of the faith and the knowledge of the Son of God, to a perfect man, to the measure of the stature of the fullness of Christ..."* (Eph. 4:8,11-13).

There has been much emphasis on those called to function in the priestly ministry of apostles in the local churches. Now, however, many more are discovering the truth that the Church that Jesus said He would build extends far beyond the walls of local churches. The true Church includes every believer being "sent ones."

All believers are equally important, whether functioning in the five-fold ministries in local churches, or in marketplace ministries in the business or professional world. The local church is to be the place to equip the saints (every believer) for the work of the ministry and then through the process of discipleship, bring them to the full measure of the stature of Christ. They then, according to their calling, are to be either set into functioning in the five-fold ministry or sent out into marketplace ministries. Yes, there are those called to the priestly, five-fold servant ministries (Paul, a servant of Jesus Christ called to be an apostle) who function as equippers, mainly in or traveling to local churches and training centers. But, that is only where the ministry begins. If we are to reach the lost with the gospel of Jesus Christ, it requires an equally important marketplace ministry as all those who have been equipped for the work of the ministry step into either the priestly, five-fold equipping ministries, or into the kingly, marketplace ministry.

All believers are equally important: in ministry, in churches, or in the marketplace.

Today, many are discovering that according to God's Word, every believer is to be equipped for the work of the ministry; therefore, every believer is a minister. Those called and functioning as equippers, and those called and functioning in marketplace ministry, are equally important.

We are all sent ones as kings and priests in the Kingdom of God. One function is not more important than another. Each is to full-fill God's calling on their life.

Jesus said to them again, *"Peace to you! As the Father has sent Me, I also send you"* (John 20:21).

Believers are discovering that they, having aligned themselves with spiritual apostolic leadership, are now functioning as sent ones into every strata of society, into every realm of influence in the world today. They are discovering that they have a kingly ministry to function as sent ones in the marketplace.

IT IS ALL ABOUT FUNCTION

The term apostle was never intended to be used as a title. Instead, the emphasis on an apostle, or a sent one, was the function to which they were sent. In the Scriptures, Paul was never referred to as "The Apostle Paul." Instead, he always referred to himself as *"Paul, a servant of Jesus Christ, called to be an apostle ..."* (Rom. 1:1). Many today are discovering that their position in the business world is a ministry, and that this, too, is a call of God. They have been sent into the marketplace as kings to forcibly advance the Kingdom of God in their realm of influence. Many are leaders in the business, professional, governmental and financial communities. They are in alignment with apostolic leadership, and are also functioning as spiritual fathers in the Kingdom of God.

Paul wrote to the Corinthians, *"I do not write these things to shame you, but as my beloved children I warn you. For though you might have ten thousand instructors in Christ, yet you do not have many fathers; for in Christ Jesus I have begotten you through the gospel. Therefore I urge you, imitate me. For this reason I have sent Timothy to you, who is my beloved and faithful son in the Lord, who will remind you of my ways in Christ, as I teach everywhere in every church"* (1 Cor. 4:14-17).

The word "instructors" used here is the Greek word *padagogos* which means a boy-leader who was one whose function was to take children to school and as one who was involved in the training and discipline of children, but not in the impartation of knowledge. Yes, we have many of these, but where are the true spiritual fathers? Where are those, who in alignment with the apostolic, are functioning as true spiritual fathers in the marketplace?

We notice the relationship between Paul and Timothy was one of an apostolic father relating to a spiritual son. Paul had mentored his faithful spiritual son and now Timothy was being sent to the Corinthians as one who had his father's DNA. Spiritual sons imitate their spiritual fathers and they mentor others to do the same.

Paul wrote Timothy saying, *"You therefore, my son, be strong in the grace that is in Christ Jesus. And the things that you have heard from me among many witnesses, commit these to faithful men who will be able to teach others also"* (2 Tim. 2:1-2).

Many feel that we are rapidly approaching the "day of the Lord" when Jesus will return for His Bride. God spoke through Malachi the prophet saying: *"Behold, I will send you Elijah the prophet before the coming of the great and dreadful day of the LORD. And he will turn the hearts of the fathers to the children, and the hearts of the children to their fathers, lest I come and strike the earth with a curse"* (Mal. 4:5-6).

His coming will be a great day for the church, the Bride of Christ, and all those who have made themselves ready.

However, it will be a dreadful day for so many who have not yet received Him both as their Savior and Lord. For the most part, those who have yet to be reached are not found within the walls of the local churches. Instead, they are in the marketplace, and this is where many will be reached for the Kingdom of God.

Malachi went on to refer to one, by the name "Elijah the prophet," being sent before the day of the coming of the Lord. Elijah was best known for the miracle-working anointing that was on his life. And even moreso, for his ability in the spirit to impart that same anointing in double-portion to his faithful spiritual son, Elisha. Elijah and Elisha had a close, personal relationship. Elisha would not let Elijah out of his sight until he could receive his anointing in double-portion. After Elijah was caught up into heaven, Elisha picked up his mantle, and with that mantle, imitated his spiritual father and parted the Jordan River.

"Now when the sons of the prophets who were from Jericho saw him, they said, 'The spirit of Elijah rests on Elisha...'"
(2 Kings 2:15)

It is interesting to note that while there were 14 miracles recorded in the ministry of Elijah, and with that double-portion anointing there were exactly twice as many, 28 miracles, recorded in the ministry of Elisha.

Today, our Father God is sending that same spirit of Elijah to turn the hearts of the fathers to the children, and the hearts of the children to their fathers. It is with that same spirit of Elijah that those in alignment with apostolic leadership are being sent into the marketplace, into the Seven Mountains of spiritual influence in society. Spiritual fathers and mothers are looking for faithful spiritual sons and daughters to mentor and impart into their lives so that they will function with an even greater, double-portion anointing both in the church and in the marketplace.

It is important to understand how one receives the father's anointing in double-portion. It is not enough to get a spiritual father to lay hands on us. It comes from an intimate, committed relationship over a period of time. One must be found worthy by being a faithful son, by being in spiritual alignment with an apostolic father. Only faithful sons can receive that double-portion anointing. Even as Elisha was a faithful son to Elijah, Gehazi could have been a faithful son to Elisha and could have received a double-portion anointing. But, Gehazi was not a faithful son.

Gehazi, the servant of Elisha the man of God, said, *"Look, my master has spared Naaman this Syrian, while not receiving from his hands what he brought; but as the LORD lives, I will run after him and take something from him"* (2 Kings 5:20).

Gehazi ran after the very financial gain Elisha had refused, and then he tried to hide it by lying to Elisha.

"Now he went in and stood before his master. And Elisha said to him, 'Where did you go, Gehazi?'

"And he said, 'Your servant did not go anywhere.'

"Then he said to him, 'Did not my heart go with you when the man turned back from his chariot to meet you? Is it time to receive money and to receive clothing, olive groves and vineyards, sheep and oxen, male and female servants? Therefore the leprosy of Naaman shall cling to you and your descendants forever.' And he went out from his presence leprous, as white as snow" (2 Kings 5:25-27).

Obviously, Gehazi could not receive the double-portion anointing from Elisha as Elisha had received from Elijah because he was not a faithful son. When Elisha died, he was buried with that fire (or anointing) still in his bones.

"Then Elisha died, and they buried him. And the raiding bands from Moab invaded the land in the spring of the year. So it was, as they were burying a man, that suddenly they spied a band of raiders; and they put the man in the tomb of Elisha; and when the man was let down and touched the bones of Elisha, he revived and stood on his feet" (2 Kings 13:20,21).

The prophet Jeremiah wrote of this fire, *"Then I said, 'I will not make mention of Him, nor speak anymore in His name.' But His word was in my heart like a burning fire shut up in my bones; I was weary of holding it back, and I could not"* (Jer. 20:9). And again when he wrote, *"From above He has sent fire into my bones..."* (Lam. 1:13a).

Anointed spiritual fathers and mothers have a fire in their bones that they should no longer hold back. They shouldn't be buried with that fire still in their bones. They need to pass it on in double-portion to faithful sons and daughters.

To receive the double-portion anointing, a spiritual son or daughter must come into a close relationship with the fathers and mothers of the faith, but this can only be done when the fathers, mothers, sons and daughters are all in spiritual alignment under the headship of Christ, the Anointed One.

"Behold, how good and how pleasant it is for brethren to dwell together in unity! It is like the precious oil upon the head, running down on the beard, the beard of Aaron, running down on the edge of his garments. It is like the dew of Hermon, Descending upon the mountains of Zion; For

there the LORD commanded the blessing - Life forevermore."
(Ps. 133:1-3)

When Aaron, the high priest was anointed, the oil was poured on his head, representing Christ, The Head of the Church, and The Anointed One. The oil then flowed down to his beard, representing spiritual fathers, and from there, all the way down to the bottom, or edge, of his garments. This pictures the anointing flowing down from Christ, being passed through spiritual fathers from generation to generation, or from double-portion to double-portion.

As the anointing oil flowed, it became thicker and thicker, and the anointing increased and increased, until it reached the hem of the garment. Matthew tells us that the multitudes reached out to touch the hem of Jesus' garments.

"And when the men of that place recognized Him,
they sent out into all that surrounding region, brought
to Him all who were sick, and begged Him that they
might only touch the hem of His garment. And as
many as touched it were made perfectly well."
(Matt. 14:35, 36)

When Aaron, the High Priest died, it is interesting to note, that they were not instructed by God, to anoint Aaron's son with oil. Instead, he was to wear the garments of his father for seven days.

And the holy garments of Aaron shall be his sons' after him, to be anointed in them and to be consecrated in them. That son who becomes priest in his place shall put them on for seven days, when he enters the tabernacle of meeting to minister in the holy place (Ex. 29:29,30).

In the realm of the Spirit, faithful spiritual sons are wearing their father's spiritual garments. It is all about the generational (from spiritual fathers and mothers to spiritual sons and daughters) increase or advancement of the Kingdom of God.

> *"Of the increase of His government and peace there will be no end, upon the throne of David and over His kingdom, to order it and establish it with judgment and justice from that time forward, even forever. The zeal of the LORD of hosts will perform this"*
> (Isa. 9:7)

Today, the spirit of Elijah that Malachi prophesied is turning the hearts of spiritual fathers and mothers to spiritual sons and daughters. No longer is the church to be considered an organization of man. Instead, it is to be about the Father God and his sons and daughters being in proper relationship to one another, and today this is being extended to the marketplace.

There are many who are still fatherless in the Kingdom of God. God sent Elijah to a fatherless family, and with the coming of the spirit of Elijah, a spiritual father, came a miracle of supernatural supply.

"God spoke to Elijah, 'Arise, go to Zarephath, which belongs to Sidon, and dwell there. See, I have commanded a widow there to provide for you.'

"So he arose and went to Zarephath. And when he came to the gate of the city, indeed a widow was there gathering sticks. And he called to her and said, 'Please bring me a little water in a cup that I may drink.' And as she was going to get it, he called to her and said, 'Please bring me a morsel of bread in your hand.'

"Then she said, 'As the LORD your God lives, I do not have bread, only a handful of flour in a bin, and a little oil in a jar; and see, I am gathering a couple of sticks that I may go in and prepare it for myself and my son, that we may eat it, and die.'

"And Elijah said to her, 'Do not fear; go and do as you have said, but make me a small cake from it first, and bring it to me; and afterward make some for yourself and your son. For thus says the LORD God of Israel: The bin of flour shall not be used up, nor shall the jar of oil run dry, until the day the LORD sends rain on the earth.'

"So she went away and did according to the word of Elijah; and she and he and her household ate for many days. The bin of flour was not used up, nor did the jar of oil run dry, according to the word of the LORD which He spoke by Elijah" (1 Kings 17:9-16).

The spirit of Elijah brings life back to dead sons. Upon the prophetic word of Elisha, the Shunammite woman had conceived and given birth to a son. When this son died later, Elisha brought life back to him.

"And when Elisha came into the house, there was the child, lying dead on his bed. He went in therefore, shut the door behind the two of them, and prayed to the LORD. And he went up and lay on the child, and put his mouth on his mouth, his eyes on his eyes, and his hands on his hands; and he stretched himself out on the child, and the flesh of the child became warm. He returned and walked back and forth in the house, and again went up and stretched himself out on him; then the child sneezed seven times, and the child opened his eyes. And he called Gehazi and said, 'Call this Shunammite woman.' So he called her. And when she came in to him, he said, 'Pick up your son'" (2 Kings 4:32-36).

Being in relationship with spiritual fathers can bring hope, faith, and spiritual and economic life back to sons and daughters in the marketplace. Prophetic downloads of heavenly wisdom can change situations from lack to abundance.

"A certain woman of the wives of the sons of the prophets cried out to Elisha, saying, "Your servant my husband is dead, and you know that your servant feared the LORD. And the creditor is coming to take my two sons to be his slaves."

"So Elisha said to her, 'What shall I do for you? Tell me, what do you have in the house?'

"And she said, 'Your maidservant has nothing in the house but a jar of oil.'

"Then he said, 'Go, borrow vessels from everywhere, from all your neighbors—empty vessels; do not gather just a few. And when you have come in, you shall shut the door behind you and your sons; then pour it into all those vessels, and set aside the full ones.' So she went from him and shut the door behind her and her sons, who brought the vessels to her; and she poured it out.

"Now it came to pass, when the vessels were full, that she said to her son, 'Bring me another vessel.' And he said to her, 'There is not another vessel.' So the oil ceased. Then she came and told the man of God. And he said, 'Go, sell the oil and pay your debt; and you and your sons live on the rest'" (2 Kings 4:1-7).

Being aligned with apostolic/prophetic spiritual leaders has resulted in many examples of desperate financial situations being turned into a release of great wealth in the marketplace. The wisdom of spiritual fathers, divine connections, heavenly downloads of creative ideas, and words of wisdom can open the doors to abundant, Kingdom-advancing finances, to those who are aligned with spiritual fathers in the marketplace. Empty vessels are being filled with the oil (anointing) of the Holy Spirit. Godly wisdom from these spiritual fathers can give the keys needed to reposition oneself into experiencing God's richest blessing.

Isaac proved God's faithfulness in the time of famine. *"There was a famine in the land, besides the first famine that was in the days of Abraham.. Then Isaac sowed in that land, and reaped in the same year a hundredfold; and the LORD blessed him. The man began to prosper, and continued prospering until he became very prosperous; for he had possessions of flocks and possessions of herds and a great number of servants. So the Philistines envied him"* (Gen. 26:1, 12-14).

Abraham had taught his physical and spiritual son, Isaac, how to enter into the blessings of abundant Kingdom finances. Many are discovering abundant spiritual blessings by being in alignment and listening to their spiritual fathers. Those who are faithful sons and daughters have learned how to sow mentoring seeds into the lives of their sons and daughters. They have discovered the power of sowing greater and greater financial seeds into the Kingdom of God. With the blessing of God, we can sow in time of famine (financial recession), and reap in the same year a hundredfold.

Others, who may have started out in the marketplace with some degree of success, seemed to have lost their "cutting edge" and are faced with economic downturns. Apostolic/ Prophetic fathers and mothers can help their sons and daughters get back their edge in the marketplace.

"And the sons of the prophets said to Elisha, 'See now, the place where we dwell with you is too small for us. Please, let us go to the Jordan, and let every man take a beam from there, and let us make there a place where we may dwell.'

"And he answered, 'Go.'

"Then one said, 'Please consent to go with your servants.'

"And he answered, 'I will go.' So he went with them. And when they came to the Jordan, they cut down trees.

"But as one was cutting down a tree, the iron ax head fell into the water; and he cried out and said, 'Alas, master! For it was borrowed.'

"And the man of God said, 'Where did it fall?' And he showed him the place. So he cut off a stick, and threw it in there; and he made the iron float. Therefore he said, 'Pick it up for yourself.' So he reached out his hand and took it'" (2 Kings 6:1-7).

This son had lost his cutting edge. But Elisha became involved in helping him, by first of all asking him, "Where did you lose it?" Once the young man could tell him where he had lost it, he could tell him how to get back his ax head. Notice, Elisha told the young man, "Pick it up for yourself." Spiritual fathers and mothers can impart the anointing into faithful sons and daughters; they can impart godly wisdom, but then these sons and daughters must take it up for themselves.

There is a God-given power when we come into proper alignment with the apostolic fathers and mothers who mentor and give godly wisdom to spiritual sons and daughters. There is a new ability as many have reached out and picked it up for themselves. They have gotten back their cutting edge in the marketplace. They have found themselves in the midst of abundant spiritual and financial blessing.

There is a new generation of faithful sons and daughters who are arising with a double-portion anointing. They are taking back the Seven Mountains of Influence in our culture and forcibly advancing the Kingdom of God in this great end-time harvest.

ABOUT THE AUTHOR

Dr. A.L. Gill is a #1, best-selling author and publisher with more than 20 million of his books in print around the world. A.L.'s first book, *God's Promises for Your Every Need*, in its various editions, has sold over 20 million copies. He has authored many other books also. His teaching and training materials in books, manuals, DVDs and CDs are in tremendous demand.

Dr. Gill's manuals are available in many languages. His 10-hour, International School of Ministry video course, "Supernatural Living and Healing through the Gifts of the Holy Spirit," is available in almost 70 languages. Already, 300,000 believers have been trained in over 15,000 training sites in close to 150 nations. Many are now continuing with his new 32-hour "Miracle Living" module, which includes five additional courses as part of the largest video Bible school in the world.

A.L.'s ministry travels have taken him to over 80 nations, establishing churches and Bible schools and preaching to crowds of hundreds of thousands. Through his apostolic ministry, he is known affectionately as "Papa Gill" to ministries and churches around the world.

He is known for his miracle ministry, and for his practical, life-changing preaching and teaching of the Word of God. His teaching, through manuals, video and audio courses, is Jesus-centered, Word-based, faith-filled and taught in the power of the Holy Spirit and in the love and compassion of Jesus.

A.L. has both a Masters and Ph.D. degree in Theology. His preaching and teaching of the Word is continually being confirmed with many remarkable signs, wonders and healing miracles.

To learn more or contact him, visit his website at www. gillministries.com or email him at papagill@gillministries. com.

CHAPTER FORTY-SIX

APOSTOLIC MOTHERS

SHARON BILLINS

According to Wikipedia, a mother is a woman who has raised a child, given birth to a child, and/or supplied the ovum that united with a sperm which grew into a child. There is no more noble work than that of a good and God-fearing mother.

David McKay stated the following: "Motherhood is the greatest potential influence either for good or ill in human life. The mother's image is the first that stamps itself on the unwritten page of the young child's mind. It is her caress that first awakens a sense of security; her kiss, the first realization of affection and compassion; her sympathy and tenderness, the first assurance that there is love in the world." Motherhood consists of four principal attributes or qualities, namely: 1) the power to bear, 2) the ability to rear, 3) the gift to love, 4) the gift to teach and educate. McKay added, "That mother who rears successfully a family of healthy, beautiful sons and daughters deserves the highest honor that man can give, and the choice blessings of God."[1]

On September 28, 2012, *Good Morning America* ran a segment entitled "Is There a Gene for Motherhood?"

ABC News anchors JuJu Chang and Mary Pflum reported the following information. It was said that researchers at

Rockefeller University did a study with mice and determined that a single gene exists that could be responsible for motivating mothers to protect, feed, and raise their young. The study's findings mean there could be a valid explanation as to why some women seem born to be maternal figures, while others come across as detached or cold or even completely not interested when it comes to children. Some are calling the discovery the "mommy gene."

I believe that the Lord has placed a "spiritual mommy gene" in designated godly women across the world. This special gene allows these Apostolic Mothers to position themselves as spiritual mothers who aid in the rearing of spiritual children in their lives.

Ps. 87:2-3 says, *"The LORD loves the gates of Zion more than all the dwellings of Jacob. Glorious things are said of you, O City of God."* Zion is the city of David and the city of God. In Isaiah 60:14, Zion is used figuratively as the people of God. Many in the body of Christ have called their spiritual mother, Mother of Zion, Mom, Mother, or Mother in the Lord. In this chapter we will call the spiritual mother an Apostolic Mother.

An Apostolic Mother is a spiritual mother to many sons and daughters in the kingdom of God upon this earth. This term is a metaphor for the loving, caring, patient and nurturing relationship that God has with His children.

CASE STUDY:
MARY, THE MOTHER OF JESUS

We will examine the life of Mary (the Mother of Jesus) to use as an example of a true Apostolic Mother, and the processes involved therewith. Following are some of the steps she experienced during her life in the order that they occurred:

1. **Impregnation** – Mary is impregnated with the seed of that Holy Thing which is Jesus Christ, the Savior (Luke 1 & 2).

    Many Apostolic Mothers are dispersed throughout this world. They are the seed carriers of great destinies in this land. It takes an Apostolic Mother to carry an apostolic seed. Heb. 3:1 says, *"Wherefore, holy brethren, partakers of the heavenly calling, consider the Apostle and High Priest of our profession, Christ Jesus."* They possess the DNA that connects or attracts to the DNA of their spiritual son or daughter. It does not matter the color of skin, race or gender. What matters is the potential to birth out purpose in someone else's life. Age, culture, and economic background do not factor into the equation of spiritual mothering as well.

    If you are willing and able, then God will impregnate you with an anointing that prepares you to become an Apostolic Mother. This mothering seed contains the innate ability to exert supernatural power during the spiritual birthing process, the ability to raise up and help you comfort, nurture and teach spiritual sons and/or daughters to mature spiritually, and to provide spiritual counseling and guidance throughout their life.

    Ask yourself these questions: "Lord, what am I pregnant with spiritually? Lord can you help me to birth out divine purpose on this earth?"

2. **Gestation** – Mary makes an extended visit to her relative, Elizabeth, who was also pregnant (Luke 1:39-56). This is the Gestation period of Jesus Christ, that

holy thing being fully developed in Mary's womb. Then, and even now, traditional customs would dictate that unwed pregnant teenagers are to be sent away to await the time of delivery of the baby. God will allow us to be positioned with people who have experienced similar testimonies to our own. These people can serve as encouragers and comforters to let us know that we are not alone in what we are experiencing.

There are thousands of Apostolic Mothers who have birthed out destinies of sons and daughters in many parts of the world. God will also strategically place sons and daughters in places whereby they can be "hidden" from the enemy. It is in this place that the Lord allows His process of gestation of purpose to be fully established within that son or daughter.

When that son or daughter comes into contact with that Apostolic Mother, there will be a leaping of their "baby" or purpose in their spiritual womb. When the apostolic mother gives them a salutation, their baby will leap in their womb and they will become instantly connected to the anointing that lies within the mantle of their spiritual mother.

Many times, various spiritual sons and daughters will call me periodically. They will leave a message and say.... "Hello Mom, I miss you and just wanted to hear your voice." A true apostolic mother will have an innate desire and ability to answer the cry of her spiritual children. The Holy Spirit will prompt you when you need to communicate by phone, email or make a visit to your spiritual children. Ask yourself the following question: Can I allow myself to walk in a new level of grace that will enable me to make time for an extended spiritual family? Lord, allow me to pray for those sons and daughters that belong to me.

3. **Presentation and Dedication** – of the baby Jesus – (Luke 2:21-40). Prior to His dedication, Jesus was circumcised. An Apostolic Mother out of love and concern helps in circumcising their children (if the father is not available) — the cutting away of the flesh. There must be a cutting away of the flesh in order that the Spirit will reign in our lives. An example of this is Zipporah, the wife of Moses, when she took the knife to circumcise their sons the night before God was about to kill Moses for failing to do so and exercise his fatherly responsibility in their family.

Mary and Joseph presented the Christ Child to a righteous man and righteous woman of God. Simeon was a devout follower of Christ and Anna was a Prophetess who interceded daily concerning the things of God. One of the foremost responsibilities of an Apostolic Mother is to ensure that their spiritual son and daughter are commissioned into the kingdom via laying on of hands, verbal commissioning, or ordination and licensing. There are too many spiritual orphans in the Kingdom of God who are running wild because they have no spiritual parents in the Lord. The Apostolic Mother makes sure that the proper steps are taken, that will give credibility to their son's or daughter's calling on their life.

Ask yourself the following questions? Do I have true spiritual accountability in my life? Lord, is there someone who I can help birth out purpose in their life? Lord, where are the sons and daughters that belong in my life and can I ensure that they have the proper earthly credentials to walk in their spiritual calling?

4. **Sequestration** – Mary and Joseph protected Jesus from the spiritual abortionists of that hour which included King Herod. Herod's order was to kill all baby boys under the age of two, similar to Pharaoh's order when Moses was born. God sent an angel to warn Mary and Joseph of this sinister plot, and they took the baby Jesus into Egypt. Jesus was hidden in Egypt just as Moses was hidden in the basket of bulrushes and then in the palace. The Lord will hide his treasures until it's time for them to be presented to the world. Thank God for true apostolic mothers who are able to spiritually protect the God-given destinies of their children in the Lord.

5. **Maturation** – Mary Expresses Love and Concern for Jesus. When Jesus was 12, and one year shy of Jewish manhood and Bar Mitzvah, Mary and Joseph took him to Jerusalem. Jesus went missing, and when his parents finally located him in the Temple, Mary was understandably concerned. She confronted Jesus, asking, *"Son, why have you thus dealt with us? Behold, your father and I have sought you in sorrow"* (Luke 2:48).

I must pause here for the sake of all mothers. If I had been Mary, Jesus the child would have gotten a good spanking on that day. Thank God for Mary. Smile. He would have gotten a piece of my mind and a piece of something else. That's all I have to say on that. Well, needless to say, both Mary and Joseph were upset. Jesus answered by asking her how she could not know that he was about his Father's business.

An Apostolic Mother expects their spiritual son or daughter to be held accountable to them. We as disciples of Christ must be accountable to Jesus and to our spiritual mother/father on earth. The Apostolic

Mother's job is to display concern and understanding of their spiritual child's Kingdom assignment and coming of spiritual age. Also, as an Apostolic Mother, we must know when to cut the apron strings to allow our spiritual children to walk in their God-given callings. Ask yourself this question: Have I been holding onto this person too long? Is it time to release them and trust them in this God-given assignment?

6. **Activation** – Mary Asks Jesus' Help at Cana – John 2. At the wedding at Cana, where Mary and Jesus were guests, the host family ran out of wine during the celebration. Mary did not ask for a miracle, but that's what Jesus performed when he turned water into wine, his first miracle. And the wine was of exceptional quality according to John 2:10. *"His mother said to the servants, 'Whatever he says to you, do it.' And there were set there six water pots of stone...Jesus said to them, 'Fill the water pots with water.' And they filled them up to the brim.....When the ruler of the feast had tasted the water that was made wine, and knew not whence it was: (but the servants which drew the water knew;) the governor of the feast called the bridegroom..."* (John 2:5-7, 9).

Activation of Destiny. The true Apostolic Mother walks in a spirit of boldness when it comes to her spiritual son or daughter. The Apostolic Mothers place a demand on their sons and daughters at certain times or seasons of their maturation process because they know what their offspring carry and what is in their spiritual DNA and their destiny and identity. It is their God-given duty to recognize the gift and the anointing that is upon their children. All weddings are to celebrate and Mary's request to her son on this family occasion, activated the miracle power and anointing resident (abiding) in her son.

There are times that a mother bird must push the baby bird out of the nest so that they can fly on their own. Thank God for the mothers who taught us how to tie our own shoe, make our own bed, put on our own clothes, brush our teeth and so forth. *"Train up a child when he is young, and when he is old he shall not depart from it"* (Prov. 22:6). Ask yourself this question: As a potential Apostolic Mother, am I willing to walk in boldness and recognize and push forward my spiritual children in their gifts and callings?

7. **Separation** – Mary Suffers and Stands Vigil at the Cross. After Jesus' three-year ministry ended with his passion and crucifixion, Mary stood vigil at the foot of his cross near the Beloved disciple, Mary Magdalene, and others. Jesus addressed Mary from the cross, saying, *"Woman, behold thy son!"* This referred not to himself, but to John the beloved. He told John, *"Behold thy mother"* (John 19:26-27). There comes a time in all of our lives that we too must bear the cross as Jesus did. The Apostolic Mother's role at this stage is to be in a posture of praying for God's grace upon their spiritual son and/or daughter.

An Apostolic Mother cannot bear the cross for the one in whom divine purpose has been birthed out. Our job as Apostolic Mothers is to encourage, edify, comfort and nurture our spiritual children during God's processing of them in their calling. Matt. 16:24 (JPB) says, *"If anyone wants to follow in my footsteps, he must give up all right to himself, take up his cross and follow me."*

Also, this stage of the process represents Jesus giving instructions to John to take care of his mother. So, John becomes the son in the place of Jesus because he now is being exalted through dying to sit on the right hand of the Father. Many sons and daughters will be promoted by the hand of God, through persecution and sufferings and must go on to produce their own sons and daughters in the spirit of multiplication.

Ask yourself these questions: Can I provide the necessary counsel and encouragement needed for my spiritual children when they have to bear their own cross? At the time of separation, can I let go, in order that promotion will come to my spiritual children?

8. **Multiplication** – Mary Joins Others in the Upper Room (Acts 1). The Apostolic Mother recognizes her human limitations. Mary, the mother of Jesus, understood that in order to truly be one with Jesus, she would have to clothe herself in humility and pray in the upper room with the other 119 disciples. Their prayers were answered and Mary and the others were baptized in the power of the Holy Ghost and fire by a sudden outpouring of God's spirit. A true Apostolic Mother prays for their spiritual sons and daughters to walk fully in the mantle upon their lives.

The Apostolic Mother is willing to eat the pure fruit of the children that she has birthed out. As Jesus poured out His Spirit upon them, it caused Mary to become an Apostolic Mother of the Apostolic Movement which was birthed out on the day of Pentecost. In Acts 1:14, all of the disciples' names are listed and Mary is the only female whose name is written and they recognize her as the mother of Jesus. Praise God for the fruit.

In John 15:16 the Lord says that He has chosen us that we will produce fruit and that our fruit would remain. Ask yourself the following questions: Am I willing to humble myself and receive from the wine that is produced from the spiritual children who were mentored by me? Am I willing for my children to go further in the Lord than I have been, or to have greater callings or destinies than me?

OTHER BIBLICAL EXAMPLES

I must mention that there are also other types of Apostolic Mothers mentioned in the scriptures. In the story of Ruth, Naomi taught her daughter-in-law Ruth, a Moabitess, the ways and customs of her people, the Jews, and discerned and gave Ruth strategy and timing to go in at night and lie next to her kinsman-redeemer Boaz at his feet. This was far more than playing matchmaker, as Jesus came through the lineage of Ruth. Their son was Obed, father of Jesse, father of David. Other biblical examples of Apostolic Mothers include Lydia, a seller of purple in Philippi, who after she and her household received Christ from the teaching of Paul, invited him and his companions to stay with her, and also the local church met in her house on a regular basis.

Aquila and Priscilla were sent by Paul to Ephesus, where they imparted to and taught Apollos a more excellent way, since he only knew and taught the baptism of John. Priscilla served as an Apostolic Mother for Apollos, an eloquent teacher and evangelist and Hellenistic Jew. Later Priscilla and Aquila led a church in their home in Rome (Rom. 16:3-5) and were publicly thanked by Paul for risking their lives for him. He went on to say that all the churches of the Gentiles owed them a debt of gratitude. Apostolic Mothers are birthed and called by God in many different ways. The Holy Spirit will choose you when it is time for you to assume your position as an Apostolic Mother to new sons and daughters.

PRAYER OF IMPARTATION & ACTIVATION OF THE APOSTOLIC MOTHERING MANTLE

Dear Lord, I receive this new mantle that will cause me to become a true Apostolic Mother to the sons and daughters that you release into my life. Impart to me, wisdom, knowledge, understanding, counsel, love, compassion, gentleness and kindness. Thank you Lord for an anointing that transcends gender, race, age and any or all other barriers preventing my sons and daughters from fully becoming who you have called them to be. Thank you Lord for empowering me with perseverance, patience and insight that will allow me to mentor, train and equip my spiritual children to be all that they can be through Christ Jesus who strengthens them. In Jesus' name I pray, Amen.

ENDNOTES

1. David O. McKay, *Gospel Ideals*, pp. 453-54. Salt Lake City, UT: An Improvement Era Publication, 1954.

ABOUT THE AUTHOR

Apostle Sharon Billins is the CEO and Founder of Palm Tree International Ministries, Inc., which serves as the spiritual covering for many churches and ministries. She is the Senior Pastor of The Remnant Church of Columbus, Ga. and The Remnant Church of Tallahassee, Fla. President and Founder of The Samuel School of the Prophets, she holds a B.S. degree in Chemistry from Florida State University.

Reverend Billins worked as a Chemical Engineer for 10 years and has taught in the Public School System. She has over 27 years of experience in management, supervision and training. She is a past business owner, having been the CEO of Diversified Training Systems. She has worked as a Consultant/ Instructor for the Georgia Department of Technical and Adult Education and the Pastoral Institute Business Resource Center. She also served as a Hospital Chaplain at St. Francis Hospital and is a graduate of the Clinical Pastoral Education Unit at St. Francis Hospital. She is also a graduate of the Pastoral Care Specialist Program at the Turner Clergy Center of the Pastoral Institute. Reverend Billins served as the first female President of the Muscogee County Clergy Association. She also served as the Chairperson of the Columbus Prison Task Force.

She is an outstanding speaker and energetic professional who is committed to service. She has hosted numerous conferences and workshops and has presented at many local events. Reverend Billins is active in community affairs and has sat on the Board of Directors and Governing Councils for many community organizations. She received an Honorary Doctorate in Divinity in 2012 for her humanitarian work from Kingdom Bible Institute, San Bernardino, Calif. To learn more or to contact her, visit her website at www. sharon-billins.org.

SECTION VIII

APOSTOLIC LEADERSHIP & TEAMS

CHAPTER FORTY-SEVEN

NEW PERSPECTIVES ON APOSTOLIC LEADERSHIP

DICK AND DR. ARLEEN WESTERHOF

One of our new church members gave us a compliment recently. He said that one of the first things he and his wife noticed when they started attending was that we do not treat our members like victims, even those with the most traumatic backgrounds. Everyone is in a growth process and moving towards wholeness, healing and their destinies. While some are further along than others, everyone is seen as someone with the potential to exert influence for good, whether it's in their own family or as a leader of a multinational corporation.

Genesis 1:26-28 is known as the "Kingdom Mandate": *"Then God said, 'Let Us make man in Our image, according to Our likeness; let them have dominion over the fish of the sea, over the birds of the air, and over the cattle, over all the earth and over every creeping thing that creeps on the earth. So God created man in His own image; in the image of God He created him, male and female He created them. Then God blessed them, and God said to them, 'Be fruitful and multiply; fill the earth and subdue it; have dominion over the fish of the sea, over the birds of the air and over every living thing that moves on the ground."* In essence, it says that every individual has the seed of greatness within them because we are created in God's image and because God has given us dominion over the earth.

This lies at the root of what Jesus referred to as the *"gospel of the kingdom"* (Matt. 4:23; 9:35; Mark 1:14). With it, God is restoring the truth back to the church that we have been given authority. This is a fundamentally different view than the church-based paradigm that we have had since the Protestant Reformation almost 500 years ago.

Dr. Bill Hamon, the founder and leader of Christian International, calls this new era we are currently in the "Third Apostolic Reformation." The First Apostolic Reformation occurred when Jesus came to earth. In it, God restored the truth that Jesus was, and is, the fulfillment of all of the law and the prophets (Luke 24:44; John 1:45). The second occurred with Martin Luther and the Protestant Reformation. The truth restored here was that we are saved by grace through faith and not by our own works (Eph. 2: 8-9). In the Third Apostolic Reformation, God is restoring the truth that apostles, prophets, evangelists, pastors and teachers are meant to equip believers for works of service (Eph. 4:11, 12). No longer will it just be "the anointed man or woman of God" who gets to minister. All of God's saints get to participate in God's Kingdom. This is going to require a radical change in how apostolic leaders think and act. Making this change, however, is imperative. If we do not, we will not see the Kingdom of God manifesting in and transforming our nations as God intended.

THE KINGDOM OF GOD
IS BIGGER THAN THE CHURCH

The Gospel of the Kingdom, which Jesus preached, says that we are called and anointed to infiltrate every sphere of society with God's glory and not just the Church. We have to move from a Church-based paradigm to one which is Kingdom-based. If God gave some to be apostles, prophets, evangelists, pastors and teachers (Eph. 4:11), then it means that most are not called to function in these ministries within the context of full-time ministry in the church.

Dick: Several years ago a fellow pastor who leads a large church in our city came to talk to me about discipleship. He was struggling and said, "I don't know what to do! God keeps giving me people with leadership ability, but there are only a limited number of leadership positions in the church. What am I supposed to tell them?" I cannot remember what I replied but I do remember what I thought: "Then send them to me!"

Arleen: When I applied to go to university, my pastor at that time tried to dissuade me. He told me that if I really loved God I would go to Bible school.

These days we discourage many of our church members from attending Bible School. We're not against Bible schools. Many young people, however, are not called to go to Bible School. Studying graphic design or studying for an MBA is just as much "equipping the saints for the work of the ministry" as is going to Bible School for those who are called to these areas.

THE SIN OF THE NICOLAITANS

Jesus talked about the Nicolaitans twice in the book of Revelation. Rev. 2:6 says, *"But this you have, that you hate the deeds of the Nicolaitans which I also hate."* Rev. 2:15 adds, *"Thus you also have those who hold the doctrine of the Nicolaitans which thing I hate."*

Jesus says that He hates both the teaching and the deeds of the Nicolaitans. The word "Nicolaitan" is made up of two parts – "Nikos" which means to overcome and to dominate and "Laos" which means the common people, or laity.

The Nicolaitans were a group of leaders who placed themselves above the laity and lorded it over them. The Nicolaitans had the knowledge and training to lead but they kept the laity ignorant and unable to walk out their callings. Unfortunately, things have not changed that much since then. While this is especially evident in the Roman Catholic and Greek orthodox churches, it is also present in our Protestant churches. In both traditional and Pentecostal churches, it is considered normal for pastors to position themselves above the laity. This was never God's intention.

1 Pet. 5:2-3 says, *"Shepherd the flock of God which is among you, serving as overseers, not by compulsion but willingly, not for dishonest gain but eagerly; nor as being lords over those entrusted to you, but being examples to the flock."* The Bible is clear; leaders should not lord it over those entrusted to their care. Apostolic leaders who think that their people are only sheep that need to be led are missing a large and very important part of God's plan.

John Maxwell says that "leadership is influence."[1] In this sense, every church member is called to be a leader and to advance the Kingdom of God in their sphere of influence.

Pastors are leaders in the Religion mountain. The word "mountain" here refers to one of the seven societal spheres of influence that determine our thoughts and our actions (religion, family, business, education, government, media, arts and entertainment). In our congregations, we have both leaders in the other mountains as well as those called to those mountains. Their callings are no less valuable than ours as pastors.

Our assignment as apostolic leaders is to encourage and to stimulate their spiritual growth and to facilitate, where possible, their equipping so that they can enter and ascend the mountain(s) that they are called to. When we start to treat people as (potential) influencers, we will no longer stand alone at the top of our mountain. Instead, we will stand side by side with our members advancing the Kingdom of God in all of the mountains of influence in our nations.

The changes required in our perspectives will, however, be difficult for many leaders to embrace, since they require a high degree of emotional maturity and another leadership style. For those who are not able to make this change, God will raise up new leaders who can.

HELPING PEOPLE BECOME ALL THEY ARE MEANT TO BE

One of the reasons why a higher degree of emotional maturity is going to be needed is that if we are called to equip the saints for the work of ministry, then it is no longer about us as apostolic leaders. It is about those we are called to serve and to equip. For many years now the Church has emphasized the importance of "serving the man or woman of God." We have encouraged people to put leaders on pedestals to become like us instead of discovering their own unique gifts and talents. The problem is that we have thought this way for so long that we think it's normal.

Almost eight years ago we started the church we pastor. Three years after we started, we consulted a church-growth specialist. When we told him that our key motivation for starting Embassy was to help people become all that they're meant to be by empowering them to have impact wherever God placed them, he just shook his head and looked at us. He then said, "You might as well close the church now. It will never work. You can't grow a church if people aren't willing to serve you and your vision." Instead, God has done exactly the opposite. The church is growing explosively as people hear what we are about and their hearts tell them that this is what they have been waiting for all of their lives!

It is important to note that this message also appeals to non-Christians. Last year we bought our own building. One of the two men who we employed to help us with this was not a believer at the time that we hired him. One day we invited him to attend a conference that we were hosting in order to get a first-hand view of what we wanted to use the building for. During the morning meeting he heard that God had created him with a purpose in mind. This was a new idea for him. Later, at another conference, he asked Christ into his heart during a prophetic presbytery.

While waiting on the Lord for revelation about his gifts and callings, the team got Rev. 3:20 for him, *"Behold, I stand at the door and knock. If anyone hears My voice and opens the door, I will come in to him and dine with him, and he with me."* That day he opened the door of his heart to Jesus. Even non-believers know in their hearts that they are here on the earth for a reason. In our opinion, this is one of the key ways in which the Church will become relevant in the future.

While there is a danger that some people will become too focused on themselves and on their callings, our experience has shown that the vast majority do not. They turn right back around and use their gifts to serve others. This was always God's intention when He said through Peter, *"As each one has received a gift, minister it to one another, as good stewards of the manifold grace of God"* (1 Pet. 4: 10).

MARKETPLACE LEADERS

From the time we started the church we pastor, God made it clear to us that He wanted us to do things differently. It started with Him choosing us to pastor the church. Neither of us went to Bible school or studied theology. We have a Master's degree in Civil Engineering (Dick) and a Ph.D. in Chemistry (Arleen). This means that we were not trained to think within the usual confines that pastors traditionally have.

Since "like attracts like" in the relational sphere, it means that many of the leaders in the church are marketplace ministers. An example of this is our church's apostolic leadership team, which is made up of several apostles, one prophet and a teacher. Everyone on the team has either had their own business in the past, or currently owns and runs their own business. This creates an atmosphere in which people are not afraid to initiate things and to take well-calculated risks. In the past four years, many church members have started their own businesses and several have started foundations. One of these is the Dutch Art Academy. The woman who started it has the vision to see a new generation of Christian Dutch Masters like Rembrandt and Vermeer come forth and take the arts mountain for God.

This is also true for the apostolic network that Dick leads. The majority of those who attend are marketplace leaders and are not involved in full-time paid ministry.

Arleen: I will never forget the day we learned just how important it is to acknowledge marketplace leaders. Several years ago at one of our first conferences, I talked to a businessman during one of the breaks. We had not seen each other for a while. I had, however, called and invited him to come because I felt that God was going to do something special for him there. We talked and he told me that he was thinking of retiring. I asked him if he would let me prophesy over him. As I waited, God said, "Tell him that I have called him to be a business apostle and that it is not his time to retire." When I told him this he started to cry. He then said something that broke my heart: "I have been a believer for 40 years now and have always felt like a second-class citizen because I am in business and not in full-time ministry. I now realize that that is exactly what I'm supposed to be doing!"

It was a simple revelation. It has, however, had a tremendous impact on his life. He went back home and resigned as an elder in his church. At the time of that conversation, he owned two small family businesses. In the four years since then, he has started eight more businesses, his inventory turnover and profits have skyrocketed, and he is busy funding large-scale projects that are advancing the Kingdom of God worldwide – and all of this in a time of deep economic crisis!

CREATING A CULTURE OF LEADERSHIP

If we say that we want to help people to use their influence for good, then we have to train them in how to do it. Within our church, we try to create a culture of leadership by offering leadership training courses throughout the whole year. These courses are open to everyone. They do not have to hold a leadership position in the church in order to be eligible.

This has had amazing results. A much larger group of people have started to think and to act like leaders, both inside and outside of the church. An increasing number of people are getting promoted in their jobs and several have started their own companies. Our church is also benefitting because people are stepping up to the plate and taking responsibility for different aspects of the ministry.

Making leadership training available to such a large group has also had a very positive effect on the unity within the church. Throughout the years, we have had very few disagreements about the decisions that we have made. Because such a large group now thinks like leaders, they understand much better why and how we make our decisions.

LEVEL 5 LEADERSHIP

In his book *Good to Great*, Jim Collins describes his findings on the factors responsible for exceptional performance in organizations throughout the generations.[2] It turned out that the number one factor contributing to a sustained high level of performance is Level 5 leadership. Collins defines Level 5 leaders as "those who build enduring greatness through a paradoxical blend of personal humility and professional will." They are humble people who do not claim credit for their successes. Instead, they give the credit to their teams. They are also the first to take the blame when things go wrong. Interestingly enough, many people outside of their own organizations do not even know their names because they do not seek the limelight. Instead, they tend to avoid it when they can. They are too busy empowering and encouraging others to move forward.

This image of an effective leader flies in the face of what we usually think of when we think of apostolic leaders – charismatic personalities who thrive on being in the limelight. One thing that we love about Collins' book is that it is based on research findings and not on his opinions. The data show conclusively that organizations run by leaders with larger-than-life personalities only thrive as long as the leader is there. As soon as they leave, however, the performance of the organization drops dramatically.

Often larger-than-life leaders will not take the time to think about succession. When they do, they very often set their successors up, whether consciously or unconsciously, for failure due to nepotism or by sabotaging the successors. King Saul is a classic example of this type of behavior. When he heard the women of Israel singing *"Saul has slain his thousands, and David his tens of thousands,"* he became very angry; *"...the saying displeased him; and he said, 'They have ascribed to David ten thousands and to me they have ascribed only thousands. Now what more can he have but the kingdom?' So Saul eyed David from that day forward"* (1 Sam. 18:8-9). Jealousy sets in and they instinctively act to claim and protect what they feel is rightfully theirs.

Level 5 leaders are not spineless. They are strong, visionary leaders who have learned to subject their egos to a greater cause. Becoming a Level 5 leader does not just happen on its own. It does not matter how talented you are. Only those who make a conscious choice to receive emotional healing will have a chance at becoming a Level 5 leader.

The more healing we receive, the more we will be able to rejoice sincerely at the successes of others without feeling threatened by them.

EMPOWERMENT IS ONLY POSSIBLE WHEN WE HAVE A LOVE ENCOUNTER WITH THE FATHER

While hurting people hurt people, hurting leaders hurt many people because of the level of responsibility that God has given them. Unhealed emotional pain causes leaders to be controlling and to not empower or release others. Their emotional wounds cause them to be more driven by a need for adulation and affirmation from people than from God. They are constantly afraid that the church may like someone else better than them. They become performance-oriented and use people to build their own kingdoms. The degree of spiritual abuse that occurs within churches as a result is tragic to witness. Sadly, we hear about these types of situations almost every week.

Several years ago a friend of ours suggested that we host a week-long Father Heart School in Amsterdam. At the time, we were not enthusiastic. We considered Father Heart Schools as something that was good for people with pastoral counseling issues, but not necessary or valuable for those of us who were "normal." By the time the week was over, however, we had changed our tune and had done a 180-degree turn in our attitude. Preaching and talking about the Father's love is totally different from experiencing it yourself.

Encountering the Father's love allows us to live lives that are transparent. We can live freely knowing that we have nothing to prove to anyone, nothing to lose and nothing to hide. Being secure in the love of the Father allows us to rejoice sincerely when others succeed and to live every day with the heart revelation that God says the same thing to us that He said to Jesus, *"You are My dearly loved son (or daughter) and you bring Me great joy!"* (Mark 1:11).

FEEDBACK: DON'T AVOID IT. WELCOME IT!

The Gospel is holistic. This means that it is not enough for us just to be able to function well in ministry. All of the areas of our lives need to be in order. Psychologists say that the number one key to aiding personal growth is being able to give and receive accurate feedback. Unfortunately, we had to learn the hard way how crucially essential this is.

Before we started our church, we were assistant pastors in another large, fast-growing church on the outskirts of the city. Four months after we started there, a scandal erupted around the senior pastor in this church. He was not only the senior pastor, but also the leader of our denomination. He had been dishonest in his business dealings and had cheated several people, especially church members, out of a lot of money. We, too, lost a large amount financially. Unfortunately, he never repented and the whole denomination fell apart.

While we were licking our wounds and helping others to work through their own pain, we had to ask ourselves some hard questions: "How could this have happened and why didn't we see it coming?" As we thought and prayed about things, one thing kept coming up again and again: in that church no one was allowed to voice criticism. As soon as they did, they became the problem and not the thing(s) that they were concerned about. This became even more obvious when soon after the scandal broke, friends of ours, a married couple who pastored a church 45 minutes from where we live, were fired by the elders of their church. The vote was unanimous. The elders and the members had had enough of their behavior.

To say we were shocked would be an understatement. This couple was young and they were strong, visionary leaders. We got along well with them because we were just like them in many respects. Dick went to one of their members' meetings during this period and he didn't have to listen very long to discover what had happened. The church had fired our friends because they had consistently refused to listen to criticism and were domineering in their leadership style. They had justified their behavior by saying that God had given them the vision and appointed them as leaders. They therefore did not have to discuss how things were going to be done. This was a wake-up call for us. We knew if we did not learn how to communicate differently with our leadership team, and with our members, that in a few years we, too, could be voted out!

We were fortunate, however, that at that time we had a psychologist in our leadership team, whose specialty was communication. For a year and a half he trained our team in how to confront us and give us feedback about how we were acting. He also trained us in how to receive their criticism without getting defensive.

Arleen: When we started this process, I was concerned that it would lead to a lot of negativity in the team. Instead, the exact opposite happened. Communication opened up because people felt free to say what they were really thinking, knowing that it would not be used against them later.

In practice, this means that during team meetings a member can say to us, "Dick (or Arleen), I feel that you're being really pushy when you talk like that and that you are not really willing to listen to what I have to say." When this happens, we stop talking about the matter at hand and start to ask process questions. For example, "What is it about my behavior that is making you feel that way?" Sometimes the root of the issue lies in unhealed emotional pain from their past, but sometimes it lies in unhealed pain from our past(s). Asking process questions helps us to discover the root issue behind the behavior that needs to change. Once this is clear, we can help each other to take the steps needed to get healed in these areas. This in turn leads to lasting positive changes in behavior.

This approach has worked so well for us that we now not only train our new leaders, but also the whole church. Learning how to give and receive feedback and to ask process questions has resulted in the church becoming much healthier. People are learning the skills they need to talk out their problems with one another instead of just allowing them to fester.

Since we started doing this we have also noticed, however, that not everyone is willing to change. Those who do not want to take responsibility for their own personal growth tend to leave our church. Thankfully, this group is in the minority. It does, however, leave us with those who want to be teachable not only in word, but also in deed.

Using this approach has also had another benefit which we did not expect – for the first time in more than 50 years of combined leadership experience in ministry, we not only feel like we have friends in our leadership team, but we know we do. Throughout the years, we have gone through thick and thin together and we know that our vulnerability will not be taken advantage of by our leaders. It is an amazing feeling.

CONCLUSION

We began this chapter by saying that the new apostolic era that we are living in is going to require radical changes in how apostolic leaders think and act. It is also going to require courage and vulnerability. The body of Christ is starting to stand up in large numbers and move out into ministry, both inside and outside of the church. As they do, they will become more vocal and less willing to tolerate authoritarian leaders.

In this time of transition, God is issuing a challenge to all apostolic leaders – equip and empower new leaders and influencers. It is no longer sufficient to just lead followers. While leading leaders is much more of a challenge, it is also much more rewarding and crucial in our post-modern age. It is only by doing so that we will see lasting reformation and transformation in our nations as the Kingdom of God impacts every societal sphere of influence.

ENDNOTES

1. John Maxwell, *Developing the Leader Within You*, p. 1. EQUIP Publishing, Belarus, 2005.
2. Jim Collins, *Good to Great. Why Some Companies Make the Leap and Others Don't*, p. 20. HarperCollins, New York, 2001.

ABOUT THE AUTHORS

Dick and Dr. Arleen Westerhof are the Senior Pastors of the God's Embassy Church in Amsterdam, Netherlands (www.embassyamsterdam.nl). Embassy is a fast-growing, bilingual church on the outskirts of the city. Dick is also the founder and leader of the Coalition for Apostolic Reformation (CAR), a national apostolic network dedicated to promoting the Kingdom vision and the Seven Mountain Strategy as essential elements in reforming society (www.coalitie.org). Arleen is the founder and facilitator of the Netherlands Prophetic Council (www.nederlandseprofetischeraad. org), a group of prophetic leaders and ministers cutting across denominations, and the Chairperson of the Board of Directors of the training foundation, Living In Your Destiny (www.liyd.org).

CHAPTER FORTY-EIGHT

APOSTOLIC TEAMS

BILL JOHNSON

For centuries the people of God have gathered together around specific truths. Denominations and organizations have been formed to unite these groups of believers. Having common belief systems has helped to build unity within particular groups and define their purpose.[1] Historically, these groups were formed from people who were usually newly saved, or were asked to leave whatever denomination they were previously a part of.

Unity based on common doctrines has a measure of success. But there is an inherent problem with this approach – unity of this nature is based upon uniformity. When God is saying something new,[2] those who are listening are usually asked by their leaders to leave the group they were a part of.[3] Their newfound convictions and beliefs are considered threatening and divisive. If the whole group doesn't move in step with what God is saying, there will be a break in fellowship. When agreement in nonessential beliefs is considered necessary for fellowship, then division is natural and to be expected. While doctrine is vitally important, it is not a strong enough foundation to bear the weight of His glory that is about to be revealed through true unity.

CHANGE IS IN THE AIR

There are major changes in the "wind" right now. For the last several years people have started to gather around fathers instead of doctrine. In the natural, it would be easy to imagine a father with two very different children – one politically liberal and the other conservative. While discussions would probably be quite lively at the evening meal, they would not bring an end to the family. Gathering around fathers gives a stability that enables people to endure differences in opinion without falling under the influence of the spirit of offense. Fathers bring an element of peace that is impossible without them.

SPIRITUAL FATHERS

Apostles are first and foremost fathers by nature. True fathers continually make choices for the wellbeing of their children with little thought to personal sacrifice. They are not jealous when their children succeed, but instead are overjoyed because of those successes. It is normal for a father to desire his children to surpass him in every way. Brothers compete; fathers do not.

In the same way that a father and mother are to bring stability to a home, so the apostles and prophets are the stability of the church. The apostle Paul calls them the church's foundation.[4] Good foundations bring stability. The concept of team ministry starts with these two. Stability is the primary fruit of the ministry of the apostolic team.

TEAM MAKEUP

Apostolic teams are not necessarily made up of just apostles and prophets. They are a group of people that carry the 'family mission' without selfish agendas. They are sent by their leadership, and entrusted with delegated authority to establish God's rule in their realm of experience and expertise. When they go with that heart, they carry an apostolic anointing because they function under the umbrella of the apostle's authority.

We can't be co-missioned until we're in sub-mission to the primary mission. This is true of every believer before God. But it is especially true of apostolic teams. Setting aside personal agendas is a big part of the success of team ministry. Many teams have failed in their mission because of an individual who wanted his/her gift or opinion to be recognized.

MEASURE OF RULE

A big misunderstanding occurs when apostles think they have the same measure of authority in every geographical location. When Paul went to Jerusalem to participate in the first Apostolic Council, he submitted his experiences to the other apostles who had also gathered there.[5] It wasn't until James, the apostle in Jerusalem, spoke, that there were any conclusions. A true apostle carries their apostolic authority wherever they go, but it is foolish for him to not recognize local authority. The same is true with apostolic teams. It is their respect for the local church and the biblical authority that helps them to serve effectively.

Authority, like favor, is for the benefit of others. It is not a title to help in building one's own self-esteem, and is never for personal gain. For that reason the Apostle is at the 'bottom of the stack' . . . the 'least of all'. The title simply recognizes function. And that function is to make others better and more complete in their walk with the Lord.

THE PURPOSE OF THE TITLE

Throughout history there have been many ordinary individuals who have become desperate for God in unusual ways, and have sought God with reckless abandon. The encounters they had with God made them appear extraordinary. Their breakthrough made them household names with remarkable gifts and ministries. But when God gives someone an unusual gift, it is never for the purpose of acquiring admiration and fame, or even drawing big crowds. Those things are normal byproducts, but they are not the purpose. The place of favor that one gets as a result of God's unusual touch on their lives is a God-given position to equip others. It is God's heart to take those high points of human experience in the man or woman of God and make them the new norm for the believer. Equipping the saints becomes the focus of true fathers.

THE SPIRIT OF REVELATION

One of the things that helped to keep the early church strong and healthy was their continual devotion to the apostles' doctrine.[6] However, you'll notice that there is no mention of a list of beliefs that the Bible declares to be the official record of important doctrines. It is safe to say the "apostles' doctrine" is referring to something other than a specific list. Peter understood this when he exhorted the church concerning 'present truth.'[7] That phrase is to direct our attention to that which the Lord is emphasizing for this season. That is the apostles' doctrine. The word coming from apostles is to bring clarification of the Father's focus for the church, and in turn strengthen our resolve to His purposes. Fresh revelation carries fresh fire, which helps us to maintain the much-needed fire in our souls.

Apostles carry a blueprint in their hearts concerning the church and God's purposes on the earth. They are used to bring fresh revelation to the church. Apostolic teams are sent to represent their spiritual father, and carry the word that has been entrusted to their 'tribe'. They help bring an understanding and establish an order needed in the particular location they were sent to.

THE NEED FOR OTHERS

God never gives the whole picture of His plan for the church to one father/apostle, or even to one tribe. Scriptures declare that "we" have the mind of Christ, not "I."[8] Dependence upon the whole is essential for us to grow up in a way that pleases Christ. As the various "tribes" learn to work together, we will see a more complete picture of the Father's intent for Planet Earth.

The revelation carried by Apostles and the five-fold ministry will result in a church coming to a common knowledge of the Son of God.[9] Much division presently exists in this area. He is our common focus. A study of the scriptures without the Holy Spirit giving understanding creates much religious conflict. Division exists because people are committed to different levels of truth that appear contradictory. Fathers are necessary to sort these things out. Variety, without uniformity, is important. These teams carry revelation to help the church to live out of a common revelation of Jesus – who He is, and who we are because of Him. God's aim is to fulfill His word in John 14:17 - *"As He is, so are we in this world."* We are to become like the Jesus revealed in Revelation chapter one – resurrected and glorified. We are not headed for the cross – we live 'from' the cross. Apostolic revelation has that in mind.

THE DAY OF POWER

One of the more notable prophets of our day recently told me that he wouldn't be able to come into all that God had created him for until the apostles came forth to their appointed place. The apostles help release the prophets into their destiny, and vice versa. In a sense they complete each other.

Apostolic order without apostolic power is to be questioned. Order based on biblical principle that is lacking biblical power is tragic at best, and deceptive at worst. Order does not exist unto itself. The wineskin exists for the wine. The wine is the focus. All order exists to house God Himself – not to restrict Him, but to accurately express Him. Wineskins need to flex in order to be useful, because of the expanding nature of the wine in the fermenting process. The Holy Spirit brings constant change, and to house Him means to embrace flexibility as a way of life. The goal is not to create a perfect structure or government. It is to create one that recognizes Him, and flexes with His changes.

LAST DAYS ASSIGNMENT

All of this serves one purpose – Jesus is returning for a bride. For this to happen the harvest must be brought in, and must be "cleaned." He's not returning for a bride that He has to heal up and put together like a puzzle in heaven. He is returning for a bride whose body is in equal proportion to her head, and whose parts work together in coordination. It's called a "glorious church, without spot or wrinkle" in scripture.[10] Anything less is an illegitimate vision.

The bride is to make herself ready for that day.[11] As Larry Randolph puts it, "it is a perversion to think that Jesus will dress the bride before the wedding." Our assignment is clear, and the gifts are in place. And they are all expressions of Jesus Himself. But they are simple in purpose. Re-present Jesus to the world!

The fire of God must rest in the souls of men. Christians without passion are almost as great a mystery as Christians without purpose. Apostolic teams carry fresh fire with divine purpose. They enlist men and women to God's dream, and in the process the church steps into her destiny.

(Editor's Note: *This article first appeared in Fresh Fire's *Destiny Magazine* several years ago and is used by permission of the author.)

ENDNOTES

1. There are three basic levels of biblical doctrine: 1. There are doctrines that are essential to the Christian faith – For example, Jesus is the eternal Son of God; 2. Then there are doctrines that are important, but not essential – For example, how we use the gifts of the Spirit in a church service: 3. And finally, there are doctrines that are good but not essential – For example, the exact nature and timing of Christ's return.

2. This is never in addition to scriptures. Instead, He unveils what is already there.

3. This is far from an absolute rule, as many leaders are in tune to what God is saying. However, some are more concerned with preserving past accomplishments over and above the advancement of the kingdom. This creates a weakness that tends to miss God's present word.

4. Ephesians 2:20

5. Acts 15

6. Acts 2:42

7. 2 Peter 1:12

8. 1 Corinthians 2:6

9. Ephesians 4:11-16

10. Ephesians 5:27

11. Revelation 19:7

ABOUT THE AUTHOR

Bill and Brenda (Beni) Johnson are the Senior Pastors of Bethel Church in Redding, Calif. Bill is a fifth generation pastor with a rich heritage in the things of the Spirit. Together they serve a growing number of churches that have partnered for revival. This apostolic network has crossed denominational lines in building relationships that enable church leaders to walk in both purity and power. Bill also has an honorary doctorate degree from Wagner Leadership Institute.

The present move of God has brought Bill into a deeper understanding of the phrase, "on earth as it is in heaven." Heaven is the model for our life and ministry. Jesus lived with this principle by only doing what He saw His Father doing. Learning to recognize the Holy Spirit's presence, and how to follow His lead, will enable us to do the works of Christ, destroying the works of the devil. Healing and deliverance must become the common expression of this gospel of power once again.

Bill and the Bethel Church family have taken on this theme for life and ministry. Healings, ranging from cancer to broken bones, to learning disorders and emotional healing, happen with regularity. This is the children's bread. And these works of God are not limited to revival meetings. The church is learning how to take this anointing to the schools, workplace, and neighborhoods with similar results. Bill teaches that we owe the world an encounter with God, and that a Gospel without power is not the Gospel that Jesus preached.

All three of their children and spouses are involved in full-time ministry. They have nine wonderful grandchildren. To learn more or contact Bill, visit his web sites at www.ibethel.org or www.bjm.org.

CHAPTER FORTY-NINE

BUILDING BRIDGES FOR KINGDOM ADVANCEMENT

DR. CARL L. WHITE JR.

"And I say also unto thee, That thou art Peter, and upon this rock I will build my church, and the gates of hell shall not prevail against it."
(Matt. 16:18)

Nothing is more important to the advancement of God's kingdom than to learn the process of "crossing over" and how to help others get across after having done so yourself. Everyone is important to God and He sees their value and appoints someone to become their "spiritual escort" to get them across to the next levels in Him. After looking back over the years of my life, I see the pattern of how God prepared me to become a "bridge" for others who would have a journey similar to mine.

I want to share a brief history of my journey to give context to why I was called to build bridges for others. As the firstborn son of a Baptist pastor, I served in many areas of ministry. Of course, it wasn't called ministry at that time but rather "auxiliaries:" deacon boards, ushers, nurses, willing workers groups and many more. I served as a junior deacon and choir director. Being around my dad as a leader was very healthy for me because I saw a "leader of leaders" close up, and it impacted my life tremendously. I saw good leadership in action, forming a base for what I would eventually come to know today.

According to my destiny and the plan of God, I was licensed on October 24, 1976 at the church and faithfully served as a youth director before being called to pastor a church in a local community. But before that, I accepted the call of God on my life in 1976 after many years of trying not to preach the gospel. The experience of serving my country in the Vietnam War during the period of July 1971 through March 1972 caused me to feel I missed something in my life and my first response after getting home, strange as it may seem, was not to come back to the church, but to turn to worldly living. I sang R&B, dabbled in drugs and a riotous lifestyle. The enemy had me to think that I deserved what seemed to be the "good life," telling me to get all the gusto you can, for you only go around once in life. Finally, God got my attention through a series of close encounters with death and things that potentially could have caused incarceration.

I was soon ordained by my father so that I could accept the appointment to a local church as pastor. The church was a small traditional Baptist church that had existed for over 40 years. I'll never forget sharing some biblical principles with a deacon who said to me, "Enough of this Bible stuff; we have a way of doing things around here."

Needless to say, it was clear that tradition had taken over. Some traditions become like those of the Pharisees and Sadducees in Matt. 16:6-7, *"Then Jesus said unto them, take heed and beware of the leaven of the Pharisees and Sadducees. And they reasoned among themselves, saying, it is because we have taken no bread."* Because they were not sensitive to the spirit dimension, they totally misunderstood the words of Jesus. Their traditional thinking had gotten the best of them. As a young pastor I found that every vision had to be voted on, packaged and sold to the majority of the Board. Many times after trying, mind you, to no avail, I just abandoned the idea for the sake of unity. But, after seven years and many days of prayer and fasting, the Holy Spirit gave me a release to leave this assignment. I soon organized a powerful, Spirit-led church with 100 members and united with the old church. Initially, healing had to take place, then the walls of tradition had to be torn down. These walls were built by religious traditions, and there were even some in my own life.

Brick by brick, we started to build upon the five-fold ministry based on the word of God. What a journey! I found out that because I had dropped "Baptist" from our name, many would not fellowship with us and those who made earlier transitions treated us like we were not a part of their reformation. It's amazing that when you want to seek for truth, sometimes condescending attitudes will alienate you.

This is when God equipped me to become an "ambassador" to begin building bridges. I had to do as Luke 14:28-32 says and "count up the cost." *"For which of you intending to build a tower, sitteth not down first, and counteth the cost, whether he have sufficient to finish it? Lest haply, after he hath laid the foundation, and is not able to finish it, all that behold it begin to mock him, saying, this man began to build, and was not able to finish. Or what king going to war against another king, sitteth not down first, and consulteth whether he be able with ten thousand to meet him that cometh against him with twenty thousand? Or else, while the other is yet a great way off, he sendeth an ambassage and desireth conditions of peace."*

ARCHITECTS OF ATMOSPHERE

This is what we as apostolic ambassadors and bridge builders must consider. As premier organizers of governmental resources and administrations, we must be able to optimize and maximize the potential of people, places and things we are charged to serve with and oversee or steward. We have to be able to connect everyone to their respective DNA streams and with our own, to have the finished product that God desires. God gave me grace, common sense, spiritual awareness and sensitivity, and caused me to be able to see the human and spiritual needs of the people around me in my district, city, former denomination, political party, and national organizations of which I am a member or leader. I couldn't leave behind the ones God gave me to "carry over."

Apostolic bridge builders have a special ability to become architects of the science of crafting laws, language and legitimacy to form an atmosphere where even the weak and disenfranchised can be brought across. They are even able to make allies out of virtual enemies at times due to the wisdom and favor of the Lord granted to them for their assignments.

I saw such a need to help pastors who knew that the Holy Spirit was empowering them for apostolic ministry. Someone had to take the time to reach back with the knowledge of where these brothers and sisters were on their journey and without condemnation, but with compassion, instruction and some transparency, do a little "boot camp" training with them. To build God's army with skilled, special, faithful leaders in the kingdom, we need the "Bridge-Building Apostles!"

This journey has offered me the opportunity to "build bridges" between the business arena, social service, political, health care, lawbreakers, offenders and those who have been incarcerated. As an apostle, I see more disconnection in some areas than connection. Who decided that we should be limited and cannot connect with politics and social services and cannot enter into the healthcare field or business arena? Today we are embarking on much more movement in all of these areas, and across societal spheres. I want to be that which God has called me to be – to build bridges for those who want to cross over. I accept my "sending" as an apostle. Kingdom-level ambassadors are essential to the proper governance of communities and their resources. We can form the right alliances and distinguish between friends and foes as we build the kingdom on earth.

As a bridge-building apostle, I began to look beyond the local church into the marketplace and governmental circles where I found the need to connect faith-based institutions and healthcare and social service organizations. It is not something I just decided to do, but because of a family health crisis with my daughter, who was diagnosed with Hodgkins Lymphoma, I found myself reaching out to these areas of needed help from those organizations. Little did I know, "bridges" were being built. Much to my surprise, I saw a need for spiritual guidance to connect resources to the faith-based organizations. This information from the Word of God helped me to channel these resources that were lacking in the marketplace and community as a whole.

We formed an organization that would bring inspiration and resources by connecting these organizations. We began monthly meetings where we were able to utilize this organization to channel the areas of necessity to each one of us. Lo and behold, the faith-based leadership provided mechanisms by which we could work together to do meaningful ministry in the community.

Building bridges apostolically with resource centers and providers in both the government and private sectors is not just denominational, but is necessary for community continuity and connectivity. The information that was gathered by connecting all three sectors, including education – now a fourth entity – brought phenomenal success and results. Our community has benefited tremendously from us connecting with one another, which has produced "lasting fruit." I know that the Holy Spirit through personal need gave movement to building bridges beyond the local church.

"And he gave some apostles; and some prophets; and some, evangelists; and some pastors and teachers; For the perfecting of the saints, for the work of the ministry, for the edifying of the body of Christ" (Eph. 4:11-12). The Apostles, along with the other four ascension gifts to the Body, are for the perfecting of the saints. The word "perfect" means to mature and equip, because until you are prepared, you cannot effectively carry out the work that ministry requires in order to edify the Body of Christ. The apostles are ambassadors of Christ, sent to areas like Crete in Titus 1:5.

Truly, I have a heart for Pastors, who like me, know that God has more to be revealed to them, but because of peer pressure, denominational and family traditions, and lack of true fatherhood and biblical church government, they remain locked in a religious system that condemns rather than explores, and stagnates rather than multiplies.

God is still speaking through His word, unfolding mysteries for the fullness of this time. Apostles are not afraid to tread on new territory in order to bring truth that has lain dormant until illumination and revelation stirs up that which God needs for this hour. So, as we follow the voice of the Holy Spirit leading us into all truth, build bridges for others to cross after you have moved closer to Him, and after you have crossed over yourself. In the end..."*The kingdoms of this world are become the kingdoms of our Lord and of his Christ, and he shall reign for ever and ever"* (Rev. 11:15).

God bless you with love and happiness.

ABOUT THE AUTHOR

Carl Lee White, Jr. the oldest of ten children, was born in Winchester, Ark. and lived there until the age of six. His family relocated to Chicago in 1957, and he now resides in suburban Chicago with his wife, Pamela and their family. A graduate of Orr High School, Apostle White continued his education at Malcolm X College, organized and directed the Kansas State University African American Choir, and the Outreach Theological Seminary, where he received his doctorate. He is married to Pamela and the father of eight children, and has seven grandchildren.

Being raised in the home of a Baptist Pastor, Apostle White acquired a love for music and the Lord at an early age, and sang in many school, community, and church choirs. His love for music afforded him the opportunity to write best-selling songs for the Savoy label and to write and sing his own music, Victorious Living and Apostle C.L. White, Jr. and Friends, featuring "According to my Faith", both on the Jasmine recording label. Apostle White has also authored two books: *My Foot Almost Slipped*, and *At Ease*. Presently, he is in the process of penning others specifically designed for ministering to pastors and church leaders.

Apostle White served in the Vietnam War and returned home honorably, knowing that it was only by the grace of God, the prayers of the righteous and his determination to do the will of God, that he survived.

On June 7, 1987 Apostle White organized Victory Christian Assembly Baptist Church in Markham, Ill. under Pastor Princeton H. McKinney and Pastor Gordon Humphrey, Sr. One hundred members united with him on that day, and the membership has continued to grow since then. The church adopted the motto "Ministering to the Total Man." From the beginning, he coined the phrase "God bless you with love and happiness," and the law of reaping and sowing has blessed him much with love and happiness.

Apostle White has been an encourager to the Body of Christ throughout his life. He has served in ministry and pastorate for over 30 years. With preaching engagements locally and across the nation, his early years of preaching were characterized as Little Thunder. Apostle White is instrumental in leading, counseling, and assisting Pastors and Churches throughout the nation. In addition, he serves on the boards of directors and/or in executive leadership of several nonprofit organizations.

His genuine love for people and wanting to please God motivates him daily. His knowledge and faith in the Word has withstood many obstacles and storms of life. His belief that God has a specific purpose for him is to encourage and bridge the gap of traditional Baptists into better understanding how this present age of the church has to minister in today's society. Although he conducts two weekly worship services, Apostle White has not forsaken his evangelistic call, and maintains a rigorous schedule of preaching nationwide. There are presently some 13 churches in the states of Arkansas, Indiana and Illinois that have decided to unite with Apostle White and his leadership through Victory Christian International Ministries, an apostolic network. To learn more or contact Dr. White, visit his website at www.vcimc.com.

CHAPTER FIFTY

APOSTOLIC APPRAISERS

DR. GORDON E. BRADSHAW

One afternoon I was having a phone conversation with Dr. Bruce Cook and a heavy prophetic anointing came upon him. We were having a discussion about the GEMS Network (Global Effect Movers & Shakers Network), which I oversee and Dr. Cook said, "God says you are an apostolic appraiser!" Right away I was taken into another place in my spirit because the words so powerfully described the mandate that God has placed on my life over the years. The logo of the network is an image of the world surrounded by 12 blue diamonds. Since 12 is the number of spiritual government and apostolic order, I knew there was more to come from this prophecy! In the ensuing weeks I couldn't get the words "apostolic appraiser" out of my mind. I began to research appraisal methods. To my surprise, I discovered that much of the way I had been leading, fathering and mentoring people and organizations over the years mirrored the science of gemology.

Apostles are "master builders" in the kingdom of God and are continuously being developed by Him to have the perception and perspective to recognize the plans and purposes by which He operates. God believes in succession, longevity, and sustainability. He believes in the evolution of process and technology and in the continual development of strategies and tactics that produce greater results. He believes in "value" and few things seem to hold value like precious stones or gems. Apostolic appraisal is much like the ability to mine, refine and define the identity of precious stones.

Nothing catches a person's eye like a brilliant, finely-cut gemstone. Apostolic appraisers are apostles whose eyes "catch" the glimmer of the purpose, the power and the potential of others and are able to identify, clarify and magnify people, places and things as they relate to the kingdom of God. It's about having an "eye" to discover the original spiritual DNA they contain and knowing how to market and present the value of God's "lively stones."

> *"Ye also, as lively stones, are built up a spiritual house,*
> *an holy priesthood, to offer up spiritual sacrifices,*
> *acceptable to God by Jesus Christ."*
> (1 Pet. 2:5)

Believers, as lively stones, are often found "in the rough" as raw diamonds and gemstones are when they're first discovered. Like natural stones, they may not look appealing at first and draw little attention. But, the plan of God is to release apostolic appraisers in the earth to discover and develop the rough diamonds into top-grade gemstones that reflect the power and purpose of God!

In the Greek text the word "stone" is *"Lithos"* and is simply described as a common stone as it would occur naturally. But, the word *"lithos"* is related to the term "lithography" which means: The process of printing from a plane surface (as a smooth stone or metal plate) on which the image to be printed is ink-receptive and the blank area ink-repellant (Webster). In other words, it's a process for transferring an image in which the outline of the image is clear and distinct from its background. One portion of Dr. Cook's prophecy to me stated that as an appraiser, people would see those who I had prepared and their value and finish would be easy for others to distinguish. This is utterly important in the full formation of God's kingdom in the earth. We can no longer remain ambiguous, unidentified and unclarified. The sons and daughters of God must rise with distinction!

Apostolic appraisers, like natural gemologists or appraisers, are able to identify four distinct areas of a gem to determine its value. They are color, clarity, cut and carat weight. There are tremendous similarities between the appraisal of gems and of God's kingdom citizens.

COLOR

"O thou afflicted, tossed with tempest, and not comforted, behold, I will lay thy stones with fair colors, and lay thy foundations with sapphires."
(Isa. 54:11)

"Now therefore, if ye will obey my voice indeed, and keep my covenant, then shall ye be a peculiar treasure unto me above all people: for all the earth is mine."
(Ex. 19:5)

Color can be described as the character and distinctiveness of someone or something as compared to others. Webster describes "color" as "a phenomenon of light (as red or blue) or visual perception that enables one to differentiate otherwise identical objects." Colored diamonds and other gems have specific traits and desirable characteristics making them either more or less valuable. Colored stones often have a more striking appearance because they are unusual as compared to clear or white stones. Even when certain colors are obvious there are other color traits that are often hidden from view. Certain colors are hidden in a spectrum of light that is invisible to the naked eye.

Scientists use an instrument called a spectrograph to view these hidden colors. In the apostolic ministry or spectrum there are certain people, places and things that have "stand out" color or characteristics also. Apostolic appraisers have the spiritual technology to detect the "color" of someone or something's future potential and purpose in God and can see their worth. Color, even when hidden from view and seemingly having no context with certain subjects, is an important part of life even when it relates to things that have nothing to do with sight. Even music and fragrances are identified as having "color." That color adds a unique quality that differentiates the music or fragrance from others.

CLARITY

*"But we all, with open face beholding as in a glass the glory
of the Lord, are changed into the same image from glory to
glory, even as by the Spirit of the Lord."*
(2 Cor. 3:18)

Clarity represents clearness or the ability to be transparent and allow light to penetrate and pass through the stone. In gemology this is best noted when the lack of inclusions or defects enhance the stone's ability to reflect light. When facets are cut into a stone, it's intentionally done to reflect light to the greatest degree and to avoid allowing inclusions or defects to be in a position to interrupt the "flow" of light through the stone. Apostolic gemologists apply the same cutting and crafting principle on people, places and things that they are responsible for overseeing or advising. Nothing will ever reach the full kingdom-level manifestation without the cutting and shaping of an apostolic instrument.

Every believer needs to experience the cutting and shaping that comes with exposure to the apostolic dimension. We are the reflection of Jesus Christ in the earth and need to be honed and shaped so there's no reduction in the original glory of Jesus Christ as it's transferred to us and made known to the earth. The Word of the Lord and the power of the Holy Spirit through apostolic vessels reveal the image and glory of the Lord in us. The revelation of God's glory is the "glass" or "*katoptrizomai*" (Greek) of 2 Cor. 3:18, which means: To see a reflection of oneself and the intensity by which one is viewed.

When we look into the glass or mirror or "stone" of God's purpose and power and view its reflective qualities, we are changed into exactly what we see. It causes us to "reflect" on how we live our lives. We are purified and cleansed to God's specifications. We are changed into the same image from glory to glory even as by the Spirit of the Lord. As we are cut and cleansed, we allow a greater passage of light through our lives. It's the passage of "glory" or light through a stone that gives it brilliance and reflectivity. The entrance of the Lord's word gives us light (Ps. 119:130).

As more inclusions are revealed and removed from our lives through the glory of His word, even more glorious light is allowed to pass through us, changing us into the same image as Christ Himself. Jesus Christ is the "crown jewel" of the kingdom of God and when we become like Him we are able to glorify Him to the greatest measure! Apostolic leaders must go through the same process, too, just to be able to craft and reveal another diamond's greatest value.

CUT

*"All these were of costly stones. According to the measure
of hewed stones, sawed with saws, within and without, even
from the foundation to the coping, and so on the outside
toward the great court."*
(1 Kings 7:9)

In the science of gemology, cut is an extremely important factor in determining the value of a stone. More emphasis is placed on this section because it is the "cut" of the stone that really gives it the visibility that draws attention. It affects how light hits the facets or cut surfaces of the stone, giving it brilliance and reflectivity. A stone with poorly-cut facets is dull and uninspiring and is unable to "catch the eye" so to speak. When stones are properly cut, light will enter, reflect from the surfaces of the facets and return to the eye to be seen and enjoyed. If the cut is poor, light will enter the stone and simply pass through it without reflecting. Gemologists call this "windowing." Stones must be cut properly to fully reveal the prismatic effect of the colors of the rainbow and the beauty that may be hidden within them.

Also, when diamonds are inspected, they are often observed from the bottom up rather than from the top down. This is a practice that directly parallels the way things are built in the apostolic kingdom dimension because it requires one to look at "foundations." Interestingly, the place at the bottom of a diamond is called a "pavilion." An amazing comparison is found in Jer. 43:10. While the text is about Nebuchadnezzar, a king of Babylon, we have to note the powerful similitude that is shown and realize that at the particular time of this Scripture, Nebuchadnezzar was on assignment from God.

"And say unto them, Thus saith the Lord of hosts, the God of Israel; 'Behold, I will send and take Nebuchadnezzar the king of Babylon, my servant, and will set his throne upon these stones that I have hid; and he shall spread his royal pavilion over them.'"

I believe the "stones" represent certain people or things that God has hidden to be released at a certain time. According to the text, the stones that God ordered to be hidden needed a proper "covering" or pavilion over them. So do the people, places and things that God has ordained for His purpose under apostolic leadership. But in the case of apostolic leadership, the covering is foundational or is actually located "under" the stones to protect them. Just as large buildings need a proper foundation to support the weight of a great structure, so do people, places and things that are on the way to greatness. The pavilion of apostolic covering is actually beneath the stones according to Eph. 2:19-20. *"Now therefore, ye are no more strangers and foreigners, but fellow citizens with the saints, and of the household of God; And are built upon the foundation of the apostles..."*

In providing proper foundations, covering and pavilions, apostolic appraisers are able, with the heart of Christ, to mentor and manage the spiritual destinies and careers of those who are assigned to them by God. They must remember that the people, places and things which God has entrusted them with are products of God's design and purpose and are not really their own. Their stewardship over God's commodities is a very serious matter. It's easy to "cut" and correct but it's also easy to damage the goods. Cutting cannot be done indiscriminately or in a "heavy-handed" way. Apostolic appraisers must be men and women of the Spirit of God who can follow the patterns of Isa. 11:2-5:

"And the spirit of the Lord shall rest upon him, the spirit of wisdom and understanding, the spirit of counsel and might, the spirit of knowledge and of the fear of the Lord; And shall make him of quick understanding in the fear of the Lord: And he shall not judge after the sight of his eyes, neither reprove after the hearing of his ears: But with righteousness shall he judge the poor, and reprove with equity for the meek of the earth: and he shall smite the earth with the rod of his mouth, and with the breath of his lips shall he slay the wicked. And righteousness shall be the girdle of his loins, and faithfulness the girdle of his reins."

It takes a proper relationship to provide the "cut" that may be necessary to develop believers into true kingdom gems. In my book entitled *The Technology of Apostolic Succession: Transferring the Purposes of God to the Next Generation of Kingdom Citizens* (Kingdom House Publishing), I wrote, "Since the office of the apostle is one of 'position' rather than 'promotion', it directly affects how a 'heritage' and its benefits are imparted to generations. The family heritage is a matter of reputation as well as the accumulation of wealth or goods. The person who is in position to pass on this heritage is the father (or mother) of the tribe."

I also wrote, "There is a certain 'koinonia' (the Greek term for 'fellowship') level that is needed to properly distribute the DNA of apostolic ministry. In this season of new technologies, we as leaders must be reachable and within the sphere of touch and relationship in order to transfer mantles. We must not fear that our sons and daughters will become 'greater' than us...in fact, that is the whole idea behind our efforts and behind the purpose of God. They are to evolve and mature and become greater than us!"

A leader must have a genuine concern for the evolution and growth of the ones they cover. Spiritual fathers and mothers in apostolic leadership are much more in position to provide the cuts that may be necessary for calibration and proper shaping than one who simply administers the blow without a relationship. When proper relationships are in place, the family, organization, corporation or community has proper foundations, pavilions are in place and the order of God is manifested. After all, the purpose of apostolic appraisal is to produce a finished product after His own design. Our finished works will bring Him the glory He deserves as the creator of all things.

CARAT WEIGHT

*"For our light affliction, which is but for a moment, worketh
for us a far more exceeding and eternal weight of glory."*
(2 Cor. 4:18)

Carat weight is the criterion by which a stone's actual physical size is measured. Usually, the larger a stone is the more valuable it becomes. However, there are stones which are comparatively smaller than others but carry a higher value because of design and cut. Similarly, size doesn't always matter in issues of the kingdom of God. Where we place value comes under a different heading when we live the kingdom life.

*"And he [Jesus] said unto them, 'Take heed, and beware of
covetousness: for a man's life consisteth not in the abundance
of the things which he possesseth.'"*
(Luke 12:15)

The Lord is often more concerned with the quality of a thing than the quantity of it. Throughout the Bible we find God intentionally using the "underdog" or a small army to win a dramatic or overwhelming victory against much greater opposition. In matters of the kingdom and in apostolic appraisal, other factors are measured than mere size.

The value and quality of a life can often be measured by the refining elements of suffering, discipline, trials and testing that one goes through, rather than by the things which he possesses. These "light afflictions" work in us to produce the color, clarity and cut that we couldn't achieve any other way. They produce "a far more exceeding and eternal weight of glory." Our true weight comes from the glory of God that is allowed to reflect through us.

The term "weight" is from the Greek word "Baros," meaning – The notion of going down, a load, abundance, authority. It implies the fact that the humbling process of life produces true wealth and value and yields a sense of authority that comes from one who suffers as Christ did and is now able to reign with him. Apostolic appraisers are those who have, themselves, been placed in the furnace of affliction and have gone through the processes of refining, molding, shaping, hardening, sharpening and honing so that they have become examples of how to submit to God and not simply taken on a position of authority to wield their power without reason or right. They understand the "weightier matters" of God's law and know how to evaluate and propagate the sons and daughters and the systems under their leadership.

In the book entitled *The Technology of Apostolic Succession: Transferring the Purposes of God to the Next Generation of*

Kingdom Citizens, I wrote, "The apostleship is an ascending movement into a greater level of responsibility, assignment and purpose in Christ. It is a key office in the kingdom of God, and one which requires its participants to fully understand the challenges which lie ahead of them. It is an important office, not in the sense of providing exaltation to those who are assigned by God to this position, but more importantly, to those who are to benefit from the 'fathering' spirit of true apostolic leaders and the governmental grace that propels those disciples into their generational heritage in the kingdom of God." Nothing should dissuade a person from assuming the apostleship is a promotion moreso than the text written by the apostle Paul in 1 Cor. 4:9-15:

"For I think that God hath set forth us the apostles last, as it were appointed to death: for we are made a spectacle unto the world, ad to angels, and to men. We are fools for Christ's sake, but ye are wise in Christ; we are weak, but ye are strong; ye are honourable, but we are despised. Even unto this present hour we both hunger, and thirst, and are naked, and are buffeted, and have no certain dwellingplace: And labour, working with our own hands: being reviled, we bless; being persecuted, we suffer it: Being defamed, we intreat: we are made as the filth of the world, and are the offscouring of all things unto this day. I write not these things to shame you, but as my beloved sons I warn you. For though ye have ten thousand instructors in Christ, yet have ye not many fathers..."

Truly, the apostolic dimension needs spiritual fathers and mothers – apostolic appraisers who can discern and sense the destinies of others and will produce the gems that God desires, and that the world needs.

ABOUT THE AUTHOR

Dr. Gordon E. Bradshaw has been a Kingdom Citizen for almost 40 years and is the Founder and Governor of Global Effect Movers and Shakers (G.E.M.S.) Network, a Kingdom-level consortium of ministry, marketplace and municipal members. He and his SCOPE Vision Group (Strategic Company of Prophetic Engineers) have been positioned by God to enlarge and expand the Kingdom influence on the earth.

Dr. Bradshaw is a published author, trainer, keynote speaker at conferences, Apostolic-Prophetic leader, and has served as a Chief Executive Officer and consultant with over 30 years in the fire service and in the educational field. His most recent books include *The Technology of Apostolic Succession: Transferring the Purposes of God to the Next Generation of Kingdom Citizens,* and *Authority for Assignment: Releasing the Mantle of God's Government in the Marketplace.*

Dr. Bradshaw is Senior Scholar of Spiritual Formation and Leadership for Hope Bible Institute and Seminary and President of the "ACT-tivity" Institute Center for Kingdom Empowerment. He resides in the Chicago area with his wife Pastor Angela Bradshaw and their family. To learn more or contact him, visit www.gemsnetwork.org or email drgebradshaw@gmail.com.

CHAPTER FIFTY-ONE

APOSTOLIC RESPONSIBILITY FOR DESTINY

WALT PILCHER

Like many of us, in my reading of Ephesians 4:11-16, about Jesus giving the gifts of apostles, prophets, evangelists, pastors and teachers, I assumed these were only for leadership and governance of the Church. "Five-fold ministry" seemed like it might be foundational and important, but not much was taught about it, much less practiced, even in churches.

My perspective on this changed when I read *Good to Great*, the popular business book by Jim Collins. For me it was a launching pad from the natural to the spiritual because it opened my eyes to the fact that the Eph. 4:11 gifts are for the marketplace, not just the Church.

I began to see that many, if not all, functions and positions on an organization chart had parallels to Eph. 4:11-16. The CEO or department head might be apostolic. If so, maybe Sales = evangelistic, HR = pastoral, Finance = prophetic, Marketing = prophetic and evangelistic, Manufacturing = teaching, and so on. This was quite a revelation.

Collins identified 11 companies that far outperformed their peers. The central question was, "What did the 11 good-to-great companies share in common that distinguished them from the comparison companies?" The answer boiled down to similarities in the characteristics of the CEOs.

They had ambition, but their ambition was mostly for their companies and not for themselves personally. They were fearless, yet humble and modest. Unlike their domineering CEO counterparts in other companies, they motivated people through inspired standards, not personal charisma or rank. They were father figures, casting vision, setting the tone for the culture of their companies and providing consistency that people could count on and identify with.

These characteristics were very much like those we would call apostolic, or apostle-like. Furthermore, these CEOs brought in people who had talents and skills that complemented their own so as to build a well-rounded leadership team. The book didn't focus on those people, but my impression was that they brought to the table at least some of the characteristics of the other gifts of Eph. 4:11, that is, prophetic or perceptive, evangelistic or spreading good reports, teaching or communicating, and pastoral or compassionate.

That's when I concluded that not only are the five-fold gifts of Eph. 4:11-16 for the marketplace, but in fact, the Church is supposed to take them to the marketplace and make them available to any organization, not just businesses. By "marketplace" I mean any organization, large or small, that is anywhere on one or more of the "Seven Mountains of Influence," which, when you think about it, is pretty much all-inclusive.

I'm happy that more and more Christian thought leaders are embracing this idea and are looking for ways to apply it. Here's what Eph. 4:11-16 says:

*"And He Himself gave **some** to be **apostles, some prophets, some evangelists,** and **some pastors and teachers,** for the equipping of the saints for the work of ministry, for the edifying of the body of Christ, till we all come to the unity of the faith and of the knowledge of the Son of God, to a perfect man, to the measure of the stature of the fullness of Christ; that we should no longer be children, tossed to and fro and carried about with every wind of doctrine, by the trickery of men, in the cunning craftiness of deceitful plotting, but, speaking the truth in love, may grow up in all things into Him who is the head – Christ – from whom the whole body, joined and knit together by what every joint supplies, according to the effective working by which every part does its share, causes growth of the body for the edifying of itself in love."*

(NKJV, author's emphasis)

The "five-fold ministry" is a team leadership model that works when all five of the leadership voices are heard, mutually respected, and integrated behind the task of equipping people to do the work they've been called or hired to do, whether in ministry or in the marketplace. In fact, it is now well accepted that *our work* is *our ministry*. The happy result for an organization that is apostolically led, especially if it is also led in the power of the Holy Spirit, is a potentially unlimited success that I call "the five-fold effect."

CALLING AND DESTINY

Among the most important functions and benefits of a sound apostolic leadership situation are helping people to get a better understanding of their gifts and talents and thus their calling and destiny. You need to see yourself as God sees you so you can position yourself to identify and move ever toward your destiny on this earth, that is, to move in the direction of what He has planned for your life.

> *"And we know that in all things God works for the good of those who love him, who have been called according to his purpose."*
> (Rom. 8:28)

> *"'For I know the plans I have for you,' declares the Lord, 'plans to prosper you and not to harm you, plans to give you hope and a future.'"*
> (Jer. 29:11)

> *"For we are God's workmanship, created in Christ Jesus to **do good works, which God prepared in advance for us to do**."*
> (Eph. 2:10, author's emphasis)

LEADERSHIP'S RESPONSIBILITY

Leaders have the responsibility to help people discover their destiny and to position themselves to walk "according to His purpose."

One very practical reason this responsibility should be fully recognized is that when people are doing what they are supposed to be doing, properly trained or equipped and in accord with their gifts, talents, passions, and calling, the enterprise in which they are engaged will prosper. If we start with the idea of equipping people as in the Eph. 4 model, everything else falls into place and the church or the company (the "body") benefits. By contrast, if we start with, "How will this benefit the company?" and look at everything from that standpoint, then we put the cart before the horse.

Another reason this responsibility is so important is that it helps a person close the gap that often exists between how he sees himself and how God sees him. The world, and religion, want people to view themselves as having far less value, significance and potential than they really do have. People are encouraged to focus on their weakness and shortcoming, or on the idea that they "don't deserve" God's grace and favor or anybody else's either. It's easy to see how this would stifle confidence, ambition, and performance in most people.

However, God never sees anybody that way. He sees only the good, only the potential, only the plans He has for each of us. If there is anything negative, or a shortcoming, God sees it merely as an opportunity. It is an area of your life the Holy Spirit hasn't helped you to deal with fully. As an apostolic leader, part of your job is to help people reverse their negative self-images, restoring confidence and making them more effective in whatever they do, for their own benefit and for the benefit of the enterprise. Our culture has no problem with people taking healthy pride in themselves when they do well. Moreover, when others notice and appreciate good work, good works, and success, there is an opportunity to give glory to God.

PROPHECY—THE FIRST STEP

There are motivational, personality, and behavioral tests that people can take to help them and their employers identify "who they are" in terms of their talents, gifts, and temperament profiles. These can be quite valuable and should be considered.

However, apostolic leaders have an additional tool, and that is to prophesy over their team members. Jesus modeled this in the way He equipped His disciples to become apostles. He guided and corrected them according to who they were, and He prophesied over them, telling them of their destiny and how to get in position for it. In this way, Jesus was intimately involved in the personal lives of his followers, but always and only for their benefit and that of the Kingdom. He still is today.

Prophesying may sound like a tall order, especially if you don't come from a tradition that accepts prophecy as a gift that is in operation today and you have never experienced it. However, in its most basic form, it is as simple as asking the Holy Spirit to reveal to you where each person might fit best on the team or in the organization to achieve an alignment of the organization's needs with the gifting, calling and destiny of that person, or vice versa.

WHY SHOULD WE "GET INVOLVED"?

Over the past 100 years or so, opinions have varied about whether employers should get involved in the personal lives of their employees, and if so, how. For a long time the prevailing thought was that it is probably a bad idea.

That began to change in the 1980s when the "Total Quality Management (TQM) Movement" was launched, led by people like W. Edwards Deming (*Deming's 14 Points for Management*), J.M Juran (*Juran on Leadership for Quality: An Executive Handbook*), and Philip Crosby (*Quality is Free*). The key and enduring TQM concepts required managers to get to know their people better, to identify and understand their strengths and weaknesses, and to risk giving them the freedom, or "empowerment," to team with each other to try to solve their own work problems and improve productivity, not by working harder but by thinking up better ways of doing things.

These ideas involved employees and management working together to develop the best processes, systems, and policies instead of having them dictated by management. It was "holistic" in the sense of recognizing that employees are capable of seeing the company as organic, an entity made up of components which, when properly related, could make the whole effectively greater than the sum of its parts.

Today there may still be a reluctance to get "too involved" for various cultural and political reasons, but the benefits of getting sufficiently involved to create effective teams are well accepted.

MY EXPERIENCE WITH TQM

In 1984 I attended a "Deming's Methods for Management of Productivity and Quality" seminar at George Washington University with several other executives from L'eggs Products Company, of which I had recently become the president. L'eggs, a division of Sara Lee Corporation, was the nation's leading brand of women's hosiery, the pantyhose in the plastic eggs. Also attending were our Marketing VP, our Manufacturing VP, and our Director of Product Development. At the time, most of Deming's famous "14 Points for Management" seemed outrageously radical and rigid. However, after we returned from the seminar and tried them at L'eggs we had substantial success. Why?

TQM WAS A FORETASTE OF APOSTOLIC LEADERSHIP

It is instructive now, over 25 years later, to look back on some of Deming's 14 Points and see how they foreshadowed the concepts that flow from an understanding of how to apply five-fold leadership principles. In the following list of eight of these points, I've referenced five-fold or Eph. 4:11-16 parallels in parenthetical italics after each of Deming's points:

1. Institute leadership. The aim of supervision should be to help people and machines and gadgets do a better job. (*Apostolic, prophetic, equipping the saints*)

2. Drive out fear, so that everyone may work effectively for the company. (*Pastoral*)

3. Break down barriers between departments. People in research, design, sales, and production must work as a team, in order to foresee problems of production and usage that may be encountered with the product or service. (*Teamwork, perceiving and discernment, i.e., prophetic*)

4. Eliminate slogans, exhortations, and targets for the work force asking for zero defects and new levels of productivity. Such exhortations only create adversarial relationships, as the bulk of the causes of low quality and low productivity belong to the system and thus lie beyond the power of the work force. (*The whole body joined and knit together, effective working by which each part does its share*)

5. (a.) Eliminate work standards (quotas) on the factory floor. Substitute with leadership. (*All five: apostolic, prophetic, evangelistic, pastoral, teaching*)

(b.) Eliminate management by objective. Instead, substitute with leadership. (All five)

6. (a.) Remove barriers that rob the hourly worker of his right to pride of workmanship. (*Prophetic, pastoral, evangelistic*)

   (b.) Remove barriers that rob people in management of their right to pride of workmanship. (*Prophetic, pastoral, evangelistic*)

7. Institute a vigorous program of education and self-improvement. (*Equipping, teaching*)

8. Put everybody in the company to work to accomplish the transformation. The transformation is everybody's job. (*Apostolic, pastoral, evangelistic, the whole body joined and knit together, effective working by which each part does its share*)

Clearly, while none of this specifically called for prophesying over people, an important strategy was nevertheless to help people and management identify their gifts, talents, strengths and weaknesses so as to help ensure they were doing jobs they were best suited to do. All of it pointed to equipping people to fulfill their purposes on their way to realizing their destinies in their marketplace endeavors (their jobs) and ultimately their lives. The only missing tool was practical prophecy.

Because those of us on the L'eggs leadership team who attended the Deming seminar had shared the challenging experience of it, and also later a three-week course on Strategic Manufacturing at Harvard Business School, a team spirit arose between the Marketing, Manufacturing, Product Development and Planning departments as we enthusiastically embraced the idea that "the sky's the limit" to what we could try and what we might accomplish. We understood at last that while it was our, the leadership's, responsibility to see to having the best systems instead of blaming each other or the workers for the company's shortcomings, it was also true that most often the people actually doing the jobs were the best sources of ideas on how to do them better and to better integrate them with each other.

We applied TQM at L'eggs, including the 14 Points, with excellent results. For the first time, sales forecasting and production planning became truly coordinated functions. There was give and take between the departments over product specifications, with Manufacturing making suggestions that Marketing actually listened to and often adopted, making way for process and materials innovations that improved gross margins, which encouraged the Manufacturing and Product Development people even more. Never again was our Manufacturing VP heard to say, "Just tell me what to make and I'll make it," which is a typical Manufacturing department response to the frustration of being left out of the leadership loop.

Although no one from the Sales and Distribution or Finance and Accounting functions had attended the Deming seminar or the Harvard course, both of those departments enjoyed a feeling of greater respect from those who did attend, which spurred them to cooperate, contribute to and otherwise support the overall endeavor. The level of mutual trust rose throughout the company.

Higher gross margins allowed investment in more aggressive advertising and promotion programs and state-of-the-art machinery and methods. That led to higher market share, economies of scale, and the ability to invest even more, and so on and so on. Reduction in the labor content of our products due to higher process efficiencies was more than made up for in sales growth, requiring a larger workforce instead of layoffs. L'eggs became an unstoppable juggernaut until Casual Friday and then Casual Every Day caused the market for pantyhose to decline in the early 1990s. While it lasted, we enjoyed a substantial "five-fold effect" without having any idea what that was. No one had ever thought of it in terms of Eph. 4:11-16 five-fold leadership.

Granted, there were other factors in our favor. These included a fundamentally sound business model to begin with, a healthy culture established by my predecessors that valued a willingness to embrace challenge and change with a minimum of office politics, good direction and support from our parent company, Sara Lee, outstanding work by our advertising agency, Dancer Fitzgerald Sample, and a growing economy. Nevertheless, I attribute the acceleration of our success during that five-year period largely to the effect of applying, however inconsistently, what amounted to an apostolic organizational leadership strategy.

Implementing TQM at L'eggs was immensely satisfying to me personally and professionally because of its positive impact on people at all levels in the company. It was as close as I ever came to establishing an apostolic leadership team anywhere. Of course, since we had no idea that is what it was because we weren't thinking in five-fold terms, we weren't able to take full advantage of it, allow ourselves to be led by the Holy Spirit, and do an even better job. I often think back and wonder how much bigger our five-fold effect might have been if we had only known about the five-fold leadership concept and applied its principles more comprehensively!

TIPTOEING TOWARD DESTINY

At L'eggs and other companies where I worked, it wouldn't have occurred to us to prophesy over people. But, we did perform behavioral and motivational testing on many employees and we did put some focus on career development. However, it was mostly geared toward not forcing square pegs into round holes and to identifying unusually talented individuals we could put on the fast track to promotion via specialized training and programmed career path moves. So, in a sense, we were going in the right direction, but without the five-fold framework as a reference. Even so, it was more about making sure the company benefitted than it was about whether employees lived lives of significance. That attitude must change if a company wants to enjoy the full five-fold effect.

ACCOUNTABILITY— BEING MY BROTHER'S SERVANT

Graham Cooke says, "Accountability is calling people to be who God says they are." A team or an organization operating according to the five-fold paradigm is an accountability group. All are accountable to one another for the edification of each other and the organization. The idea of prophesying over someone to help that person perceive his or her calling and destiny may seem daunting. You may rationalize that you don't need to do this by thinking, "Am I my brother's keeper?" No, but you are your brother's servant.

When you identify someone's gifting and prayerfully put him or her in the best place on a leadership team or elsewhere in an organization, you are agreeing with God about His plan for that person's life for that season, and you are contributing to that person's realization of his or her destiny. As a leader, and as a Christian with the ability to prophesy, you have a responsibility to pray, "God, please show me what's going on in that person's life as it relates to what we're doing here, and then tell me what You want (me) to do about it."

Depending on circumstances, it may or may not be necessary or appropriate to do this out loud, or even with the person present. As well, circumstances may determine whether and how you choose to discuss with anyone what the Holy Spirit shows you. In time and with practice and study, you will develop a feeling for how to handle these issues. Of course, the CEO can't prophesy over everyone in the company. This is a delegated function that should be performed by team leaders, team by team, just as Moses carried out his role as apostolic leader of the Israelites by delegating to group officials after Jethro set him straight with a prophetic word of advice (Ex. 18:13-26).

Here's another way to think about this responsibility. Prov. 22:6 says, "Train up a child in the way he should go, and when he is old he will not turn from it." This is not only about teaching children politeness and good values. Even more, it is about helping them to discern and position themselves to walk in their destiny – that is, the plans God has for them. That is the meaning of "the way he should go." As applied to children, we rightly think of this as mainly a parental responsibility. However, on a five-fold leadership team, and especially if you have the apostolic role, which is father-like, you are in many ways acting *in loco parentis* for your team members.

None of this absolves each person you work with from having the primary responsibility for seeking God for his or her own calling and destiny, but it is a key role of five-fold leadership to help in this process. It is not hard to ask God to give you insight into His plans for someone. He will answer you. What a privilege!

CONCLUSION

The apostolic leadership, praying and prophesying over each person, brings a higher level of discernment because of its authority and maturity. The leadership also has the benefit of knowing the vision and plans for the organization, which when shared with the people, helps the people to see how their role contributes in each progressive season, widening the scope of their own discernment about God's direction for them. Only in this way can true unity of purpose be achieved so that each part can know and do its proper work in the building up of the body or organization, resulting in a full realization of the five-fold effect.

ABOUT THE AUTHOR

Walt Pilcher is a former CEO of L'eggs Products division of Sara Lee Corporation, Kayser-Roth Corporation, and Nihon Sara Lee, KK (Japan). He holds a BA from Wesleyan University and an MBA from Stanford University and has served on the Board of Trustees of Regent University, the Board of The United Way of Greater Greensboro and as a church elder. He is currently on the Board of Directors of The Apostolic Network of Global Awakening, an international evangelistic ministry. He was a contributing editor of *In-Store Marketing: A New Dimension in the Share Wars,* by Michael Wahl and an editor of *More than We Can Imagine:*

A Practical Guide to the Holy Spirit, by Rev. Dick Robinson. Walt has recently written a book which will be a practical guide to applying the principles of five-fold leadership in the marketplace. The working title is *The Five-fold Effect: Unlocking Power Leadership and Results for Your Organization.*

Walt and his wife, Carol, live in Greensboro, N.C., and attend Grace Church in High Point, N.C., where they serve on various ministry teams.

CHAPTER FIFTY-TWO

APOSTLES & PROPHETS MAKE GREAT TEAMMATES

KEN BEAUDRY

I have an incredible story to tell about apostolic and prophetic alignment that I have experienced in my own ministry lately. But first, I want to give you a little background on my history. I am a businessman and have been the owner of Beaudry Oil and Propane in Elk River, Minn. for over 30 years. My wife, Carrie, and I have a heart to see unity in the body of Christ, and to see our cities and nations transformed by the power of the Kingdom of God being manifested.

For many years, we ministered in the Catholic Church and the marketplace through prayer and discipleship groups, seminars and retreats. Since then, we have been involved with Pray! Elk River (a transformation movement) through leading a "city intercessors" group for over 10 years, being part of a "servant leadership team," and facilitating worship in our city.

We were also privileged to write a few chapters in a book called, *The Elk River Story*, written by Rick Heeren, which tells some of the things God has been doing in our city to bring unity and transformation. Through this, we have experienced the power of team ministry as our pastors, business people, and our mayor would go out to other cities to share and minister. We would experience an increase in the anointing when we would go as a team. Besides this, Carrie and I would go and minister as God would open the doors.

In 1998, I was at a conference led by Rodney Howard Browne in Brooklyn Park, Minn. Later, in that service, Rodney had an altar call to pray over everyone there. He laid hands on me and I went down under the power of God and saw a coat come upon me from heaven. I still remember it like yesterday! I got up and I did not feel any different, though, and my ministry did not change. But, unbeknown to me, God had a different plan.

I had been praying for a few years that God would give me a nation to go to and minister in. In the winter of 1999, John Matthews of World Harvest Network, called me and asked if I wanted to go to the Ukraine and teach people there Christian business principles. He told me that many people were coming to the Lord and some were in business and needed teaching on how to function as a Christian in business. This was new to them and with all the corruption, they did not know how to operate in Christian principles. I told him that I would pray about it and when I hung up the phone, I knew inside that God was up to something and I started to weep and wondered, "What is this all about?" I called John back and told him I would go.

In May of 1999, Carrie and I went to Churches of Praise in Krivoy Rog, Ukraine to minister. We met the pastor, Gregory Suchina and his wife, Galena. He pastors the main church and she also pastors a church in the same city! At that time, they had over a dozen churches in Krivoy Rog and the surrounding areas.

At first, I ministered to small groups of business people and then, that Friday afternoon, Pastor Gregory asked me to speak to a class at their Bible school—probably 50-60 people in this Bible class. As I was speaking, the Holy Spirit fell on the people in the class. All I could do was to hang on to the pulpit as God moved and people were falling off of their chairs and holy laughter was breaking out. The Holy Spirit fell on my translator also and she was twirling and dancing and could no longer translate. I did not understand at the time, but later realized it came from the impartation I had received from heaven with Rodney Howard Browne. God had decided that day to turn the key on and my ministry and life have not been the same ever since.

The pastor was not there and I did not even know if he believed in this kind of movement of the Holy Spirit and I just thought to myself, "Oh my goodness, when Pastor Gregory finds out, he is going to kick me out; I messed up the whole Bible school!" It was God that did it, but I did not understand what was going on. I was supposed to be here to speak and teach on business protocols. I stood there for over an hour or longer—the Glory of God came upon that Bible class and I could not even speak.

Pastor Gregory found out and he invited me to speak in the main church on Sunday. At that time the church held about 500 people. On Sunday, when I did the morning service, the same thing happened! I yielded myself to the Holy Spirit and could not preach much and God moved. People were getting touched, filled with the Holy Spirit and God was moving all over the place. And all I could do was watch what God was doing. There were miracles and people that had never experienced the Holy Spirit or a touch from God did so that morning. Praise the Lord! That started a journey for me of ministering at the Churches of Praise in the Ukraine over the next 13 years.

GOD'S STRATEGY

Churches of Praise continued to plant churches and reach out to their city and in February of 2002, Pastor Gregory and I spent an afternoon brainstorming—"Holy Spirit brainstorming," I call it. We thought we could strategically make a plan to take the nation of the Ukraine for Jesus. We had all of the major cities lined up to reach, but there are 23,000 villages in the Ukraine and we weren't going to these first, because they are the darkest places in the country where there is a lot of witchcraft and extreme poverty. But, God again had a different plan. He showed us when we become strategically aligned with one another, He will move.

In that spring of 2002, there was an apostolic meeting. I was not there, but John Matthews was there and a group of pastors from the churches they had planted. They sensed that God wanted Gregory set in as the apostle over the work that God was doing there. Gregory was reluctant to be called that; he had always been the "pastor." The leaders gathered around Gregory and interceded and Gregory accepted the position of being the apostle.

God so honored that word and so honored that meeting that from there a fire broke out; a fire came from heaven for church planting! People went out and started planting churches and a church-planting movement was started. Even grandmothers and young believers were on fire to spread the gospel. They went from town to town and from village to village; it was just like in the Acts of the Apostles—signs and wonders followed them. Reports of miracles came in; they could hardly keep track of them. In the next three years, over 500 churches were planted. Some had church buildings, but most were house churches. They had the problem of brand new believers becoming pastors; it was incredible. A whole movement of new church planting began to a degree they had never experienced before! Many of them started planting churches in nearby countries: in Kazakhstan, in Afghanistan, and also Armenia. Because of the recent recession, there has been some pulling back, but the movement has continued to grow.

During this time, I continued to minister there about once a year. I believe my calling is to bring an impartation and refreshing from the Holy Spirit—a stirring of the gifts and encounters in the presence of the Lord. In Acts 3:19, Peter says, *"That a time of refreshing may come from the Lord."* John Matthews and Pastor Gregory encourage me to keep coming back to the Ukraine to bring this refreshing and presence of the Holy Spirit to the Body there.

In approximately 2006, we started doing an annual Leaders Congress at Churches of Praise. This is a three-day conference in July or August for their leaders from the different cities and nations. This was more of a challenge for me as before this, I did revival-type conferences just for the people of the congregation. In the early 2000's, I saw more signs and wonders, more healings, but it seemed like my ministry lately had the time of refreshing but it didn't have the miracles and healings that I saw at first—not to the level I wanted to see! I saw some, but now I was crying out to the Lord, "I want to see more; I want to see more." I kept pressing in.

Then, in the winter of 2012, the Lord spoke to me and said to bring a friend of mine, Craig Nelson, with me this year.

Craig is also a businessman who does ministry. Craig has a lot of the same DNA as me, but with a strong prophetic gifting. Craig is an edgy guy who wears cowboy boots and is really bold. He has a strong sense of humor that the Ukrainians loved! He holds a meeting on Thursday evenings called "Miracles in the Marketplace." This meeting is held in a business and the emphasis is to train and equip people to be a minister wherever God calls you in your sphere of work, etc. Craig challenges me and keeps me challenged, as iron sharpens iron! So, Craig and I went to the Ukraine together to do the annual Pastors' Congress in July of this year. We shared some services and in a lot of them we took turns ministering.

INCREASED ANOINTING

As Craig and I ministered together, with the apostolic and prophetic coming together, there was an amazing increase in the anointing we experienced and in the fruit of our ministry times. When we would share a service, I would do what I normally do and that is to wait on the Lord. I let the Holy Spirit move and work with the worship team to do prophetic worship and see the heavens open up and the glory of God start to fall. Then Craig would come in and start to prophesy over people and give words of knowledge and take the meeting to a whole other level. It was like the Lord was using me to open the heavens and then Craig would walk into that Glory and move in his gifts. And both of us together would lay hands on the people through healing prayer lines. In all my years of ministry—and Craig would say the same thing—we have never seen the healings like we saw at these meetings!

With me being apostolic and Craig being prophetic and aligning together, we could say, in some meetings, we saw 100 percent healed in the prayer lines! Backs were healed; tumors disappeared; we saw legs grow out; a tumor in a man's left foot—the pain was gone. Many of the people we found out later were in pain the whole service and then said, "When you prayed for me the pain was gone!" Praise the Lord! There were about 1,000 people there.

At one part of the Congress, I asked the people to raise their hands if they had been healed. Over 50 percent raised their hands. So, we believe over 500 people were healed in these services and this was just in a few days. We had incredible manifestations: when Craig was speaking, my hands got really hot. I have had this happen before, but this time it was off the charts and I started praying for people for healing and the heat would go through their body.

When I would lay hands on the part that needed healing, they would feel the heat and the pain would leave. One man I prayed with had stomach problems, kidney problems; his back was hurting; this guy was in pain, and his face was just strained from all the pain. When I laid hands on him, I said, "Do you feel that?" And he said yes, because heat was going through his whole body. When people would feel heat I would say that is Jesus because it is Jesus doing it. And the man was totally healed; all the pain left. We had a tremendous move of healing! We were so caught up in it.

After the Congress had ended, Craig and I both pondered this. We also spoke in some other churches in the Ukraine after the Congress and the same anointing of healings continued. We ministered in the Churches of Praise Sunday night service and it continued to manifest there also! One scripture that John Matthews brought to my attention was Eph. 2:20-22:

...having been built on the foundation of the apostles and prophets, Jesus Christ himself being the chief cornerstone, in whom the whole building, being fitted together, grows in to a holy temple in the Lord, in whom you also are being built together for a dwelling place of God in the Spirit."

And that is what we saw: a dwelling place of God in the Spirit. With the gifting of an apostle and prophet together, we saw miracle after miracle. And sometimes, we did not have to lay hands on people. I had one meeting where God just started to touch people during the meeting. During the prophetic worship time, Craig, John, Gregory and I would start calling out words of knowledge for healings. God was showing us what He was doing. We started a testimony line and we never got to all the testimonies because of time. But, this was the kind of thing that we had for three days in the glory and another day in the church services.

We came back home and both of us have been moving in a greater level of anointing for healing since then. Craig said that all of the meetings he has been in recently where he has laid hands on people, it was just like in the Ukraine. There is a tremendous release from heaven when we align the prophetic with the apostolic, aligning together to build the Lord's house. There is a release from heaven. In my own ministry, the same thing has occurred. Most everyone has been healed when I have laid hands on them.

So, in these end times, I believe it is important that we form teams as we go out. God is looking for unity in the body of Christ. I know many churches are already doing that and seeing much fruit. We can have a tremendous gifting and end up being lone rangers, but God is looking for us to team up the apostolic and prophetic and to align with one another in the unity of the bond of peace, that there would be no competition between us. In Luke 10:1, Jesus sent His apostles out two by two:

"After these things, the Lord appointed seventy others also, and sent them two by two before His face into every city and place where He Himself was about to go."

Jesus is about to visit many cities and nations and he is looking for teams that will go out and align with Him and with each other. If you notice in Acts 8:14-16:

"Now when the apostles who were at Jerusalem heard that Samaria had received the word of God, they sent Peter and John to them, who, when they had come down, prayed for them that they might receive the Holy Spirit…"

They sent the apostolic team. When they had come down and prayed for them, they received the Holy Spirit for as yet He had fallen on none of them. So, Peter and John had specific gifts and as a team there was a greater anointing. They could have very well each went on their own, but they knew as a team there was greater power and the Holy Spirit honored that and they had a tremendous move of God and people were filled with the Holy Spirit. All through Acts, you will see teams. In Acts 13:2-3, it says:

"As they ministered to the Lord and fasted, the Holy Spirit said, 'Now separate to Me Barnabas and Saul for the work to which I have called them.' Then, having fasted and prayed, and laid hands on them, they sent them away."

In Acts 16, Paul and Silas are together. The New Testament records numerous teams, with many of them being apostolic and prophetic. In Acts 17:14, Silas and Timothy teamed up to stay in Thessalonica. In Acts 18:5, Silas and Timothy came from Macedonia. In Acts 15, Barnabas went with John Mark and Paul chose Silas and they departed and went from city to city strengthening the churches.

We are building the body of Christ—apostles and prophets together, building foundation as they go out. Thy kingdom come and Thy will be done and the kingdom of God will be upon us.

ABOUT THE AUTHOR

Ken Beaudry is a businessman dedicated to using his companies and the resources God has given him to finance revivals around the world. Best known for financing the church-planting explosion in the Ukraine where over 500 churches were planted in three years, Ken has spoken internationally on transforming cities through the marketplace. Ken has a calling and anointing for impartation of the gifts of the Holy Spirit to release marketplace ministers into their calling and destiny in Christ. Ken and his wife, Carrie, have four beautiful children and two grandchildren. To learn more about Ken or contact him, visit his website at www.beaudryoil.com.

CHAPTER FIFTY-THREE

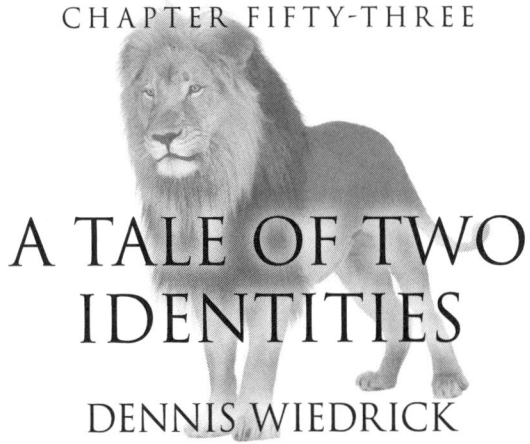

A TALE OF TWO IDENTITIES

DENNIS WIEDRICK

"It was the best of times; it was the worst of times…"
Charles Dickens

What an amazing time in which to live! There has never been a day or an hour like this. Life as we know it around the world is changing at lightning speed. Advances in science, technology, medicine, education, business, etc., are catapulting us into the future – ready or not. Knowledge is multiplying in every field. Today's "breakthrough" quickly becomes tomorrow's old news.

As Christians, we too are experiencing major paradigm shifts. The Kingdom of God is advancing so rapidly, that it has now spilled out of our churches, and is impacting every aspect of society. Our mission has changed from simply preaching the "gospel of salvation" to declaring the "gospel of the Kingdom!" Our goal is no longer to get people to "come to church," but to be the agents of change, so that eventually, *the kingdoms of this world would become the kingdoms of our God, and of his Christ!"* Finally, we are becoming as Jesus said, the *"salt of the earth, and the light of the world!"*

It's true! This could be our finest hour! The best of times!

Meanwhile, the kingdom of darkness is not idle. The enemy mobilizes his armies to go forth and deceive the nations. The news media is constantly reporting dramatic shifts taking place at an alarming pace. Economies are shaking; governments are reeling. Men's hearts are failing them because of fear. It seems as though *"all of creation is groaning and travailing"*... but why? What is going on?

In a time when it seems that *"everything that can be shaken, is being shaken,"* the world desperately looks for answers. They look for leaders. But, where will they find these leaders? Who will they turn to for the solutions? Who can accurately diagnose our societal "illnesses," and who then can prescribe the necessary medicine? Could it be that our world is *"eagerly awaiting the manifestation of the (mature) sons of God"*? Could it be that we, the church, have actually been given the *"keys of the kingdom,"* and that God is wanting to partner with us to see whole cities and nations transformed?

As those who choose to be aligned with God, we could, right now, be taking ground at an unprecedented rate. As those who advocate a "kingdom paradigm," and a scriptural worldview, we could be leading the nations *"out of darkness, and into His marvelous light."* As those who are saying "yes" to the Great Commission, we could be ushering in the beginning of a global harvest, the like of which the world has never seen before!

But, for those who choose not to be aligned with God, the days could become very dark. Nation will rise against nation; there will be wars and rumors of war. The worldly economic systems, which are already stalling, could eventually collapse, taking the hope of nations down with them.

And so we see the great divide: the best of times, the worst of times; the huge chasm that exists between what God has planned, and what the enemy is trying to accomplish.

But God.

And God is still looking for someone... a man, a woman, anyone who will *"stand in the gap,"* as a *"restorer of the breach."*

THE PASTOR

Enter: "the Pastor." For hundreds of years, evangelical Christianity has looked to the "pastor" to be God's chosen vessel to "shepherd" us into His Plan. We have counted on the pastor to evangelize, baptize, teach, and correct. To marry, bury, counsel and direct. In short, we have asked him to be and to do all that Jesus commissioned the whole Body to do. We have consequently ended up with a "shepherd and a flock," but not a functioning "body" where every member has a vital part to play. So, this pastor has valiantly attempted to stand in the gap between an ungodly culture, and *"the narrow way"* for centuries. But, the odds were against him from the beginning.

In my travels around the world, I have noticed that the vast majority of pastors have been trained to lead in a certain way. I call it the "Levitical priestly mindset." What do I mean by this? Well, we all know that 12 tribes identified the Israelites of the Old Testament. One of these was the "tribe of Levi." This was the priestly tribe. Their complete focus was on the temple... the house of God.

They were trained, clothed and anointed to serve in the things of the temple. They offered incense, made blood sacrifices, and stewarded the rituals of the law. They had to dress a certain way, speak a certain way, and function in a certain way, or risk being disqualified.

However, the greater issue was what the Levites were NOT allowed to do. Because they were "sanctified" or "set apart" for the temple, they were not allowed to be involved in the *"cares of this life."* They were to *"come apart, and be separate, and not to touch the unclean thing."* Here are some of the restrictions they had to observe:

- They could not own land.
- They were not allowed to conduct business in the marketplace.
- They could not go to war or use weapons of any kind.
- They were not encouraged to have a vision or to function in any way in the entrepreneurial spirit.
- Furthermore, they were not even to provide for themselves, but were to trust God's people to bring their tithes and their offerings for their support. Then their entire focus could be exclusively on the things of the temple.

Well, that model worked in Old Testament times, because there were 11 other tribes all involved in those other things. All the bases were covered. Twelve tribes, each having a specific assignment = "God's order."

Now, the problem comes when we take the Levitical model of the Old Testament, and make it our template for the New Testament minister. We have a NEW covenant. It is, according to Hebrews, a better covenant, founded upon better promises, by a better mediator, who offered a better sacrifice! *"The glory of the latter house is greater than the former!"* Hebrews chapters 7, 8, and 9 highlight the huge contrast between the old and the new. Had the old covenant been sufficient, there would have been no need for the new. But the old fell short. No one could be justified under the Law. We needed a new covenant.

JESUS

Enter Jesus! Now we have a better Mediator between God and man. Now we have a High Priest who entered once and for all into the Holy of Holies, and sprinkled His own blood on the Mercy Seat, forever atoning for our sins, and reconciling us to God. But notice, He did not come after the order of Levi. He is a priest forever after the order of Melchizedek!

Well, who was this Melchizedek? There has been much discussion about this unique character in the Bible. Some say he was a pre-incarnate manifestation of Christ, *"without father, without mother, without genealogy, having neither beginning of days, or end of life, but made like unto the Son of God..."* (Heb. 7:3). Others say he was a man, who manifested a Christ-like image. Either way, he was certainly very different than Levi!

He was a priest, and for that reason, had full authority to enter the Temple, and to engage in priestly activities. However, he was also a king... the king of Salem. As a king, he would be well within his sphere of authority to own land, go to war, employ weapons, steward resources, and engage in all kinds of marketplace and entrepreneurial activities.

So, we can now see how beautifully Jesus manifested the Melchizedek anointing. He had full authority as a priest to enter the temple (even at the age of 12), to teach the scriptures, to offer sacrifices, to pray, and then... to leave the temple, go out into the marketplace, to function as a Jewish businessman (carpenter), to engage with fishermen, tax collectors, doctors, etc. and ultimately to reign as a king on a throne!

Jesus is *"a priest forever after the order of Melchizedek!"* This was prophesied numerous times in the Old Testament, and declared several times in the New Testament, which leads me to my next point.

I believe the two most important words in the New Testament are, "in Christ." *"If any man be 'in Christ', he is a new creation." "There is therefore now no condemnation to those who are 'in Christ.'" "'In Christ', there is neither male nor female,"* etc. It follows then that, if we are 'in Christ', then we are not of the order of Levi, but of the order of Melchizedek!

SET APART FROM THE WORLD?

My experience, like many others called to the ministry, was to prepare by enrolling in a Bible School or Seminary, to learn how to be a "priest." We were taught theology, as well as how to walk, talk, and to conduct ourselves as "ministers." I was told that to fully serve God, I needed to abandon all interest in business, politics, or "worldly" pursuits. I was told that a real "man of God" is set apart from these activities. It was as though to be engaged in them would mean to be "defiled" by them.

But, weren't some of the apostles also fishermen? Wasn't Paul a tentmaker? Weren't Pricilla and Aquila prosperous business people? They were not restricted to things of the temple. In fact, so much of what happened in the early church happened outside of the temple! Have you noticed that most of the miracles in the New Testament did not even take place in or near a religious building? Most were out on the street where the everyday activities of life take place.

When Jesus made the supreme sacrifice on the cross, the veil that separated the holy from the unholy was rent in two from top to the bottom! No longer, God – in a box, hidden behind a veil. Now it can be "Immanuel"— God with us! No longer separated! No longer... the "sacred" vs. the "secular" (not even a biblical word). But, God *"in all and through all!"*

No longer is the Glory of God confined to a 'temple' but *"the glory of the Lord shall cover the earth, as the waters cover the sea!"* You do not have to choose between being a "priest" restricted to the temple, or a "king" functioning just in the marketplace, but you can be both! How? In Christ!

Because of our religious tradition, many of our leaders (pastors) have been trained to be Levites. They have then set the defining tone in the church as priests, and not as kings! Consequently, many gifted entrepreneurs and visionaries cannot relate to the shepherding flavor of churches that are pastorally led. They cannot get excited about entertaining or babysitting Christians. Our whole focus shifted from the Great Commission to the Church... with our programs, buildings, traditions, and priorities all directed inwardly! The body of Christ has then come "to church" to do the priestly thing, but has not been equipped to go out into the world, as kings ... to reign!

Nowhere in the Bible are we told to build the church! *"Except the Lord build the house, they labor in vain that build it!"* Jesus said, *"I will build MY church..."* We are told instead, to *"seek first the kingdom of God, and His righteousness..."* How often have we sat through church services, where the leader stood in the pulpit declaring something like this:

> "I have a vision! And you, the congregation, have the great joy of participating with me in MY vision! So, I need you from Monday to Saturday to "go into the highways and byways, earn money, and then on Sunday, bring all the tithes and offerings into the 'storehouse' to equip me to fulfill MY ministry!"

This is Levitical thinking! This is NOT the New Testament model! The Body of Christ is not called to equip the "Pastor" to fulfill his vision. On the contrary... HE, as part of the five-fold ministry of Eph. 4:11, is called to equip THEM to do the work of the ministry! Not just one vision in the house, but many, with every man or woman equipped to do his or her part.

In no way am I diminishing the importance of the local church in the plan of God. I absolutely believe in attending and supporting the local church! But, not as an end in itself. The kingdom is much larger than the church. We as the Body of Christ have a much greater assignment than just to be self-serving or maintaining the status quo!

In Ezekiel 47, we read how a mighty river flowed out from the temple, over the threshold into the streets. First, it was up to the ankles, then the knees, then the waist, and finally, waters deep enough to swim in. This is a prophetic picture of the river of life that is meant to flow out from the Throne of God, through the church, out into the streets of our cities.

Sadly, in our religious dysfunction, we have largely reversed this. We have tried to get the river to flow from the streets, into the temple, where eventually it becomes stagnant, because it has no outlet! Any river that flows into a place, and then does not flow out, becomes a swamp.

We need a transformation! We need to individually and corporately cast off the Levitical garments, and to put on the robes of Melchizedek! We need to break out of our religious traditions and learn how to reign on the earth as kings AND priests!

THE APOSTLE

Enter, "the apostle." "We are right now experiencing the greatest reformation since Martin Luther," according to Dr. C. Peter Wagner. He calls it the New Apostolic Reformation. There is a radical shift from a "pastoral" mindset of "tending the flock," to an "apostolic" mindset of taking territory! Whether that territory is geographical, political, economic, creative, or spiritual, apostles are all about "occupying until He comes!" We will no longer hide in our religious buildings and sing choruses while we wait for the Second Coming, but we will assemble to be equipped and then to go into ALL the world and subdue kingdoms.

The "pastor" is learning that he is but one of five anointed ministry gifts, given by Jesus to his Bride, after He ascended on high! Now we have apostles, prophets, evangelists, pastors and teachers, all of whom have something of tremendous value to contribute to the church. With these anointed men and women working together, the sleeping giant of the church can arise, and march through the land once again as it did in the Book of Acts.

Years ago, I had been invited to speak in a church not far from my home. As I prayed about what I would share, I saw a vision of Jesus knocking on the door of the church. It reminded me of the passage in Rev. 3:20: *"Behold, I stand at the door and knock..."* However, this time in the vision, Jesus was not on the outside of the church trying to get in, but He was on the inside of the church wanting to get out! It was as though He were locked inside. Imagine, the Son of God – a prisoner in His Father's House!

The pastor's desire is to get all the "sheep" into the "sheepfold" so he can heal them up. The apostle's desire is to equip them and then send them to the ends of the earth to impact all spheres of society! Both giftings are necessary! One does not displace the other. They are complementary. Can you imagine what could happen if we can finally grow up as the Body of Christ, and learn to function in both the priestly and the kingly? Can you envision the global impact we would have if Christ in us were allowed to be both "Shepherd" and "King?"

We could be that generation. This could be our time. The clock is ticking. The *"great cloud of witnesses"* could look over heaven's balcony and celebrate that the church has finally become that glorious Bride, adorned for her Husband. Then shall come the fulfillment of Peter's declaration that we truly are *"a Royal Priesthood."*

ABOUT THE AUTHOR

A zeal for God's house underscores 35 exciting years of ministry by Dennis Wiedrick that includes pastoring, teaching, intercession, and extensive overseas missions.

Touched significantly by renewal, Dennis brings a powerful message of reconciliation to pastors and leaders around the world. His life message highlights the priestly ministry of intercession as an absolute prerequisite to all other fruitful activity. His book *A Royal Priesthood* is an effective tool to mobilize the church to pray.

Dennis and Katie serve as Directors of Divine Exchange Inc. (www.divineexchange.ca), a marketplace corporation whose goal is the release of individuals and their businesses to fulfill their God-given mandate in the marketplace through the keys of prophetic-apostolic intercession and revelation.

Dennis and Katie presently reside near Oshawa, Ontario, Canada.

CHAPTER FIFTY-FOUR

APOSTLES FOLLOWING CHRIST'S MODEL

KENT HUMPHREYS

*"Then he appointed **twelve** of them and called them his apostles. They were to accompany him, and he would send them out ...He sat down, **called the twelve** disciples over to him...At daybreak he called together all of his disciples and **chose twelve** of them to be apostles...Taking the **twelve** disciples aside... He took Peter, James, and John with him, and he became deeply troubled and distressed."*
(Mark 3:14, 9:35; Luke 6:13, 18:31;
Mark 14:33; NLT, author's emphasis)

As apostles and as leaders, God has called us to follow the model of His Son Jesus. As Jesus prayed in John 17, He had primarily spent His time on this earth investing into the lives of 12 men. Apostles must realize that all the leadership that provide to other leaders and the masses, pales in comparison to the investment that they must have with those "12" they God has given to them. We forget that most of the teaching and preaching will soon be forgotten, but the investment that we have made into the life of a key leader will last for generations. Any leader who does not make himself vulnerable to others will soon find himself all alone.

We were created by God to need the community of those of like heart and passion. Jesus preached and taught in the temple, in the marketplace, and out on the hillside. But, most of His time was spent with the twelve in constant discussions and training situations. The legacy that a leader leaves will not be in great public accomplishments as much as in the investment that she or he makes in those closest to them.

THE SMALL GROUP

You as a leader must be involved in a small group of your peers on a regular basis. This can be with *other leaders* who have similar responsibilities as you do or with those that you are seeking to train. We need to in either case be vulnerable, teachable, and transparent. We need to share the real issues that we are dealing with whether they are in our family, our job, our finances, or our ministry to others. You may look at your schedule and ask how you could ever have time for such a group. The fact is that you cannot live without this experience of community. Jesus modeled it for us so strongly that we cannot miss it. Leaders cannot live a solitary life. We desperately need community and were created for such companionship.

I have been in numerous groups over the years in my responsibilities both in the context of the church, leading a ministry, and leading a business. I have been in groups that met weekly, bi-weekly, monthly for a half day, monthly for a full day, and quarterly for 48 hours. In the quarterly group, we had 10 men who not only owned businesses, but most of them also led ministries. These times together for several days every few months became lifelines for these leaders that had huge responsibilities. These groups have been the lifeblood for my growth and accountability. I have been challenged both by my peers and those that I was supposed to be training. We as leaders must have this time of intimacy. We cannot live without it regardless of how we may try to avoid it. And if we are not vulnerable, then we will experience the consequences of our actions.

A weekly group can have a time of teaching through a written lesson, a Biblical passage, a chapter in a book, a DVD, or any other form of curriculum. There should be a time of catch up in the beginning, a time of discussion of the lesson, and then a time of application. There may be one member of the group that may want to bring up a critical issue for the group to discuss briefly. There should be a time of prayer where the group gathers around that one person, lays hands on them, and prays for God's guidance or protection or healing. The group should have a time of community prayer before closing. As leaders, we must not get too far from this basic form of ministry that Christ modeled. It is the best form of teaching, of training, and of relating scriptural principles to real life.

Every year your group may change. As you move or change positions in the ministry or in your workplace, you will have to adjust your connecting times with the key peers with whom God has called you to be in relationship. What is critical to you as a leader is that you not let this form of fellowship and accountability be taken out of your schedule. Remember to have such a group with your peers and/or such a group with those that you are currently being asked to train. Each of these groups will serve different purposes in your life but may be similar in form and purpose. We never get too old or mature for the basic needs that God has put into the hearts of each of us. These groups may take even unusual forms as we get older and go through different stages of life.

We just met for the 20th year with seven other couples in our "empty nester" group. We meet each year for a long weekend to fellowship with the couples that are totally invested into every area of our lives. All of these couples are true followers of Christ and have key positions of leadership in their churches and communities. We are committed to each other for the long haul. We want to finish well and be there for each other as we face the tough times of life, family, ministry, and aging. One member of the group lost her husband five years ago to a heart attack. Another lost his wife after she dealt with cancer for seven years. Last year the two of them were married, which consolidated our group from nine to eight couples. Do you have a group of committed followers of Christ who are standing with you for the long term?

AN INNER CIRCLE

Not only did Jesus model to us the small group of twelve, but He modeled to us the inner circle of the three. From time to time Jesus would pull aside the three – Peter, James, and John – in order to give them a specific teaching or truth. We as leaders will not survive over the long term without an "inner circle" of two to four others who care about our soul. These do not have to meet as a group. They may even live in a different city or state. These are the people that you would call if you have a crisis in your life at 2 a.m.

You need to have someone who knows you well and can give you biblical advice, comfort, and wise counsel. We need other leaders who can call us back onto His pathway when we falter and those who can warn us of the potholes ahead.

I grieve because probably 50% of the Christian leaders that I meet do not have even three other leaders that they can turn to. Many pastors and leaders are alone and are becoming more alone each year. I find that as I get older, I need these relationships even more, but they take time. As we move geographically, change positions, and transition in life, we lose some of these people and have a hard time replacing them. It takes years to build these close relationships which have real intimacy.

God has called me as a workplace leader to represent Him through my business. He has called me to a global calling of teaching and encouraging business leaders to represent Him in and through their businesses and in their communities. I have been given opportunities as a leader in the workplace move of God to encourage and teach leaders in churches, universities, seminaries, denominations, and in other ministries.

As a vulnerable leader with physical limitations and human weaknesses, I cannot assume any of these responsibilities without a number of key men and women who are committed to me as a person, as a leader, and as a fellow member of the Body of Christ. As they stand by my side, pray for me, and hold me accountable, then I am able to continue forward as just one of the soldiers in His army. Who is standing by your side? Who are those with whom you are having regular times of refreshment?

Just as Jesus sent out the 12 apostles to fulfill His Great Commission as they went to the nations, He is calling you and me today as leaders in His army to be trained in the same way that He trained the twelve and the three. We are not only to listen to and obey His words, but we are to follow Him as His true disciples and followers. He tells us to pattern our lives after His example. We are to consistently disciple those that He has given us in practical everyday living. He has modeled for us to sit at His feet with up to 12 others and listen to His Word, discuss it, and apply it to our lives. We are to take those special times apart with the three to get a special word from Him.

Do not get so busy with all of those responsibilities that you have as a leader that you "shortcut" your key relationships. Only one-third of the leaders in the Bible finished well. About one-third of the leaders today finish well. If we are to be one of those few who finish well in His race while representing Him, then we need to be in and consistently use the small group to train and have community for ourselves. We need to take the time over the years to find and to keep an "inner circle" of others who will care about our soul and keep us on track. May God help us to follow the example of Jesus and not neglect this important teaching.

A FINAL LESSON

As Jesus faced the Cross in His final days, He spent some time earlier in the week teaching in the temple. Then on the final night He decided to spend it with the twelve. We read the story in Mark 14. Jesus gathered the twelve together for that last supper (verse 17). After Judas left the group (v20), Jesus took the remaining eleven to the garden with Him (v26). He then asked the eight to remain and took the "three" with Him.

The Scriptures relate what happened next in Mark 14:33-36 (NLT): *"He took Peter, James, and John with him, and he became deeply troubled and distressed. He told them, 'My soul is crushed with grief to the point of death. Stay here and keep watch with me.'"* He went on a little farther and fell to the ground. He prayed that, if it were possible, the awful hour awaiting him might pass him by. *"Abba, Father," he cried out, "everything is possible for you. Please take this cup of suffering away from me. Yet I want your will to be done, not mine."* Jesus wanted to make sure that we as leaders did not miss this important point. Look closely again at chapter 14 of Mark.

Jesus had modeled to us the importance of teaching to a large group in the temple. Now on that last night, He modeled three other important lessons. First, He was spending the time with the twelve. If I knew that tomorrow night would be my last night, then I would throw a big party and have all of my friends and family over for a huge celebration. But, Jesus spent time with the twelve. Then, for one more time, He modeled the time with the chosen three. Do not let others keep you from playing "favorites." Do not miss that special ministry with the three that God has given to you.

Finally, notice that Jesus went a bit down the pathway and fell on His face before the Father. He poured out His heart to His Father. Look carefully at what Jesus had planned. Jesus had allowed the "three" to hear every word of His prayer to His Father. Are you doing the same? Are you allowing those closest to you as a leader to see your personal relationship with your Father? Are you vulnerable and allowing those to see your innermost struggles? Are you allowing them to experience with you the great personal victories?

Jesus intentionally allowed Peter, James, and John to be with Him in that crucial moment. He wanted them to hear his prayer in John 17, which included praying for us today. Jesus wanted them to hear his Heart as He was soon going to the Cross. Few leaders, particularly religious leaders, allow others to see them in vulnerable positions. Make it your priority to allow just a few to see you as you are before the Father.

CONCLUSION

We as leaders will be better used by God if we follow the example of His Son Jesus. We need to have the twelve and the three in our lives. We need to make time for the ONE, the Father. We need to allow His Holy Spirit to flow through us as we are in the group of the "twelve," experiencing time with those in the "three," and having the sweet time with the "One" and only God the Father. My prayer for each of us as leaders is that this example of our Master, Jesus Christ, will burn in our hearts for all eternity. I pray that we will never be able to get that example out of our conscience. May we truly follow His example and bring glory to Him as we represent Him to others.

ABOUT THE AUTHOR

Kent Humphreys has been a business leader for 40 years. While owning and operating a nationwide general merchandise distribution business for 25 years, he worked with the nation's largest retailers. After selling the family business, Kent continued to be involved in commercial real estate and the medical distribution businesses. From 2002 through 2007, he was president of Fellowship of Companies for Christ International, an organization that equips and encourages Christian business owners who desire to use their companies as a platform for ministry. Kent now serves them as a worldwide ambassador for FCCI (Christ@Work).

For many years, Kent has spent much of his time ministering to business leaders, pastors, and students across the country through speaking, writing, and mentoring. He has spoken in seminaries across the United States and at numerous international conferences. He traveled extensively overseas for many years. Kent and his wife Davidene have written a number of books including: *Show and then Tell* (Moody Press, 2000), *Shepherding Horses*, 2006, *Christ@Work Opening Doors, Impacting Your Workplace for Jesus Christ* and *Christ@Work in Your Transition, from the Campus to the Workplace*, 2010, and *Letters to Workplace Leaders* and other titles of the *My Heart to Yours* series, 2011. Kent and Davidene have three children and eight grandchildren, and make their home in Oklahoma City. To learn more or contact Kent, visit his websites at www.ahpartners.com and www.fcci.org.

EDITOR'S NOTE:

Kent Humphreys graduated from this life on Jan. 30, 2012 after a three-year battle with a rare lung disease and will be greatly missed, deeply mourned, and joyfully celebrated by all who knew him. His was a life well lived. He finished well.

CHAPTER FIFTY-FIVE

MARKETPLACE APOSTLES: RAISING UP TERRITORIAL LEADERS

ED TUROSE

One word from God can change your life forever! There are many business men and women who are not leading churches as Pastors but instead are chosen to impact the marketplace within their sphere of influence and build the cause of God's Kingdom. Below is an example of such a word.

"And the Lord says son, I'll promise you that which I have begun in you, I am able to bring forth. And I see a pulling within the midst of you. And I see at times where you say, 'God, I don't even know if I like business anymore. And my heart is being so drawn to things of ministry.' And the Spirit of God says, 'Son, right now, I am going to settle it within your heart. I have called you a businessman.'

"And the Lord says, 'Son, I am not going to break your heart. Son, I am going to put you in an arena that most Pastors would envy the results that can be brought forth in the business world.' And the Lord says, 'Son, I am not going to break your heart, but son, I am giving you a pulpit,' says God, 'that is bigger than that which is tied down to a church. Son, I am giving you a pulpit,' says the Lord, 'that has greater dimensions than one geographical area.' And the Spirit of the Lord says, 'There has been a wrestling even

within your heart like Jacob with the angel and you say bless me God, bless me God. Do what you said you were going to do. But at the same time, your heart was pulled in two different directions.' The Lord says, 'Son, I am settling some things in the midst of you. You will know ministry, but you are business.'"

—Prophecy given to Ed Turose by Dr. Sharon Stone
Christian International, 9/23/1995

As one who is chosen in this arena, I have my attention and focus on my specific gifting and anointing as it relates to the Kingdom Cause. When I began to eliminate the distractions in life by staying focused on the building of God's Kingdom by bringing heaven to earth in my business on a daily basis, I saw the hand of God back me, according to Mark 16:15-20.

"And he said unto them, Go ye into all the world, and preach the gospel to every creature. He that believeth and is baptized shall be saved; but he that believeth not shall be damned. And these signs shall follow them that believe; In my name shall they cast out devils; they shall speak with new tongues; They shall take up serpents; and if they drink any deadly thing, it shall not hurt them; they shall lay hands on the sick, and they shall recover. So then after the Lord had spoken unto them, he was received up into heaven, and sat on the right hand of God. And they went forth, and preached everywhere, the Lord working with them, and confirming the word with signs following. Amen."

God is on the move and He is raising up leaders within territories that have a gifting in the marketplace to change their local culture. Many marketplace leaders that are not in full-time ministry need to understand that the foundational gift that they have is to operate in business and fulfill their role as an influencer in the marketplace and use the marketplace as an outpouring for their ministry.

When I realized I had a gifting and anointing to impact the marketplace, one of the major conflicts that I encountered was what to focus on most, business or ministry? As Dr. Sharon Stone spoke over me that I am business but will know ministry, that settled it for me. My business is my ministry.

PERSONAL TESTIMONY IN BUSINESS

I want to relate to you my personal story of how God has positioned me into the place of my destiny. Since 1977, I have worked for two Fortune 500 companies – 10 years with Uni-Lever, the largest package goods company in the world, and over 22 years with the Coca-Cola Company. Both of these companies have impacted the world and gained influence in many different nations. Why did God position me with these companies that have an apostolic mindset to globally influence the lives of so many people? I manage millions of dollars on a daily basis, so when it comes to managing wealth for the Kingdom of God, I have been trained and equipped in how to handle it.

I believe that God has positioned many Marketplace Apostles by allowing us to work for secular companies to bring Kingdom principles into the marketplace and see success. As God is transferring the wealth to us to build His Kingdom, we are ready to transition into the role as Ministers of Kingdom Finance.

In the past 30 years, I have received many prophetic words about millions of dollars flowing through my hands to build the Kingdom of God. Isa. 61:6 says, *"But you shall be called the priests of the Lord; people will speak of you as the ministers of our God. You shall eat the wealth of the nations, and the glory [once that of your captors] shall be yours"* (AMP).

Marketplace Apostles are Ministers of Kingdom Finance. They are ones chosen to finance and build the Kingdom of God territorially through their sphere of influence. They have an anointing to affect all or a specific number of the Seven Mountains of Society: business, government, education, arts and entertainment, media, family and religion.

There is a cry coming forth throughout the earth to unite business people to take over the mountain of business in the marketplace. However, many want to enjoy the covenant blessings of Abraham, but refuse to answer the call of that covenant to be a blessing. Every day as I enter the marketplace, I need to understand that God has blessed me to be a blessing!

Deut. 8:18 says, *"But you shall [earnestly] remember the Lord your God, for it is He Who gives you power to get wealth, that He may establish His covenant which He swore to your fathers, as it is this day"* (AMP).

You see the covenant that he is referring to is the covenant of Abraham that you and I are under and according to Gal. 3.29, we are heirs to this covenant...and if you are Christ's, then you are Abraham's seed, and heirs according to the promise" (AMP).

As a child of God, we all have a responsibility to answer that covenant call according to Gen. 12.2-3:

"...and I will make of you a great nation, and I will bless you (with abundant increase of favors) and make your name famous and distinguished, and you will be a blessing (dispensing good to others). "...and I will bless those who bless you (who confer prosperity or happiness on you) and curse him who curses or uses

insolvent language toward you; in you will all the families and kindred of the earth be blessed."

I believe there are two keys that I have incorporated into my life to enter into my destiny as a Marketplace Apostle. The first key is in the area of positioning. In 1977 when I started my career in Fortune 500 companies for 10 years I worked for the Unilever Corporation and was able to do things out of my natural ability, but I was not positioned correctly under a true apostolic ministry. In 1988 the Lord began to speak to me to get repositioned under a church that was preaching present-day truth.

This church was in the beginning of the apostolic movement and I was just getting into the place of understanding the apostolic. I began to get equipped and trained for my destiny. I spent many years serving that man of God and was equipped, but was still not positioned correctly to fulfill my destiny. God had a higher place in the apostolic for me that would satisfy the longing of my heart. I was using my gifting of training leaders, overseeing cell group ministry and leading worship which were all priestly functions but did not know that my kingly call was the apostolic in the marketplace. We are to operate as both a king and a priest according to Rev. 1:6.

In 2004, a good friend of mine, Patrick Ondrey, an internationally-recognized author and speaker, and President of Patrick Ondrey International, told me to begin to pray for strategic apostolic relationships. It was in September of that year that I was in a local meeting and met Apostle John Kelly, President of LEAD and Convening Apostle for ICA. Apostle Kelly took me under his wing and opened the door of opportunity for me. He saw the apostolic marketplace gifting in me and offered me specific platforms to speak and minister throughout the nation.

In another meeting of marketplace leaders which I was invited to in January 2005, I was able to meet another man of God who had a tremendous impact in my life. Bishop Bart Pierce, Bishop of Rock City Church, in Baltimore, Md. took me under his guidance and fathered me in specific areas of the marketplace calling in my life.

For me, the kingly gift of a marketplace apostle, was triggered and manifested when I submitted myself to a true apostolic father. This is where the doors of my gifting were completely opened and I was able to move to the next level.

Since I have faithfully served and submitted to my spiritual fathers, I have seen the fruit of the Lord opening the platforms for my anointing to be a blessing to many others.

I was able to develop a father/son relationship with both Apostle John Kelly and Bishop Bart Pierce. They became my spiritual fathers and began to give me insight into where I needed to go to fulfill my destiny. However, these men lived hours away from me and my current Pastor that I was under was following me into the Apostolic rather than me following him. It was out of order, but God opened the door to another local fellowship in 2008, I was able to connect with and get positioned under Apostle Dr. Mark Kauffman, Jubilee Ministries International, in New Castle, PA.

I found my DNA! His vision for the territory matched the vision God gave to me. I was now positioned under an Apostolic man of God where I could now focus on being a territorial marketplace leader within my local area. The key was to be correctly positioned, find my right spiritual DNA, bone of my bone, and submit to that vision and see success. The Kingdom Cause that I was after became a reality!

The second key is submission. I have traveled and spoken throughout the United States and I see many business men and women who have an independent spirit, not submitting to the set man or woman of God. Although there have been past situations in the Body of Christ that might have misrepresented the area of submission, today is a day where covering is critical. When I got submitted to the authority God placed in my life, I became free to allow those men to speak into my life and make changes because I could trust these fathers in the faith.

ROLE OF MARKETPLACE APOSTLES

Before we identify the role of a Marketplace Apostle, we need to understand that we are sons of the Most High God and our marketplace gift is what we do. 1 John 3:1-2 says, *"Behold, what manner of love the Father hath bestowed upon us, that we should be called the sons of God: therefore the world knoweth us not, because it knew him not."* Rom. 8:14 says, *"For all who are led by the Spirit of God are sons of God."*

I am a son of God! As a son I have the right and authority to change the atmosphere in the marketplace, which is my sphere of influence. In my career, I have been down-sized twice, made promises that were never kept, been lied to, and had a few million-dollar ideas stolen from me. However, if everything in this world falls, one thing will stand forever; I am a son of God! By knowing that I am His son, I can then do what He has called me to do. Please remember it is not what you do but who you are that truly matters.

A Marketplace Apostle must understand their functioning role in the marketplace within the company they work for or if they own their own business. I refer to this as operating in the Business Anointing. There are four key areas that the Spirit of God directed me to incorporate in my life to help me fulfill the calling as a Marketplace Apostle.

- Understand that I have been chosen.

- Operate in my covenant both vertically and horizontally.

- Make a full commitment to build the kingdom of God.

- Submit to my covering to be protected in my days of battle.

By operating in this Business Anointing, the fruit is distribution. In 1999, I was driving to Buffalo, N.Y. when God told me to pull over to the side of the road and write down what He was telling me. I heard that the calling on my life was to build distribution centers through my marketplace gifting to be a blessing to others. I then heard that I was to begin to mentor sons and daughters to be distributors of the anointing in their spheres of influence. God then gave me the messages and books to write on focusing on specific areas to see results.

Let's begin to discuss how you can incorporate these four key areas into your life.

Chosen: (Matt. 22:14) *"For many are called, but few are chosen."* Many are called but I believe few are chosen to enter into the role of a Marketplace Apostle as a territorial leader. The word calling and chosen according to Webster's 1828 Dictionary are very different. Calling means those summoned. Many are called or summoned to enter into their destiny in the marketplace. However, the word chosen means those selected from a number;

picked out; taken in preference; elected; predestinated; designated to office, distinguished by preference.

John 15:16 says, *"You have not chosen Me, but I have chosen you and I have appointed you [I have planted you], that you might go and bear fruit and keep on bearing, and that your fruit may be lasting [that it may remain, abide], so that whatever you ask the Father in My Name [as presenting all that I AM], He may give it to you"* (AMP).

You have been chosen, picked out by preference, selected and highly favored. From the very beginning of my days at a small Christian College in the mid '70s, I knew I was called to finance the Kingdom Cause. I started sowing my tithes, offerings, alms and eventually my firstfruits when I was in college. In 1988, I received my first prophetic word about God using me in business and a year later received this prophecy:

"Brother, you've got a burden for men. I see you being used in the business world. I see God raising you up to pray for businessmen. I see you as one who is going to be working with a lot of businessmen. And I see you as one to open up the door of their heart and you are going to leap over the walls of pride and male ego and you are going to get down and hear men confess things to you brother that will shock you and blow you away. But, God is going to make you like a shock absorber before He releases that type of ministry through you. And when men begin to pour out their heart to you of how they have cheated on their wives, how they have stolen from their funds and how they have cheated on the IRS and the government, the Lord is going to begin to use you brother to pour in truth and the mercy and truth God is going to pour through you is going to bring a deliverance and bring stability in their lives. It is going to bring forth restoration in their homes.

"I see training and disciplining and for you all to be raised up and branched out in this area. Brother, I see the dollar sign written all over you. The Lord has an increase for you. The enemy has come in and he has tried to steal; he's tried to rob you; he said it would never work; you'll fail. But the Lord says, 'Son, I've got prosperity in store for you, My storehouses are full and the vats are going to overflow for you,' says the Lord. 'For yea the time and season are in My hand. You walk with Me and I'll open up the windows of heaven,' says the Lord. 'There is no shortage with me,' says the Lord. 'Press on; keep fighting the battle for yea the Lord says the battle is not yours; the battle is Mine.'"

As I related before, I was called to be in the Kingdom. However, for years my five-fold gifting was not being used in the marketplace. I was operating in biblical principles in the companies I worked for, but my Pastor did not understand how to deal with me when my heart longed to build the Kingdom in the local marketplace. It was not until an Apostolic Father came into my life, stirred that specific gifting and established a platform for my gift to work at a greater level of executing the Kingdom Cause both nationally and within my local territory.

My focus as a chosen vessel in the marketplace is to equip, train and mentor business people both nationally and internationally. Secondly, I am submitted to my local Apostle to have influence within my local territory by being part of a local team changing our culture. What are you chosen to accomplish? Who is God calling you to minister to and bring life to?

The second area of focus was to understand the covenant I have with God and with man. A covenant is a mutual consent or agreement of two or more persons, to do or to forebear some act or thing. Covenant means I will enter into a formal agreement and bind myself to that covenant. The key to walking in the covenant is both vertical and horizontal.

We have a covenant with God that we need to tap into and utilize daily. I am empowered to prosper to be a blessing so God's covenant provides the blessing that I need to then impart or apply this blessing to others in the marketplace. This is an example of vertical relationship.

Covenant love must be applied to others in the Kingdom. You must establish horizontal relationships with those people who celebrate you, not those who tolerate you. I have developed peer covenant relationships with those who I can trust with my battles and can help me in overcoming my weaknesses. I need to be held accountable through a covenant of love with people who will be able to stand with each other. The greatest relationships are those who are covenanted together and will sacrifice all to keep that relationship strong and successful.

I have a covenant relationship with individuals who stand with me while I am operating in my marketplace gifting. Once I was in a slump situation in my business with one of the most upscale and fastest-growing grocery chains in the northeast. I needed to reverse the negative trends and get my business with this customer back on track. I reached out to two covenant brothers for prayer and agreement. The first brother was a local relationship and we got together and began to pray for wisdom and solutions for this customer. Since this customer was three hours away and I had a relationship with a couple who lived in that area and knew they had spiritual authority in that area, I reached out to ask them to pray for the territorial spirits to bow their knee when I came into this area.

In a short period of time, great favor was given to me by this customer. I was able to apply the solutions the Spirit of God provided for me during the time I spent with my one covenant brother. Secondly, the airways from the prayer of the local leaders lifted any oppression and I was able to turn my business around, gaining new distribution and providing a plan that reached my volume objectives.

In order to walk in the covenant of God and man, you must exercise your God-given authority (Gen. 1:26-28) and apply your vertical relationship with the Father to hear His voice and then apply your horizontal relationships to gain agreement to achieve greater success and productive results.

Commitment: "To engage; to pledge; or to pledge by implication." The cause of the Kingdom demands a commitment. Many people are afraid to commit. Is He just your King or is He your Lord? As my Lord, I have a responsibility to commit my talent, time and treasure into His service.

Let me give you an example of the word commitment. I committed myself to become a member of a church that was preaching present-day truth and then made myself available to be equipped and trained in biblical principles. It was then that I saw greater levels of success when I applied those principles into the marketplace where I was employed.

But, God also wanted to use these talents in the local church. My wife and I submitted ourselves to our leaders and got into a cell group system where we were trained, raised up and held accountable. We were quickly moved into cell group as leaders and our group grew from 10 to 50 adults and 25 children in a short time. We were chosen and were committed to being used for the Kingdom Cause. After a few years we became the leaders over the entire cell group system.

I was part of the worship team and then God raised me up to be a worship leader in our church. However, I knew the hand of God was on us to be big givers in the house of God. We have always been givers, but God was talking about building His Kingdom with the wealth of the wicked, which is millions and billions of dollars. You need money to build God's Kingdom and change the culture of poverty, sickness and disease! We began to confess health and wealth. 3 John 2 says, *"Beloved, I pray that you may prosper in every way and [that your body] may keep well, even as [I know] your soul keeps well and prospers."*

My wife and I have been debt free since 1993. But, in late 1999, I was in prayer and I told the Lord I was going to enter into making a demand on His supply to build His, Kingdom. I asked the Lord to bring me an additional $10,000 so I could sow that money to local projects since the tithes and offerings from our congregation were not getting the job done and allowing us to impact our local territory. I heard the Spirit of the Lord say, "It's about time somebody made a demand in the financial arena."

In March of 2000, I was supposed to get a bonus from the company for the past year's sales achievement. I gave a seed nine months prior to the time I was expecting the yearly bonus. We believe in the principle of seed time and harvest. My boss called me and informed me that we would not be getting a bonus because the company did not make the volume objective or the gross profit number for the past year. I told my boss that I believed we would get a bonus, explaining to him in terms he could understand that I sowed for that bonus and worked hard for it. He laughed and said there would be no bonus this year.

I went to God and told God that before the year started I made a demand on His finances to come into my hands to build His Kingdom. Within the week the company called my boss back and told him that they gave us an unachievable volume number and that we would each receive a bonus. The company sent me a bonus check for $20,000. Again, I believed God for an extra $10,000 to bless and build His Kingdom by using my marketplace gifting.

A few months later in August, my wife and I were in a faith convention in Fort Worth, Texas. During one service, the man of God who was preaching began to explain that in this covenant of Gen. 12:2-3, we have the coat of the blessing on us. The coat of the Abrahamic blessing is on each and every one of us so we began to make a declaration that God's super would come on our natural in the financial realm to build the Kingdom. We have been empowered to prosper to be a blessing to others.

I made my declaration and as I walked out of the arena in Fort Worth, I went back to my hotel room and called my voicemail exchange for any messages. I heard the following message. The company for the first time in history had made their profit projections and wanted to give each individual a second bonus check this year! A check for $10,000 was on its way to my home and arrived before I got home from the conference. I now had $30,000 in my hands when I asked God to give me an extra $10,000. God was not done yet; a few months later in the month of October I was in New York

City for a sales meeting and my boss got up and began to tell us that the company was reviewing our salary compared to other competitive companies. Our company decided to increase our salaries so they gave me a $12,000 raise retroactive for that particular year. This increase totaled $42,000 for the year because I made a demand on the wealth of His Kingdom to be a blessing to others!

God gave me more than enough in just one year and since that time my income has doubled and my giving has tripled. Not only do I have the resources to build His Kingdom locally, but I now have the financial resources to empower God's marketplace warriors. I have the resources to write and print books, empower people with CD series and workbooks through my website. God has blessed me with the resources now that I can be a blessing to other people and take what I've gleaned out of my Fortune 500 experience for the last 30 years and put that into your hands so that you can be raised up as a territorial marketplace leader.

In the early 1990's a great woman of God named Fuchsia Pickett who has written many books on the Holy Spirit came to our church and spoke this word over me.

"You have been one that has been saying I want the Teacher to teach me the Book. You say I want to be able to hear what He said, not what somebody else said. You have cried out to want to know revelation; well I have news for you. My Father says Ephesians the first chapter; beginning to the 15th verse is going to be yours. He is going to grant unto you not a word of wisdom, not a word of knowledge, but the Spirit of Wisdom and the Spirit of Knowledge. The Spirit of Wisdom and the Spirit of Knowledge. And the Teacher is on duty. Don't stay out of the classroom; don't stay out of the classroom; the classroom is inside of you! Go in, read that Book and have

Him to teach it to you. Because He said there is open to you a
Spirit of Wisdom, not just a word. The Holy Spirit will move
in you in wisdom and knowledge and revelation. And when
you stand to preach ... do you preach? When you stand to
preach; it won't be your words it will be what He taught you."

When I entered into the quiet place with God, everything that I have created in the marketplace such as books, CD series and workbooks, have been developed in me while spending time with Him. I challenge you to get into His presence and He will provide you with all you need from innovation to concepts to execution to solutions to gain greater levels of success.

Covering: "To shelter; to protect; to defend." In this day, you need to have spiritual covering over your life. It is not just a suggestion, but it is a mandate in the times that we are living in. When a Pastor or Apostolic leader begins to cover you in your endeavor to build God's Kingdom, each believer will experience God's government being activated within their life and they will begin to experience greater success and a protection from the hand of the enemy.

I want to relate a final story to you about how I was covered in a specific battle that the enemy had assigned against me to take me out of my position within the company I was working for.

After spending many years with a major Fortune 500 company and receiving very favorable performance recaps, I hit a major distraction. There was a severe accident that involved my son and we had to personally take care of him as caregivers. During this time, this accident got me so focused on him that it affected all other areas of my life. I realized that he took preeminence but I had to stay focused to maintain my job and my other family relationships.

The company I was working for had a grading system as follows:

- 5.0 – Best of class – (very few received this performance rating)
- 4.0 – Above Standard – (some were able to attain this)
- 3.0 – Standard – you are doing your job effectively – (most received this grade)
- 2.0 – Below Standard
- 1.0 – It gets ugly!

Under a previous manager, I was averaging 3.0 and 4.0 ratings in all 5 of my key areas of focus. I got a new manager and our personalities were very different. Although his thinking processes were different from mine, he was one of the best managers I have seen in creating processes that produce great results. During a visit into my area in the fall of that year, he graded me very highly and we had a positive work experience together. Six months later as I was in the company HQ getting my final review for the previous year, he asked me what kind of year I had. I told him it was a great year compared to my peers coming in second in volume achievement and number one in financial management which was a major focus area of the company.

THE BATTLE

The manager's response to me was that even though it was a good year for me, he did not like the way I got my results, so my performance rating became three 3.0's, and two 1.0's. I was now on 90 days probation and would be terminated after 90 days if I did not make some changes. I was in shock since he had not worked with me for over six months and the last work together was favorable. What should I do? I personally know the Vice President of the company and I thought about calling him to complain. I could call Human Resources and complain. I could defend myself and show him to be in the wrong or I could shut up and get focused. I thought it out and decided not to defend myself to upper management and instead get focused! I called my Pastor, my apostolic covering, and we prayed for protection that this would be resolved and that God would redeem me. I submitted myself to the covering God had in place for me, took authority and began to stand on God's word as I went to work to see God's hand of redemption. I stood on this scripture during this battle:

"But no weapon that is formed against you shall prosper, and every tongue that shall rise against you in judgment you shall show to be in the wrong. This [peace, righteousness, security, triumph over opposition] is the heritage of the servants of the Lord [those in whom the ideal Servant of the Lord is reproduced]; this is the righteousness or the vindication which they obtain from Me [this is that which I impart to them as their justification], says the Lord" (Isa. 54:17).

During the next 90 days, I refocused on my processes and areas where I might need to improve on. I had to provide weekly updates and follow through on areas that he felt I needed to change. A former peer of mine was promoted and given the task to hold me accountable on making the necessary changes. One of the greatest areas to improve focus is when someone can hold you accountable. After working with me for six weeks, his conclusion was I just needed a few tweaks in just one area. He reported back to my manager to change both 1.0 ratings back to 3.0. I worked hard for those 90 days and in the end I knew if I stayed focused, I would see a great result. After 90 days I was pleasantly praised by the words "great job" from my manager.

The following March I was in the National Sales Meeting when they announced the Sales Manager of the Year award winner for the prior year. That's right, my name was called and I was honored along with my food broker as the Manager and Broker of the Year! How could that be when I was on probation for 3 months? I was covered in my day of battle and according to the word I was standing on, I proved my boss to be in the wrong.

These four areas have helped me stay focused on my gifting as a territorial marketplace leader. My call now is for distribution. I am a Kingdom Distributor and I was made to change my local territory into the area of His blessing. Health and wealth are attached to me as I fulfill God's Kingdom cause. How about you?

Are you chosen to fulfill your destiny by becoming equipped and trained as a territorial marketplace leader to impact and influence the area God has called you to live in?

Are you living in the covenant of God both vertically and horizontally so you can be empowered to prosper to be a blessing to others in your local territory?

Have you made a total sold out commitment to use your time, talent and treasure in seeing the Kingdom cause manifest within your local area?

And finally, are you submitted to a spiritual covering that will protect you in your day of battle?

These four areas have positioned me for success. If I am not operating in all four then I am missing a critical part of the fullness God wants us to walk in. Take time to examine your life today and see what you need to do to make the necessary changes and become one of God's Kingdom warriors taking the mountain of business for His glory!

Additional marketplace resources are available at www. FocusCoach4U.com

ABOUT THE AUTHOR

Utilizing the gifting of exhortation and empowerment, Ed Turose bridges the gap between the workplace and ministry, and has a gifting to release finances and empower people to experience greater levels of success. Ed has over 30 plus years of business experience as a people manager, trainer, and strategic planner for two Fortune 500 Companies: Uni-Lever and the Coca-Cola Company.

Ed Turose is also President of Peak Performance, a marketing, training, and strategic planning consultancy serving corporate, government, and nonprofit clients which offers strategic business solutions that will increase profitability, productivity and efficiency.

He has authored two books and workbook series entitled, *The Focus Fulfilled Life,* which helps individuals to get focused to achieve better and greater results. He also has authored many workbooks/CD series called "Business Keys to Succeed," "The Business Anointing," and many other marketplace resources. He is an Elder under the ministry of Apostle Mark Kauffman at Jubilee Ministries International, New Castle, Penn. To learn more or contact Ed, visit his website at www.FocusCoach4u.com or by email eturose@ zoominternet.net or phone 724-748-1065.

CHAPTER FIFTY-SIX

APOSTOLIC IMAGINATION: A PREFERRED FUTURE FOR APOSTOLIC MARKETPLACE INITIATIVES

DR. JOSEPH UMIDI

APOSTOLIC IMAGINATION

The battleground for the Apostolic in the church has been waged on several fronts. With reformation Protestantism, it has been the poverty thinking over the centuries that de-legitimized the apostolic role by replacing it with the canon of scripture. Within the Roman Catholic, Eastern Orthodox and some Pentecostal liturgical traditions, it has been the institutionalism of transferring the apostolic role only to the office of Bishop or beyond. Within our current attempts to rediscover the apostolic legitimacy both in and outside the church, there has been the tendency toward a superstar, CEO, hierarchical approach (Matt. 20:25-28). None of that has created a compelling case for an energized focus on receiving, raising up, and releasing the Apostolic in the marketplace, so that leaders can respond to the overdue need in the nations at this 11th hour.

It is time to re-imagine our approach to the apostolic that reenergizes waves of apostolic gifts, ministries, and leaders in the marketplace. To do so requires another language that frees us from circular group thinking, tired categories of definitions, and the stale bread of yesterday's manna. In short, we need a fresh perspective on how to define and express an Apostolic Intelligence, as well as an Apostolic Office. We need to honor and hone an Apostolic Imagination that gets us outside of our categories and into a future governed by creativity. Einstein summed it up well when he said, "The only thing that interferes with my learning is my education."

Apostolic Imagination is recovering an Apostolic Intelligence. It is applying the language of metaphor, story, dream, and prophetic word pictures that give us new categories to see what God is up to with the Apostolic in today's economic environment. It gives us another perspective other than EQ and IQ that help us measure the kind of intelligence that God is providing to establish His kingdom purposes in the vocational spheres that are shaping our nations. In short, Apostolic Imagination is the application of an Apostolic Intelligence that results in a Brilliance @Work, expressing the creativity and the character of God in the way that only Apostles can steward.

Before we present this brief overview of an Apostolic Intelligence (AI) in the marketplace, we need to be sure that our language for spirituality in the marketplace is not tethered to the confines of stain glass thinking. Here is a plain glass approach to a Spiritual Intelligence (SI) that lays the groundwork for our call to the AI in the marketplace.

SPIRITUAL INTELLIGENCE

A legitimate question to revisit here is to ask, "Just what makes a person spiritual, and what difference does that make at work?" That is the first question I encounter whenever I mention this topic to executives. It is a question that is well worth the time it will take to read this chapter for a unique frame of reference.

There are as many definitions to spirituality as there are tribes that express certain aspects of their traditions. With the unique SI approach being presented, there is an ability to redefine and reframe this perspective. God's relationship with us, our integration with ourselves, our ability to live that out with our family, and then expressing that on the job, brings a fresh approach to this topic. These are areas that everyone can relate to despite their particular spiritual heritage.

It is an integration that people are longing to see no matter what expression we adhere to because people prefer that we be real and not religious, no matter how much devotion we may have in a particular expression. At the end of the day, people only want to know how real we are with ourselves, with our family and with the people we work with. That is the litmus test for a spiritual quotient in the vocational mountains. Spiritually intelligent men and women create a culture of honor in the workplace.

We should start with first things first and that is what we are calling Spiritual Intelligence or the Spiritual Quotient in our lives. This SI or SQ is not about being religious. It is not about being denominational. It is not about a title or an Office we occupy, including the Apostolic. It is really about being what we already are. We are spiritual beings with the capability to increase our SI in ways that make the difference for a Brilliance @ Work.

Prov. 20:27 says, *"The spirit of man is the candle of the Lord."* All of us then, as spiritual beings, have the potential in God's design to be "bright" or "brilliant" and can have a light that shines in us and through us at home and at work. The spiritual intelligence quotient is what we use to develop our longing and capacity for meaning, vision, and value. It allows us to dream. It is in essence what makes us as fully human as Jesus was fully man.

I love our God-mandated capacity for dreaming: *"Faith is the substance of things hoped [dreamed?] for..."* (Heb.11:1). SI gives us permission to dream or even dream again. I have come to see from over 15 years of coach training around the world that the pathway to transformation comes through our life-long dreams. Re-awakening and re-connecting to our dreams will cause us to be energized, keep us motivated, and keep us looking for the best even in difficult times. It also drives us to look for the unique role of the apostolic to bring them forth.

There is a large international hotel chain in which I had a coach-training contract that wanted to be number one in customer service excellence. They had already determined that the best way to do it would be simply to come up with a list of excellent behaviors for their front line staff and to make sure those workers checked off as many of those as possible each day to reach this goal. In our first manager meeting I suggested to them that in addition to having that list, they could actually come at it from a different angle.

I recommended they approach this goal in terms of what most motivated their workers to be creative in serving customers, and emphasized that they first discover the dreams of what their front-line workers had regarding their job and why they were there. It was the beginning stage of developing a culture of honor, but it was met with resistance initially.

Most of these managers thought that was kind of odd. They had not operated that way before. Quite frankly, many of these managers looked down on their front-line staff in a condescending attitude. They were not as educated. They certainly did not have the same social-economic background. It created a stir, but they took a chance when they hired me that I was on to something. That is when I gave them their first assignment.

I trained them on how to shift the culture of their supervisory meeting with their staff by asking questions. In the very next staff meeting they were to ask, "When you kick your feet out of bed in the morning, before they hit the ground and you think about coming to work, what excites you the most about working here?" To their surprise they discovered that there was 75% of their front-line staff that were motivated because they were fulfilling a dream to send money back home to their relatives, parents, children, and spouses, to be able to help them in the village and lift them out of their poverty.

That is when the culture shift began. Something transformational happened to these managers. First of all, they realized that their dreams for coming to work were not nearly as big as their front-line people. They also realized that their staff had family values that were deeper than theirs and a sacrificial living that challenged their own self-centeredness. A subtle shift began in the hotel work atmosphere as we began to move forward. The managers became more than supervisors with a check-off list. They became dream managers helping their people fulfill their own SI. Today this hotel chain is approaching number one in customer service excellence because they honored the spiritual intelligence of their front line staff. Even though they are not educated, they had the same longing for meaning, significance, and for dream fulfillment, as does the most educated of all of us.

KEY 1: INTIMACY

First, and most importantly, there is a desire in each of us in SI to have a sense of Intimacy or sensitivity to the creator, to God personally, that we would have an ability in some way to know that God has uniquely and lovingly created us for a purpose, and that this purpose in us is close to God's heart. However we express this, we are recognizing that many of us, even before we were religious or involved in any particular faith subcultures, had moments where we had awakenings or connections and had a sense of the nearness of God. This is an intimacy and sensitivity in many ways that is beyond just religious talk. It is really about a relationship, a personal relationship with a Personal God.

Intimacy means we can hear God on the job and in the midst of some difficult circumstances, conflicts, no-win options, double binds and insurmountable odds. God does a great job of communicating to those that simply desire to listen. The key is to have a sensitivity that is tuned to hearing God. Most of us want to be more productive at work. The counter-intuitive principle that I have learned is that "productivity is really a byproduct of intimacy."

KEY 2: CREATIVITY

The second key to SI is Creativity, which we are defining in our context as the ability to have insight onsite, to have a solution or a perspective that may be an alternative to opinions not being presented at the table. Creativity is a critical piece, the ability to approach things from other angles, and the openness to avoid the circular group think in a management system or in a worker's discussion.

There is always another way to approach a challenge or an opportunity, and creativity is giving permission to us to do it. Simply asking some powerful questions such as: "If you were able to ask anybody for their opinion who is not in this room, who would you want to ask to see how they would approach this situation?" You may call to mind one of your mentors, a historical person, or an author that you have read. There may be creative solutions that come when we actively listen for the ideas coming from a trained ear that hears God's voice, sometimes opening up a way where there seems to be none.

Many people today are hungering for a creativity that has eluded them for years. A recent survey revealed that 85% of people are not fulfilled in their jobs, including 50% of CEO's. Most are bored and are not getting out of bed each morning with a passion for their life on the job. Their creative juices have dried up and they are on autopilot just going through the routine of a day. The same old beaten cow path has become worn and weary, and they need a bridge to a new pathway to look at their development and fulfillment in the workplace where they spend most of their lives. They need a SI that doesn't simply help them to do their job better, but to view their life at work more creatively.

In a recent study at California's Stanford University, researchers came to the conclusion that the number one inhibitor of consistent creativity, the primary thing that holds back creative expression in people, is a judgmental attitude. Most are judging themselves, judging others, and being fearful of being judged. The product of this is an inhibited creative expression in an individual and in an organization. People can't be themselves on the job and so are looking for more time to be themselves off the job.

Research has also shown that consistent creativity does not come from tired people. When we look at the historical patterns of great breakthroughs in science, apostolic pioneers and architects, we usually see hardworking men and women at the laboratory or at the workbench who put in heroic hours looking for a solution. Yet many times the creative breakthrough came when they got away from the work environment and were playing tennis or taking a swim or perhaps even taking a shower, and then it all came together—the divine ah ha!

It all began to make sense when they had removed themselves from the work environment. Why? The reason is simple but profound. They actually were able to enter into a disengaged mode, a place of rest and restoration. Then and only then were they able to experience the creative flow that was locked up when they were so focused only on producing and on the work itself.

KEY 3: PERSPECTIVE

The third key to SI is called Perspective and "perspective power" is being able to reframe the context of what we are facing. Many times when we look at a situation we may have one or two or three options and they all seem to be negative or limiting, but through coaching or an "honoring conversation" we can go to a place of looking at what would it be like from other perspectives not seen initially until we look for them. By aligning ourselves, quieting ourselves down, and stepping out of the box in our approach, we can come up with four, five, six, or seven different options that were not there initially. Perspective power many times becomes the breakthrough idea that enables a way through where there seems to be none.

I can recall situations where it seemed like everyone had exhausted all options until we facilitated people to get in touch with their sense of connection with God, their adjustment to the alignment that He brings, and disengaging from the situation to come back at it later. Many times they returned with a fresh approach: one that did not seem like it was there before, and it made all the difference.

When we are ascending a mountain, the dangerous times are when storms may hit us trying to reach the summits and some of the great stories and heroes that we honor have come out of these seasons. These stories are really the stories of spiritual people who were able to live that out under extremely difficult circumstances.

Taking that metaphor from the mountain climbers, we believe that the ability to be a spiritual person who is assessable, have a spiritual model that others can feel is attainable, and live a spiritual lifestyle which is relevant to others around us, will be the common practice at healthy workplaces. That is the real deal: not the religious ideal for some, nor is it the religious ordeal that has become the unpleasant reality for others. That is the new deal that people have longed for and when they see it, when they taste it, and when they touch it, they know that this is the kind of a person that they want to work with. This is the person that they can give their best with. That is you and I who are operating with Spiritual Intelligence in the workplace.

People really do not leave jobs; they leave relationships. If you and I would aim for excellence in our spiritual quotient, and see ourselves making some progress along this assessment, then we are going to be the type of person that people want to be around. I want to spend my hours on the job with people like this. As we assess ourselves at home and at the workplace, the question of the hour is how can I be on all eight cylinders in terms of my spiritual intelligence and where do I need to be able to shore up in some areas that may be tripping me up and keeping me from being my best. That is the spiritual quotient on the ascent of our cultural mountains. That is the foundation for what we are calling for in an Apostolic Intelligence.

APOSTOLIC INTELLIGENCE

On the foundation of SI the unique role of AI in the marketplace can be described both in its absence and in its fullness. The absence of AI in the marketplace results in a culture of management/control instead of multiplication/ empowerment. Without it there is a failure to reproduce and transfer that results in poor succession and one generation impact. When AI is weak the end result is blurred identity and purpose without strategic alignment to core values and purpose.

Apostolic Intelligence is expressed in leaders who demonstrate the courage to interrogate reality. They do that by matching founding assumptions with current running reality by consistently asking questions such as, "What values do we stand for, and are their gaps between these values and how we actually behave?" Going beyond their apostolic name tag they have enough AI to have learned that the person who can most accurately describe reality without laying blame, will emerge as the leader, whether designated or not.

I am presently engaged in executive coaching with franchise owners who have drifted into mediocrity and stagnation. There was an absence of AI in their organization. When God spoke that to me with Intimacy and Insight, I was able to get a Creative plan that gave a new Perspective to the Senior Executive team.

That plan included working with these owners to determine what needed to be called forth from them back into the DNA of their franchise organization. After several training/consulting sessions with them we distilled several key themes to train and coach their franchise owners over a five-month period. As of this moment we are seeing significant results and ROI with the reawakening of the AI that was in the founders themselves, but had become diluted throughout the organizational structure.

The presence of AI in the marketplace is manifested when we focus the core role of marketplace apostles to emphasize their qualities as Pioneers, Entrepreneurs, and Architects. These word phrases are crucial to the fundamental role of DNA custodians that those with AI must steward with excellence. They imply leadership styles that are decisive, strategic, bottom-line measured, and designed focused. Yet these words and their styles applied without AI can result in a driven, demanding, insensitive approach to others.

AI is having the courage to take responsibility for the emotional wake that we may leave behind our daily work-paths. An emotional wake is what you remember after I am gone...what you feel. It is the aftermath, the aftertaste, or the afterglow. In fact our emotional wake determines the narrative that is being told about us, and our organizations. AI is learning to deliver our alignment messages without the emotional load or baggage that has too frequently been part of organizational cultures that have missed their apostolic opportunities.

APOSTOLIC LANGUAGE

A preferred future for the Marketplace Apostolic influence is one that will require an increased Apostolic Intelligence. The "river that runs through" this intelligence is the role of a language that can free itself from the past limitations and describe the terrain with a new perspective. The frequent quote of, "He that controls the language controls the culture" has great implications for what language we choose for this future.

Culture counts and language matters. The famous Colombian Shuttle disaster was not due to individual error, as determined by multiple hundreds of hours of analysis. Rather, it was in the way NASA conceived and articulated their own organizational management culture. The language they used meant that they did not even have the categories to see the problem coming, let alone resolve it!

The language of metaphor, story, and prophetic word pictures can serve an AI release into a future that will cause a multiplication of marketplace apostles that are built to last. One way is to provide an Apostolic Profile as a beginning template, though not as a "one size fits all." Here is a start:

POTENTIAL LANGUAGE FOR A MARKETPLACE APOSTLE PROFILE:

This person can see the future as well as align an organization pragmatically to get there. He/she is a self-confident pioneer with an assertive entrepreneurial influence that embraces risk while building foundations that will support trans-local multiplication. As the conductor of the orchestra they are able to interface and piece the puzzle together, utilizing every tool available, including the supernatural. With their keen sense of people motivation they are able to assess and evaluate personal character and discern healthy group dynamics. Every aspect of the organizational culture they touch is moved with high influence and synergism with all the other parts.

Another way to give language to this profile is to create a script or narrative that describes a typical future in the life of an apostolic marketplace leader or organization such as the following:

> "Bill had another great week of living his dream as a kingdom advancer in the marketplace. On Monday he was able to extend his market influence into a multi-cultural niche that has the potential of going viral. Even though he suffered from the competitor's smear campaign opposition running up to this breakthrough, he was warned in a dream of what to say at a critical juncture that tipped the scales in his favor. The decision to avoid a potentially devastating merger came when Bill influenced the partners to stay true to the values foundation that had been formed in the beginning. His read on the timing and the pulse of the market enabled the alignment of all the stakeholders and established a clarity and order that had begun to drift apart. Bill

knew that this new momentum would fuel the alliance of his company with the missionary thrust of the orphanage development that several of his employees had scouted out during their business trips overseas. He now envisioned putting out the call to the other marketplace apostles to form an alliance to appeal to the national government to release its resources to those who had been without a voice for generations. He slept well that week dreaming of the Five-Fold teams that would be received, raised up, and released in this developing nation because of the breakthrough his company had just seen."

We need a passionate core of apostolic networks, churches, and businesses to fund and fuel the kind of movies, dramas, art, You Tube and internet stories that paint the picture of these kind of scenes to call forth emerging apostles into their marketplace destiny. These case studies can become part of our five-fold equipping and allow those who have not found their apostolic voice to re-script their lives around a compelling narrative that keeps them playing a bigger game and living a bigger life.

APOSTOLIC METAPHOR

One of the most powerful roles of our media is to capture the imagination of a group so that the culture is shaped and formed by the metaphors they have created in the hearts and minds of a critical mass of early adapters. This works both for good and evil purposes and is a key to the purposes of God to establish His kingdom through the marketplace apostles. Here is an example of the metaphor that describes my apostolic role as the founder and president of an international movement of Transformational Coach Training centers in 24 countries and 14 languages.

"As a Father of a transformational coaching movement, I am a Watchman on the Wall who watches over the gates of leaders' hearts and a community's dreams to give them courage to welcome a move of the Holy Spirit into their personal and organizational destiny and legacy."

The key word picture or metaphors here are the words "Father," "Watchman," and "Dreams." These have captured my apostolic imagination in the ways that *Braveheart* captured the word "Freedom," or that *Field of Dreams* captured, "If you build it he will come." More than just words, they have become "burning bushes" to a sight and sound generation that, like Moses himself, is compelled to turn aside and gaze (Ex. 3:3). They capture the imagination to become fuel for the smoldering flame of apostolic dreams that have been doused by the voice and tapes of the border bullies that have hemmed us in to our traditional thinking.

Prophetic coaching conversations have been the tool that God has given me to speak into the bound Lazarus inside many marketplace apostles who need a powerful phrase or word picture to come out of their tombs. The prophetic ministry awakens us out of our graves but we still need coaches who can unbind us and let us go into our destiny.

Our preferred future is one that will empower and release an Apostolic Imagination. The marketplace is ready. Here am I—send me.

ABOUT THE AUTHOR

Dr. Joseph Umidi has served as Professor of Ministry at Regent University for the past 28 years while serving in senior leadership roles of several churches in Virginia during that time, including 13 years of Pastoral leadership in Canada prior. For the last 14 years he has served as the Senior Director of New Life Ministries International, a church network, church planting and missions organization based in Virginia Beach, and Founder and President of Lifeforming Leadership Coaching, Inc., the largest Christian Coach Training ministry worldwide in 22 countries and 12 languages. He is also Co-Founder of Equityforming Performance Consulting.

Dr. Umidi has authored numerous articles and books dealing with Church, Organizational, and Personal Transformation and is working in community and international transformation strategies with several ministry organizations in the developing nations. He is married to Marie, Founder and President of TMCJ, Inc., an international Gospel Arts ministry, and the delighted grandparents of three grandchildren. To learn more or to contact him, visit his web sites at www.lifeformingcoach.com or www.equityforming.com or www.newlife.cc.

APOSTOLIC CREATIVITY & INNOVATION

CHAPTER FIFTY-SEVEN

THE ART OF FAITH

MAX GREINER, JR.

INTRODUCTION

God made me an artist when I was born in December of 1951. I have been told my entire life that God put an abundance of creativity in my DNA, along with the artistic skills necessary to express my imagination.

By the grace of God, I have made my living from my artistic gifts since 1974, when I graduated from Texas A&M University, with an architectural design degree. I began my professional fine art career in 1978, after first practicing architecture in Dallas and advertising in Los Angeles.

Many times throughout my life, people have asked me what must they do to have success. By the grace of God, my professional work experience in the fields of architecture, advertising, commercial art, fine art, photography and writing allows me to speak to this question with some degree of experience.

My life journey as an artist has taught me many things about life and God. I pray my story will bless your life. Jesus Christ expects His children to be a blessing to others.

The Bible also says that if we give, it shall be given back to us. I have learned this spiritual principle is true in every area of life.

DESTINY

We all have a God-given destiny, totally unique from anyone else who ever lived. We serve a creative God. In this life, we can walk into our God-given destiny, or away from it. The choice is ours. We can use our gifts, talents, intellect and skills to build God's Kingdom, or we can use them to build our kingdom. Some may even use their God-given gifts to build Satan's kingdom. Jesus said a wise man builds his house upon the Rock.

God has a good plan for our lives. Like any earthly good father, God wants the best for His children. He wants us to prosper spiritually, financially, socially and physically. This is why the Bible clearly instructs us how to live a righteous life, and tells us how to pray for God's will in every circumstance. However, God's ways are not our ways. His ultimate objective is to make us into the likeness of His Son, Jesus. As a result, in this fallen world, we are all allowed to go through some very difficult circumstances in our walk to eternity. God perfects His children in this life, in preparation for Heaven.

God is the Master Sculptor and we are His sculptures, fashioned uniquely for His glory. We can yield to the Sculptor, or we can resist Him. However, no matter our level of submission and obedience, God patiently chips off the parts of us that don't look like Jesus. God wants people to see Jesus when they look at us.

I know from my own life that this can be a long and painful process. Trials, tribulations, and disappointments are always hard. During God's sculpting process, many things don't make sense. This is where faith in God comes in. Ultimately, we have to trust Him.

The good news is that the Holy Spirit always makes a way for us to make the right choices in every situation. He also brings good out of bad, for those who love Him and are called according to His purposes.

My advice is to yield to the Master Sculptor. Allow Him to fashion you into a vessel of honor, just as He desires. Then, when He is finished, people will see Jesus in you. Choose God's plan for your life, not your plan or Satan's. God's plan is always the best, and fastest way to live a fulfilled, successful life. True joy, peace, fulfillment and satisfaction can only come from living out your God-given destiny, whatever that looks like.

FAST TRACK TO DESTINY

There is a fast way to unlock God's destiny, and there is a slow way. The key is to pray and obey. I learned the hard way, not as hard as some, but still hard for me.

By the grace of God, I was saved at age seven at Calder Baptist Church in Beaumont, Tex. From that point on, I knew God had made me an artist and that I was His child. Thanks to godly parents and grandparents, I grew up in the blessing, instead of the curse. Basically, everything was good in my life until age 32.

My prayers up until 1983 went something like this: "LORD, PLEASE HELP ME DO WHAT I WANT TO DO TODAY, IN THE NAME OF JESUS, AMEN." Today my prayers have changed to: "LORD, PLEASE HELP ME DO WHAT YOU WANT ME TO DO TODAY, IN THE NAME OF JESUS."

SCULPTING THE SCULPTOR

In 1983, for the first time in my life, things took a serious downward turn. Everything had been great up to that point. I had a beautiful wife named Sherry, who loved God and me. I headed several state and national non-profit archery and conservation organizations. Bowhunting, camping, backpacking and canoeing were my hobbies and passions. I successfully bowhunted deer, elk, bear, lion, caribou and antelope across North America. I had a profitable fine art career creating drawings, paintings, sculpture and jewelry.

By the age of 35, our family art business had sold over a million dollars worth of my fine art. My drawings, paintings and bronze sculptures of wildlife sold for thousands of dollars each. We owned a beautiful ranch in the Texas Hill Country, with the dream to build a unique, passive-solar (green), earth-sheltered home/studio.

Everything was great, I was living MY dream. Then, during the mid '80s our world collapsed, almost overnight. First, Sherry and my dad were diagnosed with serious, life-threatening illnesses. Then, the Texas oil, gas, agriculture and real estate businesses collapsed. About 95% of my art collectors went bankrupt in that recession. Many came to us wanting their money back since at the time, we were offering a 100% money back guarantee on my art to collectors. So, we refunded art purchases until our money was gone. As a result, we could not make payments on our beautiful land, or the "temporary" mobile home we were living in at the time.

I was shocked. Everything had been good my entire life, and then suddenly everything was going wrong. I was losing everything important to me: my wife, my marriage, our business, our art collectors, our land and home, and my dad. Bow hunting wasn't even in the picture anymore. There was nothing I could do; all the hard work, optimism, talent and education I had could not fix any of my problems. For the first time in my life, I felt hopelessness and despair. I cried out to God for help. I asked for instant miracles, but God chose a slower path. He had a few things He wanted changed in me before I could finally walk into my true, God-given destiny.

A VOICE CRYING IN THE WILDERNESS

Jim Beard, a Methodist friend and minister from my college days, after learning of our predicament, called and prayed for us. However, even though I read the entire Bible at Jim's suggestion, our lives continued to spiral downward, as I tried to fix everything myself. It wasn't working. At the lowest point in April of 1986, when we were out of money, and had not made our land and mobile home notes in months, the Holy Spirit spoke to me clearly as I drove onto our driveway.

God said to my spirit in His still, small voice: "MAX, I WANT YOU TO MAKE A SCULPTURE OF JESUS WASHING PETER'S FEET." I immediately said, "BUT GOD, WHAT ABOUT ALL THESE OTHER THINGS I AM DOING?" I disobeyed Him, not seeing how creating a sculpture of Jesus could solve all of my problems. That was a bad mistake and a very costly one, which delayed my God-given destiny for two more years and kept me stuck.

LIFE LESSON

If you are sure you are hearing God correctly, obey Him immediately, even if you don't understand what is going on. Unfortunately, at the time I disobeyed God, since I could not see how creating a small sculpture of Jesus washing Peter's feet could help anything, except teach me about humility. I figured that could wait. As a result, our lives got worse, on every front. Despite repeated promptings from the Holy Spirit, and my wife, Sherry, I refused to do the sculpture and continued to work my plan.

Finally, in May of 1987, God started speaking louder and stronger to our family friend, Jim Beard in College Station, Tex. The Holy Spirit repeatedly told Jim to tell me to stop what I was doing and to obey. However, each time Jim delivered the prophetic word, I rejected it. I stubbornly continued to do things my way. The Bible calls this being stiff-necked.

Finally, in April of 1988, Jim gave me a hard word which I finally received. God told Jim to tell me: "UNTIL YOU DO THIS WORK, NOTHING ELSE YOU DO WILL SELL." That got my attention since we were out of money at the time. The fear of God came over me and I finally yielded and started working on the small 1/6 life-size wax sculpture. Immediately thousands of dollars in sales started to pour in, saving the Greiner Art Gallery, home and land from foreclosure.

WASHING FEET

On May 3, 1988 in order to better understand Christ's foot-washing example, Sherry, Jim and I washed each other's feet. It was a profound and humbling experience. Finally,

I had given the LORD a teachable spirit so He could reveal His destiny for me.

In February of 1989, I completed the small 1/6 life-size sculpture which God told me should be called "Divine Servant"®. At the time I did not have the money to cast it into bronze or print literature. So, Sherry and I mailed letters to our clients who were not bankrupt and within a week we sold 24 bronze sculptures at $1,200 each! God instantly solved our financial crisis to our amazement!

A few months later, in July of 1989, after I surrendered fully and made Jesus Lord of my life as well as Savior, God began to implement His plan for my life and destiny. At the Christian Booksellers Convention in Atlanta, Ga., Herman Baily, a TV show host with the Christian Television Network in Florida, was drawn into my small 10' x 10' exhibit booth. When Herman saw the "Divine Servant"® sculpture he prayed that God would make it possible to create the composition full-size. I had never dreamed of making a large bronze sculpture, due to the expense. Herman, a stranger at the time, prayed that God would raise up the buyers to make the monumental bronze possible.

EMPOWERED FOR DESTINY

At the end of the CBA convention, on the last day, and the last hour of the week-long show, through divine providence, Sherry and I prayed with a total stranger in his booth for the Baptism of the Holy Spirit. As Southern Baptists, we did not believe this spiritual experience even existed. The man from St. Louis, Mo., full of wisdom, power and humility, was named Bill Banks, a gentle servant of God from a Presbyterian background. Within minutes of his prayer, Sherry and I knew our walk with God had somehow changed. Within seven hours, this Southern Baptist was praying in Tongues. Within 36 hours I had to cast a demon out of someone. Within 72 hours Sherry and I prayed for a neighbor in the hospital and she was instantly healed. Within three weeks I prayed for a Methodist man going into surgery the next day. God healed him, and his wife and a Baptist missionary just holding hands with me! I never even prayed for the wife and missionary, but God healed them anyway!

Then, seven months after the CBA show and the Baptism of Power, God sent two strangers who wanted a life-size "Divine Servant"® bronze sculpture. They were Jim Buick of Zondervan and Bo Pilgrim of Pilgrim's Pride Chicken. Despite the fact that I had never created a large sculpture before, both servants of God paid $25,000 advance deposits so I could afford to do the job!

MULTIPLICATION OF FISH AND LOAVES

Because I finally gave my fish and loaves to Jesus, He began to feed the multitudes. As a result, I walked into God's destiny for my life. Today, Sherry and I live in the supernatural realm every day and have literally experienced thousands of genuine, authentic, supernatural miracles. Over the years since then, there have been battles, challenges and disappointments along with the victories. But, we have been fighting to build God's Kingdom, not ours. In the years since, there is nothing I would rather do, than God's will. This has resulted in the peace, joy, satisfaction, and the power mankind has sought for thousands of years. Everything is in Christ Jesus.

What God will do for one, He will do for another, so let our testimony challenge you to discover your own unique destiny in God. It is never too late and you will never be sorry!

FULFILLING OUR DESTINY

If we yield to God soon enough we can fulfill our destiny in this life. I believe I am in the process of that now, in my later years. I am amazed by what God has done with my few fish and loaves.

One of the main reasons God created me is to accomplish my current assignment. I have been called with the help of other Christians, to build free, Christ-honoring Sculpture Prayer Gardens across the U.S. and world. The purpose is to bring glory and souls to Jesus Christ. The Coming King Foundation (TCKF) is currently building the first proto-type garden now, on IH-10 northwest of San Antonio, near the Hill Country town of Kerrville, Tex.

THE VISION

On December 9, 2001 my wife and I traveled several hours to hear a man from North Carolina speak at Cathedral of Praise Church in Austin, Tex. The guest speaker was Dr. Mahesh Chavda. Pastor Bill Hart introduced us to Dr. Chavda as we walked in. To our surprise, later during the service, Chavda stopped in the middle of his message and asked us to stand. Then, he spoke a prophetic word over us, in front of the entire congregation. He said that we would be involved in the restoration of the Tabernacle, and that the art I had created during my lifetime would now be used to decorate this last days Tabernacle. Chavda said God would be sending others to help us do this thing.

We were confused. As everyone in the room clapped, I whispered to my wife, Sherry, "GOD IS NOT GOING TO REDO THE TABERNACLE. THAT GUY IS NUTTIER THAN A SQUIRREL!"

Eight months later, another stranger emailed me from Beaumont, Tex. saying that God was calling me to create a 77'7" crucifixion cross over IH-10. The man, Marlon Quibodeaux, said no one else could do this project for God. I called the businessman in Southeast Texas and he explained his prophetic word to me and then asked that I pray about doing his project. I have learned in my old age to always pray before accepting or turning down any deals.

I explained that he did not need a sculptor, since all you had to do to make a cross was put two sticks together. I told him to call an engineer. Marlon insisted that I was the one called by God to create this special work. At the time, Marlon thought the Crucifixion cross would be on IH-10 near Beaumont. I asked if Marlon had any money, since I knew a 77'7" cross made of anything would be very expensive. He said no, but he might be able to find a donor. We prayed over the phone for God's will. I fully intended to do my obligatory prayer and then tell the man, no thanks!

However, when I prayed after the call, to my amazement I received an open vision. I saw a 300' long, cross-shaped garden, with the Gospel presented in multiple languages on tiles, in a pathway that led to a giant open cross! The name God gave me for the biblically-symbolic, resurrection cross was "The Empty Cross®." It was and is the Door, the Narrow Gate, the Mighty Fortress and the Strong Tower that the Light Of The World could shine though.

I saw my life's work of Christian monumental bronze sculptures in the points of the cross-shaped garden and people walking toward the giant 77'7" cross. I saw cars backed up along an access road, waiting to get into the garden Tabernacle! My spirit leaped as I immediately recognized this idea was from the Throne Room of God.

WHERE DO YOU PUT A LAST DAYS TABERNACLE?

God put this project firmly in my spirit, though it had no funding, support, organization or location. However, after receiving numerous confirmations, I proceeded to form a 501c3 organization called The Coming King Foundation (TCKF). The Holy Spirit instructed me to form the new tax exempt, nonprofit organization as an art museum rather than as a ministry so it would be protected in the last days.

When I shared the vision with our Prayer Intercessors, I got two prophetic words back saying that the first garden would be on IH-10 in Kerrville, not Beaumont. First, Dallas financial planner, John Meder emailed me on May 5, 2003 saying God would place the first garden in Kerrville. I responded back and said the money was in Beaumont!

Then, on June 26, 2003, Nazarene evangelist Richard Schumann said the first garden would be at "THE GATES OF THE CITY." We would later learn that the first garden would be located in Kerrville, adjacent to the interstate highway in a small, special area which was designated by the City of Kerrville as "The Gateway Zone"!

GOD PROVIDES THE LAND

On Dec. 11, 2003, I was sitting in my Suburban at a stop light facing IH-10 in Kerrville, when suddenly the Holy Spirit spoke and said: "LOOK UP, THIS IS THE LAND I

WILL GIVE YOU." After months of praying and doing the "natural," God finally revealed the location for the first garden. It was ideal, an undeveloped piece of land at the main entrance to the city on the interstate highway facing the city. And it had a high place for the cross, a 1,930' hill.

I immediately drove to the land, which was covered with Juniper and Oak trees. However, there was no "For Sale" sign on the property. So, I drove to the Tax Appraisal Office and learned the owner of the 23 acres of prime highway frontage land was Clifford Reeh, of Pipe Creek, Tex. When I got home I called Reeh and heard a phone recording, so I left a message. Then, I wrote a letter to Mr. Reeh. Both my phone message and letter basically said: "GOD WANTS TO USE YOUR LAND TO BRING SOULS TO JESUS CHRIST. WILL YOU PLEASE SELL US YOUR LAND, OR GIVE IT TO US?" Clifford Reeh never returned my two calls or answered my letter. I assumed I must have missed God again.

However, on April 24, 2004, Mr. Reeh called and asked to meet me at the land. To my amazement, I learned Reeh was a Christian, that he had bought the land purely for investment years earlier, but that God would not let him put it on the market for some reason. I learned that Reeh was also an art collector. Then, I learned he was MY art collector and that he had purchased my $1,500 bronze sculpture, "Divine Servant®," in December of 1990!

We then prayed together, realizing this was a providential meeting. Clifford, who was of modest means, promised to pray with his wife, Dorothy, about giving The Coming King Foundation their valuable land that was worth millions of dollars.

Clifford called back and told me to draw up the legal papers and they would donate their land for the glory of God. I was ecstatic! The vision was coming together!

However, shortly after the legal documents were drawn up, my dream was shattered. Clifford told me that he had to back out of the deal because his two adult sons wanted money for the property, since the land was their inheritance. I asked how much the sons wanted and Clifford said $500,000. This was a great price for the land, but when you don't have $500,000 that is still a lot of money!

Disappointed, but knowing God would provide a way, in my kitchen I wrote out $500,000 on a sheet of paper, and the comparable land prices next to it. Then I prayed: "LORD, DO YOU WANT US TO MAKE A COUNTEROFFER, OR DO YOU WANT US TO BELIEVE YOU FOR $500,000?" Immediately, a sparkling particle formed on the paper as I watched, right above where I had just written $500,000!

The Shekinah Glory dust particle (Ex 34:29, Isa. 60:1) looked like a piece of glitter. I put a piece of transparent tape over the particle and called an emergency Board meeting. The seven Trustees voted to believe God for $500,000 and not make a counteroffer to Reeh, since we considered this a major, supernatural confirmation.

So, the land contract was written and we paid an earnest money deposit in faith. Since the Board had previously voted that we would never borrow money to build God's garden, we all prayed for funds. By the grace of God, Sherry and I were able to make a $250,000 gift, but it was not enough. The Coming King Foundation did all the normal fundraising appeals, but we barely raised enough money to pay for the printing and postage!

MIRACLE ON THE MOUNTAIN

On Sept. 16, 2005, with time running out on our land contract, 19 Christians gathered at the property to pray for the land, and a million souls for Jesus. We anointed a 17" wooden cross made from an Ash Juniper tree on the land. We anointed it with oil and water from the Holy Land. As I planted the cross in the ground, and claimed the land for Christ, a three-inch scorpion appeared and charged the cross! My wife, Sherry, crushed the scorpion under her foot.

Then, my nephew Sam, who had come in from Austin with my brother Mark, proclaimed, "LOOK UP, THE SKY IS FILLING WITH HAWKS! To everyone's amazement almost a dozen wild Northern Harrier hawks began to circle over our heads! The entire event was recorded on videotape by Trustee Rebecca Jons.

We all recognized the symbols of a spiritual power encounter in the heavens, but we still did not have the $500,000 we needed. Snakes and scorpions and flies represent Satan and his demons, prophetically speaking, while eagles and hawks and doves represent God and His angels.

THE VISION DIES

Following our time of prayer, the seven TCKF Trustees met to decide what we would do, since the contract was expiring and we were still short about $250,000. We prayed and several prophecies were given by the Trustees. I remember Pastor Jack Rothenflue prayed and said: "GOD, NOT ONLY DO WE WANT THE MONEY, BUT WE WANT A GREAT STORY, TOO!" Since we had previously agreed not to borrow money, or make a counteroffer, we had no options. With tears in my eyes, I thanked the Trustees for their service. The vision died that night.

THE VISION IS RESURRECTED!

When Sherry and I got home that night, about 10:30 PM, I noticed the phone recorder light was blinking. I pushed the button and a voice said: "MAX, THIS IS HERSHEL. GOD SAID TO GIVE YOU $500,000." I was stunned. The next morning I went out to the ranch of Hershel Reid, a man of God and the heir to a well-known American company. I asked Hershel what had happened. He was one of the 19 people who had prayed on the mountain the evening before. Hershel had said then he could not give us a dime since God had not released him to do so, and he wanted to tell me the bad news in person.

However, when I planted the 17" wooden cross in the ground, Hershel put out a fleece to God. Hershel asked his Heavenly Father to put a hawk in the sky if his family was to donate $500,000 to buy the land to build a Sculpture Prayer Garden for Jesus. When he opened his eyes at least nine wild hawks were floating over his head! The Hershel Reid family donated $500,000 through their charitable trust, which acquired the land, and then the land was given to TCKF by the trust.

THE LAST DAYS TABERNACLE IS BUILT

In the years since 2005, there have been many battles and victories on the journey to complete the evangelistic project. When the atheists and others opposed to the cross learned of our plans to erect a 77'7" cross on our private land, over the transcontinental highway, they became enraged and organized to try and stop us.

Their tactics were a combination and mixture of legal, illegal and even immoral and unethical devices and maneuvers. First, they wrote hateful letters to the local newspaper and attended City Council meetings, attacking me and the project. When these efforts failed, they began using "dirty tricks" such as creating false News Releases in our name and distributing them to the print and TV media. They sent pornography to our ministry office and even purchased mail order products in our name on a C.O.D. basis (Cash on Delivery) of which we had no knowledge.

Finally, they eventually filed false charges against us with different state agencies and the IRS, resulting in an audit of our nonprofit organization. We passed the audit with flying colors and I prayed for the Lutheran IRS agent to receive the Baptism of the Holy Spirit. God also sprinkled the agent with the Shekinah Glory dust when we prayed on our property! When these tactics failed, the atheists stirred up neighboring landowners against TCKF and filed a lawsuit to stop the cross, which cost us $200,000 to fight and took 15 months to settle. In an effort to keep the Christian legal defense firms out of our legal battle, the frivolous lawsuit was filed and positioned as a zoning case, rather than a constitutional rights case. This legal battle severely tested us, but we prevailed by God's grace.

VICTORY AT THE CROSS

On July 27, 2010 the reddish brown $2,000,000 cross was raised over IH-10. The cross sculpture was donated by my family, and Monte and Beverly Paddleford, owners of Eagle Bronze in Lander, Wyo. Thousands of people learned of

"The Empty Cross" when state, national and international media covered the story.

As the cross went up, most of the people gathered at the site were instantly sprinkled with the Shekinah Glory dust. The phenomenon was even witnessed by an Associated Press reporter that day. That night, hundreds of worshippers celebrated the victory at the foot of the cross. They were again sprinkled with the Glory Dust, as they praised God inside the 7' wide center space of the massive cross. That evening, and subsequent evenings, the sparkling particles formed on the hands, faces and clothing of hundreds of worshippers at the cross.

In addition, thousands of round balls of light were photographed by dozens of people in attendance. These globes of light seemed to hover around the cross and worshippers, ascending and descending on the cross. These so-called Angel Orbs are believed by some to be the angelic beings described by Ezekiel (Ezek. 1:15). These signs and wonders continue at the Sculpture Prayer Garden in Kerrville to this day. They have been witnessed and experienced by thousands of people, and even documented by CBS News local affiliate station KENS 5 in San Antonio, the San Antonio *News-Express*, the Kerrville *Daily Times*, TBN, CBN, and many radio stations.

In addition to these miracles, now that the Garden front entrance was opened to the public on July 19, 2012, thousands are visiting. Hundreds of visitors to the Garden are getting born again, baptized in the Holy Spirit and healed at "The Empty Cross." Four large plaques inside the cross lead visitors in prayers for salvation, empowerment, healing and miracles. Even though we are still raising funds to finish the Garden, thousands of visitors are being touched by the Holy Spirit.

Other miracles have also been documented at the modern Garden Tabernacle. People have been physically and emotionally healed. In addition, during construction of the Garden, contractors reported seeing snakes leaving the property. A week later, on June 30, 2006, a pure white dove descended in front of the workers and walked toward where the cross would one day be located.

Later, after the cross was raised, our LIVE security camera recorded a white vertical cloud that appeared behind the cross for 45 minutes on a clear day. The Kerrville Fire Department was called but no fire could be found, even though at least five people witnessed the white, stationary, cloud-like form on the video camera, including the 911 operator!

Thousands of miracles of all kinds are now being reported by visitors to the unfinished Sculpture Prayer Garden. It appears to be a "type" of last-days Tabernacle predicted biblically in Amos 9:11 and Isa. 2:2.

It is also providential that this Garden is located at the same latitude as Israel, and is approximately halfway between the Atlantic and Pacific Oceans on IH-10. The Garden also looks like the Holy Land, with thousands of massive 1.25 ton, quarried limestone blocks that have been used to decorate the Garden.

Over three million dollars worth of monumental Christian sculptures have been donated by three internationally-collected artists, including Beverly Paddleford, David Broussard and myself. About 100 to 300 people a day are now coming to the most symbolic cross in the world to find God and/or to pray, meditate and view the monumental Christian art sculptures. The presence of God is on the mountain!

FULFILL YOUR OWN DESTINY

God has a unique destiny for each of us. Don't allow anything, or anyone, to stop you from doing what God has called you to do, once He has confirmed His will for your life. Satan will do whatever he can to keep you from obeying God. Satan will even use scripture and Christians to stop you from doing God's will. Watch out for his schemes.

If you are truly doing God's will for your life, there will be resistance. Satan will always put a snake in your path. I call these Negative Confirmations. Dispatch the snake using the name, power and blood of Jesus Christ!

Remember, it is God's desire that we each use our gifts, talents and abilities, whatever they may be, to bring glory and souls to Jesus Christ. In this life we can choose who, or what, receives glory from our gifts and talents. Choose the King of Glory!

PRACTICAL ADVICE FOR
THE DESTINY SEEKER

Here are some things to consider if you want to find and live out your God-given destiny:

1. **Get Saved** – You have nothing without the saving grace of the LORD Jesus Christ. He is the foundation, the Rock that everything must be built upon. Without Him, you have nothing.

2. **Become Empowered** – Don't try to "do the stuff" as John Wimber used to say, until you are fully clothed in power, and have asked for the nine supernatural Gifts listed in 1 Cor. 12. All Believers receive the Holy Spirit as soon as they make Jesus the LORD of their life. However, they don't experience all the power they need to serve God most effectively until they ask for and receive this Empowerment Baptism. Don't worry about what you call it; just get it! This is what enabled a bunch of fishermen 2000 years ago to become world changers for Christ.

3. **God's Plan** - Each day, ask the Holy Spirit to live His life through you, and then expect God to answer this prayer. Watch for His divine appointments everywhere you go. Then, be willing to step out in faith to help someone else. I ask God daily to let me meet who He wants me to meet, and not to do anything fun without me!

4. **Do the Natural** – We do the natural; God does the supernatural. The heavy lifting is up to God. Yes, prepare, study, practice and get all of the education, training and equipping you can, in the natural. Work to become excellent at your craft. However, realize that God's involvement is required before the work can be anointed. Once it is anointed, anything can happen! Consider Paul's handkerchief! Also, don't try to fake the anointing.

5. **Use GPS (God Positioning System)** – Know the written Word of God and then seek confirmations of His will for you. Be sure you are going God's direction. Make sure your dream is God's dream for you. Ask for supernatural confirmations before you step out of the boat! If Jesus is calling you, then you can walk on the

water; if not, you could sink. The Bible says not to put God to a foolish test. Seeking God for His direction is not a foolish test. The proper use of fleeces can help determine God's will in a specific situation. Some of our most incredible miracle testimonies involve fleeces, which were used to determine God's will on a particular matter.

6. **Journal** - Keep a Prayer Journal of God's activities in your life. This allows us to give God the credit accurately after He works miracles in our lives. Always give God the glory for any miracles He works. Don't stretch the testimony. Try to be as honest and accurate as you can. Journals help keep track of the details which are often forgotten over time. My stack of Prayer Journals is about 8' high, because I started keeping records in 1989, shortly after my Baptism of the Holy Spirit experience.

7. **Get Intercessors** – It is vital to pray for God to raise up Prayer Intercessors if you want to do big things for God. These are people called by the Holy Spirit who will pray for you and your family daily. Pray for them also. Their prayers will keep you alive. I have learned that no matter how much anointing God places on any individual, Satan's constant attacks must be thwarted by Holy Spirit-directed Prayer Intercessors specifically called to pray for you in unity.

8. **Serve** – Be willing to serve others in whatever capacity the LORD desires. Use your gifts, both natural and supernatural. Be the best you can be, and then give God the glory for your success. Stay humble and under God's established authority. Stay submitted to your pastor or local spiritual leader unless he or she quenches the Holy Spirit, or teaches against the Holy

Spirit. God will lead you to a good church if you ask Him. Accountability is critical to the body of Christ.

9. **Test the Fruit and the Root** – Jesus asks us to be wise and discerning about what is going on. We can do this without having a Pharisee's judgmental spirit. Always test the fruit to see if it is good, and then test the root. Some people who appear to have good fruit actually have the wrong root. Make sure Jesus is the root. At the same time, some who have the true Vine may not have fully developed fruit yet. Remember, producing good fruit takes time. Always extend grace to others.

10. **Keep Your Eyes On The Prize** – Jesus Christ is the prize, so don't let fame, riches, miracles, influence, favor or adulation from men cause you to take your eyes off of Jesus. Many have fallen because they were distracted and lured into the snares of Satan. Maintain a teachable, humble spirit. None of us have it right all the time.

GRAVEN IMAGES, BEZALEL & THE TEN COMMANDMENTS

Finally, don't allow anything, or anyone, to stop you from doing what God has called you to do, once He has confirmed His will for your life. Satan will do whatever he can to keep you from obeying God. Remember, if you are truly doing God's will for your life, there will be resistance. Satan will put a snake in your path. Dispatch the snake using the name, power and blood of Jesus!

Satan may even try to use scripture and Christians to stop you from doing God's will. The Second Commandment tells us not to worship anything other than the one true God. The issue is who, or what, do we worship.

Right after God gave the Ten Commandments (Ex. 20:3), He then commissioned and gifted an artist named Bezalel to create art (Ex. 31:4) which honored God and reminded the people of their God.

God has not told mankind to avoid making art with this commandment. He is the one who gives talent and ideas to mankind. God loves artists because He is one. According to the Bible (Ex. 31:3), the artist Bezalel is the one who was first "filled" with the Holy Spirit. In a way, we are Christ-like when He inspires us to create something from nothing.

It is God's desire that we each use our gifts, talents and abilities, whatever they may be, to bring glory and souls to Jesus Christ. Therefore, in this life we choose who or what receives glory from our gifts and talents.

ABOUT THE AUTHOR

Max Greiner, Jr. is a professional artist in Kerrville, Tex. and a graduate of the College of Architecture at Texas A&M University. Max's artwork is collected in all 50 states and over 65 nations. His testimony and artwork have been featured on CBN, TBN, CTN, TCT, INSP, Daystar and the secular networks. His art has been owned by Billy Graham, Franklin Graham, James Dobson, Pat Robertson, Bill Bright, Oral Roberts, Charles Stanley, Rick Warren, Hal Lindsey, John Hagee, Jesse Duplantis, June Hunt, Tony Perkins, Mike Huckabee, President George W. Bush and the late Pope John Paul. Thousands of ministries, colleges and seminaries use Max's art. In 2005, Max founded The Coming King Foundation with his wife, Sherry, and five other Christians for the purpose of building free Sculpture Prayer Gardens across the U.S. and world, to bring glory and souls to Jesus Christ. To learn more or contact him, visit Max's web sites at www.maxgreinerart.com, www.greinermemorials.com or their nonprofit web site, www.thecomingkingfoundation.org.

CHAPTER FIFTY-EIGHT

APOSTOLIC INNOVATION

AXEL SIPPACH

LEADERSHIP REQUIRES CREATIVITY

The New Apostolic Reformation (NAR) started to gain traction as a heaven-sent mandate and movement in the late 1990's as God began to awaken a remnant in his church to present-truth revelation that He was not only restoring the gift and office of apostle back to the church, but also desiring his people to become an apostolic people that would powerfully walk in the apostolic dimension. This reformation and restoration movement has not only begun to incredibly transform the church, but God has also mandated that the apostolic have tremendous influence to exponentially advance and expand the Kingdom of God through the marketplace around the world to see the transformation of nations.

We are living in times and seasons of great change and transition around the world. In fact, things are changing so quickly, that the way we did things 20, or even 10 years ago, will not necessarily work in this season. IBM conducted a survey of 1,500 top CEOs around the world, with one of the questions being: what is the number one characteristic you are looking for in leaders you are recruiting today? Almost all of them answered "creativity." This is the new currency of global competition. Because of the fast pace of change today, old wineskin maintenance management styles will not be able to quickly adapt to the changing times. Without creativity and innovation, not only companies, but also churches will become obsolete and soon vanish away. The future belongs to a new breed of innovative leaders able to discern the season and trends, and not afraid to be pioneers and trendsetters that seize the greatest opportunities of this time. This is not only for the corporate world, but also for the church and ministries.

For some years now my hair and beard have become white, giving me a bit of the Moses or Abraham look. I have had the privilege now of doing apostolic ministry in more than 80 nations and traveling around the world 5-6 million miles or more for the Kingdom of God. I joke that the white hair is not old age, but mileage. But even though I have a few years under my belt, I will never allow that "geezer" old age spirit to come on me. I have a great passion to see next generation apostolic leaders raised up, and I've discovered by being around young people, it helps keep me younger. Psalm 110:3 speaks of receiving the dew of your youth. Dew can represent energy and refreshing, and I've found out that by hanging out with them, it will definitely rub off on you.

I've written a number of songs over the past three decades, and recently I broke out into a new genre: rap. In 2011 I put up a post on my Facebook page with the photo of a dinosaur exhibit from a museum. I said this is what happens to ministry leaders who don't innovate – they become a dinosaur center stage in a museum. I said, "I ain't goin' out like that!" Then I put some rhymes with it and jokingly said, "Wow, I feel like rappin." Some of my

Facebook friends commented, "We would love to hear you rap." I felt challenged and within a few days wrote my first rap. Let me share a few lines with you:

"If you don't change you be lookin' strange.
Like a dinosaur exhibit they - rearrange.

You don't innovate, you gonna - stagnate.
You just might even terminate.

You be stuck in a rut. Spinnin' your wheels.
You put the pedal to the metal, but you can't even peel.

You just kickin' up dirt, makin' lots of noise.
Wasting your gas with your homeboys.

Suck it up, change your strategy.
Cry out to the Lord down on your knees.

And say, Lord, I need, a word from you.
I got to get unstuck or else I'm through."

Hook (audience repeats each line):

"It's my time. My time to shine.
If I stop the whine. Get a spine and align.

I won't frustrate. Procrastinate.
Got to innovate. And accelerate."

CHANGE AND INNOVATION
ARE PART OF LIFE

My rap style is a bit old school '80s or '90s, but it does get the attention of young people. I did this rap a couple of weeks later before speaking at Kingdom Innovation 2011, the annual conference of the IMPACT Network for which I function as Executive Director. I think it went over pretty well. I've written a few more since then, and hope to lay down some professional tracks in the near future. My point in sharing this is that we need to be open to new things and not be afraid to risk and experiment with them. In fact, a big part of the culture of innovation you find in cutting -edge companies like Apple, Google, Facebook, etc. is experimentation. They are not afraid to try new things, and strongly encourage the regular submission of new creative ideas from their team.

Companies that have lost this creative and pioneering edge in the time we are living in quickly can become dinosaurs in a museum. Here's an example of a company that was for a century the world's most successful typewriter company – Smith & Corona. They believed they would always be on top of their game but could not see the future. They believed the world would always need their product, and since they made the best, their success and prosperity would always be assured. Their old website even said, "On the eighth day God created Smith & Corona." But they got stuck, and couldn't reinvent themselves. Their greatest strength also became their greatest weakness.

From 1991-92 they had a partnership with a small obscure company called Acer, Inc. But Smith & Corona's board could not see the future merits of this relationship and separated. Acer went on to become the world's fourth largest PC company, and shortly thereafter Smith & Corona went bankrupt and became defunct. After 100 years of identifying opportunities, they could no longer see the future. Their pride caused them to miss it, and they paid dearly for it. When was the last time you typed on a typewriter?

Change is in the air! There's no way around it. Embrace it, or become obsolete and a museum dinosaur. Companies must innovate. The church must innovate. Ministries must innovate. And we as individuals must innovate. We need the prophetic insight and anointing of the tribe of Issachar that had understanding of the times and knew what Israel should do. We must discern the times and the trends. We must see the next big thing on the horizon – the next "new big thing" God is about to do. He asked in Isa. 43:19, *"Don't you perceive it?"* Apostles and apostolic people have this kind of prophetic discernment available to them, whether for the church or the marketplace. Wherever their sphere of Kingdom influence is, God desires to give them this kind of insight. We should seek it and expect it. And when He reveals it, expect apostolic grace to step into it by faith.

Innovation is from the Latin "innovare" meaning to renew or change. It's about new ways of seeing and doing things. It can flow from shifts in mindsets that can recognize new opportunities and generate new patterns, blueprints and models. It requires having enough humility and flexibility to shift in times of monumental transition. The proud, arrogant and rigid will find themselves locked into the old order that is vanishing and soon to become obsolete.

Many times when things are beginning to shift, it is not obvious and recognized by everyone. There is much change and shifting taking place in the Kingdom of God today. But, it is usually only discerned by a remnant walking in humility and spiritual hunger for the things of God. God has always moved in times and seasons to bring forth revival, reformation and restoration with a remnant that He has had in a place of preparation and separation, many times in caves and deserts. A remnant will become an apostolic voice for the new thing God is birthing, ready to cry out like John the Baptist, *"Prepare the way of the Lord."* A remnant has been or is equipped to challenge religious systems with an apostolic pioneering and warring anointing for breakthrough that will greatly expand God's Kingdom in their generation. A remnant - like David's 400 men in the desert in a cave called Adullam...

APOSTOLIC PRINCIPLES AND PROCESSES FROM THE LIFE OF DAVID

I want to share some apostolic principles from the life of David in a time in Israel's history when they were in a monumental transition period. Their king, Saul, had become a demonized tyrannical leader oppressing the people, and God was preparing a young man he had chosen named David to become the new king and establish his kingdom throughout Israel. Most reading this are familiar with the story of David, the young shepherd boy that the prophet Samuel had anointed when he was a teenager to become the next king of Israel. As David grows up he develops his fighting prowess and achieves some "street cred," first by taking down a bear and then a lion as he is protecting his father's sheep, and then later taking down the giant Goliath who was defying the armies of Israel. That really enhanced his "street cred," obtaining him favor with the king, along with his daughter in marriage, and a lifetime of no taxes.

But as the people began to sing songs of David's military conquests, Saul became enraged with jealousy and sought to kill young David. The ax was already laid to the root of Saul's kingdom because of his disobedience. But, even though the old was still in power, the new was about to · eclipse it. The prophetic word that David would be king was now being severely challenged as he had to flee for his life. It's always good to remember that when we receive prophetic words or visions and dreams from God concerning our future destiny, that we may go through times of perhaps severe challenge, as God will also use that word to process, prepare and transform us, so we might also have the corresponding character that will sustain us where the word will take us.

David could see the future, and perceived that this was the season that God would establish his kingdom and fulfill the prophetic word. But, he must stay alive as God works out the details, and he must have an "apostolic team" of faithful warriors that will help him at the right time to succeed on his journey to the throne and then expand his kingdom over all Israel. As he is fleeing in the desert, he first comes to Gath (1 Sam. 21:10-14), and fearful that King Achish of Gath will kill him, he pretends to be insane, and then escapes to the cave of Adullam.

ADULLAM BECOMES A MODEL AND SPARKS A MOVEMENT

Adullam means "refuge" in Hebrew, but interestingly, it can also mean "justice of the people." This is very prophetic in that King Saul now stands for injustice, but David stands for justice. The household of David's father and his brothers hear about where he is, and Scripture says 400 men who were in debt, distress, and discontented came to join with David (1 Sam. 22:1-2). These men saw just enough of the future to risk everything to join with David. They also perceived it was his season. You could say they "spotted the trend" and risked their lives to come to Adullam. They were in a mess, but were going to be transformed into messengers. They knew this was the next big thing God was about to do and they made their choice. There was no going back for them. If they did, they would be killed by Saul. They got behind the word of the Lord that David would be king. They perceived this was the time. They "apostolically aligned" with David, and the results were truly incredible. The fruit of their decision to "align in the right time" was absolutely, supernaturally exponential.

So Adullam becomes an apostolic model of an environment incredibly conducive to innovation that has the potential to produce exponential Kingdom results. It becomes a shelter — a safe haven from the world to meet and connect with God and destiny. It's a place of inspection, evaluation, measurement and focus. It becomes a spiritual womb so to speak, where God's ideas and plans would be birthed in them, igniting a powerful flame of Kingdom passion and purpose as their true identity would be revealed and come forth. Their true identity was to become mighty men of valor – mighty Kingdom "apostolic" warrior leaders – sent ones sent forth to establish the Kingdom.

But, they had layers of "stuff" that were hiding their true potential, gifting, and destiny. They had to get past their pain. The cave was to get them healed, delivered and transformed. And it worked! It's important for leaders to understand that if you are willing to work with people no one wants, you will in time get those everyone wants.

The Adullam factor – these apostolic dynamics of Adullam helped initiate the beginning of a movement. When these men came out of the cave, they were ready to step into the destiny of a nation. They had found the word of the Lord. They had found the next move of God. They had found a greater cause. They had found the right apostolic alignment.

They had found their gifting. And they had found their destiny. They were in the right place, at the right time, doing the right thing, with the right people, hearing the right message that inspired and impacted them for greatness. David, at the end of his life as he is thanking the Lord for all He has done, says in 2 Sam. 22:36, *"You stoop down to make me great."* And what God did for David, He also did the same for all of David's mighty warriors, including the 400 in the cave of Adullam.

Recently I put up a post on Facebook that got a lot of response. I wrote: "If an apostolic leader can mobilize the collective gifts, talents, strengths, and anointings in the local ecclesia (church) he/she leads, through passionate vision casting, the effective result will be the initiation of powerful synergistic movement and momentum creating tremendous leverage to accomplish great things for the Kingdom of God." This is exactly what David as a type of an apostolic leader was able to achieve at Adullam with those that had aligned with him and the word of the Lord.

It's so vital for us to become Holy Spirit "time travelers" that can step into the future and see what God is about to do. And it is incredibly important for us to get past our pain and present circumstances to see where God is leading us to apostolically align. These 400 men found a greater cause beyond themselves and their own pain and circumstances, and aligned with God's Kingdom cause by faith, risking all. Something inside of them must have stirred in their spirit and motivated them to act and do this. It was all or nothing. They were ready for change. So David really becomes a type of an apostle with a Kingdom destiny and vision from the Lord to whom those in a mess can gather in this apostolic cave of Adullam for worship, deliverance, healing, consecration, teaching, revelation, impartation, fathering, activation, glory encounters and transformation. Someone might say, "Where did you get all that from?" From Psalm 34.

APOSTOLIC PRINCIPLES FROM PSALM 34

As I began to study more about Adullam, I discovered that not only were Psalm 57 and Psalm 142 written in the cave, but also Psalm 34. Adullam is where David escaped to right after he feigned insanity in Gath, and where he wrote this Psalm. I want to encourage you to read it in several translations, and as you read and meditate upon it, envision David in the cave with these 400 men sitting around him. Psalm 34 really is a very prophetic, apostolic, Messianic and Kingdom psalm. It is filled with so much revelation from which you can mine so many gold nuggets of truth. And just when you think you have discovered everything, you find even more. That has been my experience studying and meditating in this psalm over the past year or so. I would like to share just a few of the apostolic principles I have discovered from Psalm 34 that I believe will bless your life:

- **WORSHIP:** David opens this psalm in verses 1-4 with blessing or extolling the Lord. The Hebrew is "barak" which can also mean kneel, adore, thank, salute, greet, and this one I particularly love – befriend. We are to bless and worship the Lord at all times – the good and the bad times with our entire inner being – all of our thoughts and emotions. He is teaching them to worship the Lord intimately as he had learned in those years of solitude in the fields tending the sheep. In verse 2 he calls these 400 men "the afflicted" and this certainly fits if you are in debt, distressed and discontented. In verse 4 he says, *"I sought the Lord, and he answered me."* The Hebrew for sought is "darash," meaning to diligently inquire and seek the Lord through worship.

That's powerful. You can definitely expect the Lord to answer when you are seeking him in true worship. When he says in verse 3, *"My soul will boast in the Lord,"* the word boast in Hebrew is "halal" meaning to be clamorously foolish; to celebrate; to shout. We're not talking about "quiet time" here! In verse 3 "glorify" or "magnify" means to "declare his greatness." So, in these verses we see a powerful picture of David teaching and showing these 400 men how to worship intimately and passionately as a "friend of God" would, and also how to worship in unity together, expecting in faith God to respond.

- **DELIVERANCE:** God responds to David and these men worshiping in this apostolic cave. He answers by first delivering them from all of their fears. The word for fears is "megowrah" meaning the haunting apprehensions that one holds deep within. It also has the connotation of storage or dwelling place. So, deliverance from the influence of demons of fear is actually taking place here. Plus, God supernaturally has begun to intervene in the "troubles" of David and these men.

The word "yasha" here means to defend; avenge; rescue from your enemies; give victory in time of war; compassionate aid in time of need. It also has the connotation of the protective duty of a shepherd. David is called the shepherd of his people Israel. He is the shepherd-king. Apostles are kings, but also shepherds. As we shepherd those God calls to apostolically align with us, whether in the church or the marketplace, God will also bring victory to the troubling circumstances that are out of alignment with their true destiny. What happens next?

• **GLORY ENCOUNTERS:** *"Those who looked to him are radiant"* (NIV). Verse 5 here is speaking of the effects of God's presence and glory powerfully invading the cave. Heaven is kissing these men. The invisible realm is touching the visible. A portal to the third heaven is open here and their faces are shining with God's glory even as did the face of Moses after having stepped into the invisible realm on top of Mt. Sinai. This is awesome! Verse 8 calls this a "taste and see" encounter of the goodness of God.

Their faces were "sparkling like jewels," which is what the Hebrew "nahar" implies. Apostles need to be able to lead those called to align with them into encounters with God and his presence that will radically affect those they are called to lead. Such "taste and see" encounters will go a long way as they bring deliverance from fear, and encourage and strengthen potential followers with the presence of the Lord during times of great challenge and conflict, producing a supernatural confidence of faith and fearlessness.

- **ANGEL**: In verse 7 "malak" can mean messenger from God; an angel; a prophet, priest or king; ambassador; teacher; to dispatch as a deputy; one sent on business or diplomacy; deputyship such as ministry. Now in most translations this is translated angel. But this word is very similar to where in the Book of Revelation, the message to each of the seven churches is written: "To the 'angel' of the church of..." That word in the Greek is "angelos" which can also mean messenger. Theologians are divided as to whether to interpret this as angel or messenger.

  Many in the apostolic movement feel "messenger" implying "apostle" is the more correct understanding here. The same argument then can be made in Psalm 34:7 regarding "malak." In that light, we could use the following as a paraphrase: "The messenger (apostle) of the Lord encamps around those who fear the Lord, and the Lord delivers them." David, a type of an apostle, has pitched his tent to live with those who "reverence the Lord and acknowledge his good intentions" in order to bestow kindness and favor upon them, which results in them receiving deliverance.

- **EQUIPPING**: The word "deliverance" in verse 7 is "chalats" and actually can mean not only deliverance, but to equip for fighting; to strengthen; to make fat; to prepare. It conveys significantly the notion of taking up arms for battle or preparing for a general state of military readiness. It also conveys the idea of drawing out as in breast feeding which will strengthen and fortify. These are all apostolic expressions.

Paul said he had come to the church of the Thessalonians as an apostle who was gentle among them like a nursing mother nourishing and cherishing her own children (2 Thess. 2:6,7). This speaks of apostolic impartation as when he states in Rom. 1:11 that he longs to see them to impart a spiritual gift to them to make them strong. And of course in his epistles, Paul has much teaching concerning equipping of the saints for the work of the ministry along with becoming well prepared for spiritual warfare.

So, I believe we can make this same application to Ps. 34:7 concerning what the ministry of David, the soon to become shepherd-king "apostle", is accomplishing in the lives of these 400 who have aligned with him at Adullam. They are becoming nourished and "fat" drinking from the prophet, priest and king anointing upon his life, along with becoming equipped as he is apostolically preparing and equipping them for war. Interestingly, Isa. 10:27b in the NIV says: *"the yoke will be destroyed because you have become so fat (because of the anointing - KJV)."* The yoke of Saul's oppression is about to be broken off of them because of the fatness of the anointing they are receiving.

- **FATHERING**: One of the core values of the New Apostolic Reformation movement is the principle of apostolic fathering – raising up spiritual sons and daughters. And we see that principle here with David. In verse 11 he is addressing the 400 as his spiritual children – his spiritual sons. The Hebrew word here is "ben" meaning son – one who is a builder of the family name. This is a relational term, not just a biological one.

  David is entering into a father/son relationship with these men. These are not just followers, but also sons who will build the family name. What a powerful principle. This subject is a message I love to preach on, and could write many chapters about. But, I wanted to at least briefly highlight it here, and also say that I believe it is one of the most important core values of the current reformation. I have learned years ago, that one of the most effective ways for me to disciple a nation is to identify and raise up apostolic sons in that nation and father them by pouring my life into them. I believe that the end-result of all ministry that I do – all of my preaching and teaching, prophesying, etc. should be to raise up sons for my heavenly Father. God planted His son in the earth in order to reap a harvest of sons and daughters that would be with him for all eternity. This must also be the priority of every apostle.

- **TEACHING**: In verse 11b David is teaching his sons the fear of the Lord along with many other things pertaining to life. Apostles both preach and teach. David is teaching by word and example in this cave. The lives of these men will never be the same. The potent Adullam-factor combination "chemistry" of worship, deliverance, glory-encounters, apostolic impartation, equipping, fathering and teaching is setting them up for the main event – the birthing of new things.

- **BIRTHING OF NEW THINGS:** In verse 18 it says that the Lord is close to the brokenhearted and saves those crushed in spirit. The word "brokenhearted" in Hebrew also means to burst; to break; to tear; expressing bursting or breaking; to bring to the moment of birth. This word is also used in Isa. 66:9 regarding Zion (Jerusalem) birthing a nation in a day — in a moment. So what is God saying here in Ps. 34:18? He is saying that He is close to these men who are crushed, humble and contrite in spirit – close to these with the heart of David who are about to birth something new out of their brokenhearted condition.

  He is about to be a mid-wife to them and help bring to the moment of birth the baby which his prophetic word (seed) has created – a new nation that is about to burst forth on the scene out of the "apostolic womb" of Adullam. Likewise, apostles are also mid-wives called to help bring to birth the new things God is bringing forth in every season and generation. And those who are called to apostolic alignment with true apostles like these 400 men were with David, will also see new things birthed in their lives as the apostle takes his or her place to be used as God's midwife when the apostolic womb is ready to burst open.

APOSTOLIC TEAM BUILDING IS A PROCESS

There is so much more I could write about the powerful apostolic revelation in this psalm. I encourage you to do a word study of the main words and meditate on them. You will be amazed at what you see. Adullam is such an incredible picture of what an apostle in such an apostolic atmosphere can expect to see happen in the lives of those aligned with him and the word of the Lord. Whether you are an apostle called to the church or to the marketplace, these principles can help you build a powerful apostolic team of gifted, innovative leaders committed to expanding the Kingdom of God through the word of the Lord given to them. They will see and experience the birthing of new things God has promised even out of the challenges and perhaps ashes of what they have passed through. As they align with a greater Kingdom cause, their own destinies will begin to come forth and exponential advances of God's Kingdom will be realized.

When these 400 men came out of the cave of Adullam, they were completely transformed and became his mighty men of valor – his mighty warriors ready to help him succeed to the throne and establish his kingdom. Soon after leaving Adullam, they went to a place called Ziklag where they camped about a year. It was here they experienced a severe test. While David and the men were off fighting, the Amalekites raided and burned Ziklag and took captive their wives, children and possessions. It was a terrible time. Some men even lost their cool and talked of stoning David because they were so distraught. This was such a hard test of David's leadership, and of these men's faithfulness. David inquired of the Lord, and strengthened himself in the Lord, and the Lord said to go after them. They pursued the Amalekites and recovered all.

Then they settled in Hebron — a place where small beginnings turned into greatness. David was there for seven years. King Saul had consulted the witch of Endor and then committed suicide during battle the following day after being severely wounded. His son Jonathan, the royal heir to the throne, was killed as part of God's judgment on the House of Saul. His other son Ishbosheth became King of Israel. The House of David grew stronger and stronger, and the House of Saul weaker and weaker. Hebron's dynamic is that it is the place of covenant. Hebron is the highest place in Israel – even 500 feet higher than Mt. Zion. Hebron means "seat of association" – being joined together for fellowship. Hebron is not as easy to get to as Adullam. You have to climb up 3,000 feet above sea level through difficult rocky terrain. It takes effort to get there.

While in Hebron, more men began to come to him day after day until it was a mighty army — "like the army of God." They came to make him king. In 1 Chron. 12:17-18, David basically asked them why they had come — in other words, what their motives were. After they convinced him that they were truly with him, he received them and made them leaders. David ruled in Hebron for seven years only as King of Judah, one twelfth of Israel. Then after Saul's son Ishbosheth was assassinated, the elders of Israel came to him and David made a covenant with them, and they anointed him King of all Israel.

Then David and his army marched to Jerusalem to take the stronghold of Zion that had been under the control of the Jebusites. Joshua had not defeated them when he came into the land. It was a very strategic place in Jerusalem – a high, steep, rocky place easily defended – an impenetrable fortress never conquered before. The Jebusites mocked David, saying, *"You'll never get in here – even the blind and lame will push you back."* David issued the order to his army, *"Whoever leads the attack will become commander-in-chief."* The men rushed on the mountain stronghold and conquered it. David took Zion by delegated authority. The kingdom was established. His throne was established. Mt. Zion became the City of David from which he ruled and reigned. His palace was built there. It became the seat of God's government.

Zion also became the place where the Ark of the Covenant would be placed into a cloth tent to be called the Tabernacle of David where for a generation (almost 40 years), 24 hours a day, 7 days a week prophetic worship would take place. The glorious presence of God filled this tent. It was a prophetic picture of the New Covenant church. Jerusalem began to be built up and grow from Zion. Zion, the place of worship and seat of government, became a beachhead from which David's kingdom was expanded all over Israel.

I don't have space here to go into all the Messianic-Kingdom implications of this prophetic scenario except to briefly say that Jesus, the greater David, has been for the past 2,000 years seated on the Throne of David, and rules the Kingdom from there. The Kingdom has been established in the first century by Christ, and now the mission of the church is to advance and expand it. Every expression of the ecclesia – the called-out ones – whether gathering in the church or the marketplace, is an embassy of the Kingdom, an extension of the heavenly New Jerusalem.

There is a principle here that if apostles can establish strategic Zion beachheads in their village, town, city, region or nation, then from those beachheads the Kingdom of God can greatly expand. But, it all begins at a transformational apostolic cave called Adullam, where a movement is conceived and initiated. This movement gains great traction and momentum through covenant-making at Hebron, and then sees victorious establishment at Zion. His Kingdom endures forever and ever – from generation to generation. Nothing can defeat it. Nothing can stop it. The covenant God made with David is still in force through Jesus, and innovation is still an ongoing necessity and requirement of apostolic leadership.

In closing, why don't you ask the Lord if you are where you need to be in this season of your life? Ask him if you have the Kingdom relationships and apostolic alignment God needs you to have at this time in order to take you where you need to go in him? If you cry out to him in earnest, he will show you. And not only show you, but he can push the "fast forward" button of your life and quickly take you to where you need to be in this season. It's called apostolic acceleration, and you will definitely become a candidate for it when you find the proper apostolic alignment God has prepared for you regarding your destiny in this time and season.

ABOUT THE AUTHOR

Axel Sippach is Founder and President of Liaison International, and has traveled five to six million miles in international apostolic ministry since 1985, ministering in over 80 nations. Much of the first decade of his international ministry was focused on nations where the church was severely persecuted. He is also the Executive Director of the Chicago-based IMPACT Network, an apostolic global network of leaders, churches and ministries. God has used Apostle Sippach over the years as an apostolic father to be a blessing to many spiritual sons and daughters. His passion is to see young, emerging, five-fold ministry leaders raised up, equipped and sent to influence and impact their generation.

He has a strong apostolic and prophetic anointing, and preaches and teaches present-truth revelation to prepare the way for revival, reformation, and restoration. He is a highly sought after national and international conference speaker, and also serves as an apostolic consultant to churches, ministries and leaders. He has been a member of the International Coalition of Apostles (ICA), and has served on the International Advisory Board of Vision International University. He was awarded an honorary Doctor of Divinity degree in 2001. He resides in Seabeck, Wash.

CHAPTER FIFTY-NINE

THE FIVE R'S FOR THE APOSTLE IN BUSINESS

DR. NICK CASTELLANO

COMMANDING ANGELS

In the beginning, God created (*baraw*, to create from nothing) the heavens and the earth. How did He do this? He thought of creation, planted the thought in His heart, saw it done, and He spoke: *"Let there be . . ."* (The same way we create.)

We were created spiritually (*baraw*) and physically (*awsaw*) in God's likeness and image. Within and without, we were created both spiritually and physically in His likeness and image. We have all power, dominion, and authority over all things on earth because God Himself created and made us and we came out of God and are a piece of Him that represents Him on this planet.

Can we handle that? Can we believe it? I know man fell, but he was redeemed by Jesus and put back in the position he was created for—that we are created for. We bring light and life into every situation. We bring order to chaos and, with the world market in the state it is, order and light are what is needed today.

Dan. 10:12-14 shows us how angels move to do our bidding in the unseen. They are our "hands and feet" in the spiritual realm as we are God's on this earth. These angels move when we command them with the "word." We are not to beg or ask nicely, but command them. Too many times in the Word, humans fall to their faces when they see an angel; yet, the angels are there to work for and assist humans. That is why angels immediately say to people they visit to "get up, stop this worship of me for I am not worthy of worship . . . I serve as you serve." We don't worship angels (Col. 2:18)! They serve us in the spiritual realm when we speak in Power. They work for us when we speak the word with authority because we are the King's children (Heb. 1:14). Angels are our hands and feet in the spiritual realm as we are God's in the physical realm and the angels obey the word of God when spoken by someone who knows who he or she is as a Son of God.

God created the universe for our enjoyment and our dominion so we could be like Him. We are the righteousness and aroma of Christ, the head and not the tail. We are an example of goodness, strength, and morality. Our light does shine brightly and we are Kings and Priests on this planet. God, by His own hands, planted a beautiful garden for us to tend and created it as a place of fellowship for His greatest creation and Himself (Gen. 2:8).

When God wanted grass and plants, He spoke to the earth. When He wanted planets and stars, He spoke to the heavens. When God wanted creatures to live in the sea, He spoke to the water; when God wanted animals, He spoke to the earth. All creation came from the source of that creation. For example, plants and trees came from the soil of the earth, animals from the earth, fish from the dirt and water of the sea. He made them (*awsaw*, to make from something that already exists). Likewise, when God created man, He spoke "to Himself." We came out of God; God is our source.

He said, *"Let us make (awsaw) man in our own likeness and image, after our likeness and let them have dominion over the fish of the sea, and over the fowl of the air, and over the cattle, and over all the earth, and every creepy thing that creepeth upon the earth (Gen. 1:26). So God created (baraw) man in His image, in the image of God created Him; male and female, he created them."* We were both created from him and out of him as a spirit being *(baraw)* and made from the dust of the earth *(awsaw)*.

God has created everything for a godly purpose. He creates "no junk." Everything He creates has a reason, a why, and this purpose lines up with the bigger purpose of bringing the Body of Christ back together and being the light to the world so all can know God through His son, Jesus Christ.

Typically, as an apostle of God moving in the business realm, we as businessmen tend to forget the supernatural tools we are given for business to glorify and honor God. We may only see and use the natural tools used by everyone in the world. We may have a tendency to look and act in business just like our fellow businessmen that do not have that Holy Spirit's creative power working in them. Because of this lack of utilization of the Holy Spirit in business, we get about the same results the world gets. We don't set ourselves apart in the place of Shalom (health, prosperity, peace, complete, lacking nothing) that God has laid up for us in our Purpose.

We go into meetings with all the possible scenarios of what could go wrong in our head with a contingent plan for all scenarios. Instead, we should be going into the meeting sending angels ahead of us to create the Kingdom environment and declaring how the meeting will go and accepting nothing less because we represent the King of Kings and our Joint Venture partner is Papa God. Our Business vehicle is how we carry our ministry. We are a King/Priest in the business we are called to and a King doesn't "ask;" he "declares"!

A $42M CASE STUDY

Several years ago my brother-in-law was in heavy preparation for an important meeting he had the following day and I noticed the tension on his face and all the stress he appeared to be carrying. This meeting could profit his company (a commercial construction company) $40 million dollars and he was the owner and CEO of this company. He is a brilliant man and a very good manager of money. He had been considering all the options and possible concessions he could make during the meeting the next day so no matter what the scenario, he would be ready to move in the direction that could keep the opportunity alive.

I noticed his stress and began to speak with him about this and that and then I asked him, "What would the ideal outcome be in this scenario?" He paused and replied that he really hadn't given that much thought because he was so busy concerning himself with the direction they would go. He never considered what it was that he exactly wanted. We talked for about 15 minutes and he wrote down his ideal scenario, which would glean his company a $42 million profit.

I then said to him, "Now, allow yourself to accept nothing less." He seemed amazed at this simplistic concept but continued to listen. I said, "First, let's get into a place of peace, joy and love (The Kingdom Environment) so we can create for God's glory what He would want his son to attain." It took a while to get there but once in peace, the pressure seemed to leave him and he was smiling with gratitude for all he and his family had been given to steward over. He then began to see the meeting the next day exactly as it should go and then when his vision was clear, he began to speak what he had seen. At first he spoke softly and then over and over until he was very passionate about the meeting and its outcome and he was to the point that if it were not exactly how it should have been, he was willing to walk away. He was there. It was done. This is Faith! This is the Action step! This is how a King/Priest creates.

The next day at the meeting he walked in with confidence, knowing that he knew that they needed him and not the other way around. He heard their offer and then presented his. They were quiet (First to speak loses). Then the CEO of the other company spoke up and tried a few scenarios on my brother-in-law that looked like relatively fair compromises, but he did not waver. He quietly and calmly declined all alternatives to the best plan, "God's Plan" for him at this meeting. Finally, after a long quiet period, the CEO of the other company said with a sigh, "Alright, I guess we can live with this agreement....let's get started" and they signed the contract and began their business relationship.

My brother-in-law was so excited that he called me to celebrate the victory. I once again reminded him of his creative power through Christ Jesus. When he did not accept "good enough" but stood fast for the overflowing abundance God had laid up, the Kingdom was furthered and God glorified through his business vehicle.

Since this time, my brother-in-law has sold his company for a large sum of money, has become an instrument-rated pilot, bought a plane, and flies people for fun (he does get paid but doesn't need the money), declaring the Glory of God and doing what he loves to do.

So, how do you do this in your life? It's actually quite simple, so keep reading.

THE 5 R'S OF APOSTOLIC BUSINESS

In this chapter, you will learn about the 5 R's and how to apply this knowledge to bring the "unseen to the seen" and expect nothing less than God's best for you in your business and your meetings. So, here they are and let's get started.

1. **RELAX** physically and emotionally to create an environment of joy, peace, and love. In this relaxed state you are vibrating at the highest frequency and creating positive energy. In this environment you will attract things into your life that bring joy, peace, and love to you. Don't stop reading. This is not a New Age teaching; it is the Word of God and how it works. How do you get to this relaxed state? Slowly breathe in through your nose and out through your mouth for 10 to 15 minutes or however long it takes for you to become "quiet." You cannot pretend to be relaxed. If you have inner tension, it will nullify your creative power (Jas. 1:6-8).

2. **RECOGNIZE** that God exists and He has all power, and through Jesus Christ He has given us stewardship of this planet, and this stewardship is best served when we work jointly with God and each other. You must recognize that we are surrounded by God and God is in everything. God is in each of us and He created everything through the Word. All things are held together by His mighty Word.

You must recognize that we were given all power, dominion, and authority on this planet through Jesus Christ and we were created in God's likeness and image. Therefore, you have creative power in you and working through you.

You must recognize that we have the answers to all of life's questions through the Holy Spirit. This is a hard concept to grasp because most people like to go to the victim statement: "I don't know." Therefore, you must seek the Holy Spirit's guidance and listen to that small voice within you. You must recognize that we never create anything from nothing. God allows us to act as co-creators by bringing things to the "seen or natural world" that were previously in the "unseen or Spirit world." *"For by Him were **ALL** things created, that are in heaven and that are in Earth, visible and invisible, whether thrones, or dominions, or principalities or powers"* (Col. 1:16, author's emphasis).

All things were created by Him and for Him. In this case *created* comes from the Greek word *barah* which means to "create from nothing." We are to create using *awsaw*, which means to "create from something." He has already created everything that will ever be needed or ever will be in our universe and is waiting for us to take our authority and manifest it into the seen world.

3. <u>REALIZE</u> we are to be one with God and not separate from Him. We know that everything is composed of energy and we create matter (seen) from this energy (unseen) through our belief (faith) that it can be done. God has given us the power to do this! We realize that we are connected to everything through God since God is in everything and that it is only an illusion that we are actually separate from one another. Since

we all come from one source, we are all part of that source (God) and therefore part of each other. We realize that God is not *my* God or *your* God, He is just God. He is the God who will not be put in a box (calf, church building, religion). He is the God who chooses to reside in us.

You must realize that your thoughts will be transferred into things by the focusing of those thoughts, the belief in those thoughts, and the words you speak. You must realize that it works every time with *no exception*. You created it by your beliefs. If you have the faith of a mustard seed, you can command that the mountain be tossed into the sea and it will be so (Matt. 17:20).

4. **REASON** why you are creating. What is the purpose for wanting it? The purpose (your why) should be greater than you. Ask yourself, "Why do I want this money, influence, house, etc.?" As Ps. 35:27 says, *"Let the Lord be magnified, which hath pleasure in the prosperity of his servant."* In this case, *prosperity* means shalom. You should create all these things for *His glory* and the betterment of mankind so that the world may know *Him.* You, as His child, honor Him so that the entire world may see God through you. Jesus said in John 17:1, *"Father the hour is come to Glorify thy son that thy son also may Glorify thee."*

You must further understand that your conscious mind, or your left brain (as many instructors call it), is your "thinker." The subconscious mind, heart, or right brain is your "creator." This is where the power lies, where the Holy Spirit dwells. The creator (right brain/heart) does not care what the thinker thinks; its only function is to make the thinker right. You must "take every thought captive" and see if it lines up with what the Word says. If it does, then plant the thought in the good soil of your heart, where it can be nurtured and grow. You must then focus these thoughts through meditation because "focused thought is the food for ideas" and it must line up with the truth because "What You Focus on You Serve."

Remember that whatever you put into your subconscious mind, right brain, or heart and hold it to be true will manifest in your life. It works this way every time! There are NO exceptions! This is why in Luke 6:45 the Word says, *"A good man out of the good treasure of his heart bringeth forth that which is good, and an evil man out of the evil treasure of his heart bringeth forth that which is evil: for out of the abundance of the heart his mouth speaketh."*

When your thoughts and/or words appear to be going negative and you are concerned about what you are creating, listen to the Words in Phil. 4:8: *"Finally brethren whatsoever things are true, whatsoever things are honest, whatsoever things are just, whatsoever things are pure, whatsoever things are lovely, whatsoever things are of good report, if there be any virtue and if there be any praise, Think on these things."* (Fix your mind on these things.) Another excellent Scripture to memorize from Solomon is Prov. 4:23: *"Keep thy heart with all diligence (guard your heart) for out of it flows the issues (boundaries) of life."*

5. **RELEASE** knowing that your desire is planted in your subconscious or heart as a truth; let it go! Trust that it is done. Do not dig up your seeds of thought to constantly inspect them. Let them grow and create. When you truly know it is created, you don't think on it or act apprehensive toward it any longer. You walk, talk, and act *as if it were already done.* This is faith, the faith that brings the unseen into the seen; or

as the quantum physicist says, "This is collapsing or popping the quiff."

One of the toughest parts of creating, but necessary to master, is to stop trying to dictate "how" it will be done. This is key. The "how" will come about. Your focus should be seeing yourself in the done, finished, completed place. Again, you are creating an environment of peace, love, and joy around the image of you in this done place. God is a gentleman. He will not supersede your will. If you tell Him how, you limit His abilities and increase the time for your desire to manifest.

Why put limits on God when Eph. 3:20 says, *"Now unto him that is able to do exceeding, abundantly above all that we ask or think, according to the power that worketh in us (Holy Spirit)."* The word *abundantly* uses three words in the Greek to describe what it truly means (*Huper, ek, perissos*) which translates to "over and above and superior to; from out of place, time or cause to super abundance." This is the abundance I dare to step into when glorifying my God. Don't figure out "how it will be done," just "how it looks and feels" in that place of having your desire fulfilled. Turn the "how" over to God and know what belongs to you. The only delay that can be experienced is the time that exists between you speaking and creating and the time it takes for you to truly accept your desire as truth and spiritually getting yourself ready to receive it.

Many times we desire a thing that our vessel (flesh) cannot handle. There are too many weeds to steward and rule over such a thing properly. The desire would end up running us over. Does this mean the answer is no? Absolutely not. The word *desire* means "of the Father." If this desire lines up with the Word, then God wants it for you. Unfortunately, His answer will be yes. Why is this unfortunate? Because, in order to steward over this desire, you will go through trials to clean up the junk in your heart. You must pull up the weeds to properly house the desire. He did not say no; He said yes, and not yet. He loves us so much He doesn't give us more than we can handle and what could lead us away from Him. He gives us what drives us closer to Him.

Let's recap the process of bringing the unseen to the seen:

1. **RELAX** – and create an environment of love, peace, and joy

2. **RECOGNIZE** – God exists and is in everything

3. **REALIZE** – you are connected to everything through God

4. **REASON** – and know the purpose behind what you are creating/desiring

5. **RELEASE** – your creation, knowing it is done

This simple process can set you on your way to creating a new life for you and your family and be a curse breaker for you and your children's children.

I have learned some things to be careful of while in this process. When a negative situation occurs, I have a tendency to buckle down or to be forceful with my will, thus assuming that my will or "thinker" has power. The will has no power. Eventually this tactic will overload the nervous system and stress will exist in the body. Stress is when you believe you cannot overcome an obstacle, that you are not enough, and that the God in you cannot guide you to overcome. Stress is a "no power" situation. When you feel stress, STOP! Get refocused and create the outcome you want to see. This is not an excuse not to work but it helps to tie no negative emotion to the legwork that must be done to resolve a situation. Your job is to stay in peace, joy, and love and then do what you know to do and SEE the outcome DONE in peace, joy, and love.

A final reminder: Power flows to what is focused on. What is not focused on and is ignored dies. All thoughts require food and the energy of your focus is the food they need to be brought from the unseen to the seen. If there is no food, the thought, whether good or bad, WILL die.

In my case, I was so consumed with *my* success and building *my* kingdom, I focused all of my energy on it. I began to lose my wife and family. I was seeking my success for them—well, that was the lie I told myself. By focusing only on my business, I began to lose those things that I cared about the most. I could not understand my wife's anger and my children's distance. I thought they were the selfish ones because in my world and to my understanding, I must be right.

I finally spoke to a friend who walked me through the principles of focus I teach for business—but he related them to relationships. I began to focus on my wife and her love language. Her love language is very different from mine. Imagine that! I began to make my family and their needs a priority, my focus. Usually all they wanted was time with me. Almost miraculously, our marriage began to heal and we began to live in the Kingdom marriage I had always desired. By focusing on the relationship, I was changing and creating a Kingdom relationship with my wife and children.

Whenever you desire growth and power in your business, marriage, children, and relationships, you must focus on those areas. Do not think negatively. Focus on Phil. 4:8.

Thoughts that do not receive attention will dry up and not grow in your heart. Move into your God-given power and create your day, your business and the life God has destined you to live. There are no cop-outs, no victims, no junk, and no excuses. There is no retirement or free pass in the Kingdom of God. All must participate in order to grow the light in this world. We only have 120 years to do what He has called us to do on this planet as Man and we will be judged for all eternity based on what we have done with those talents He has given us for our Kingdom purpose. Let us not "bury" those talents.

ABOUT THE AUTHOR

Dr. Nick Castellano was trained at Virginia Poly Technical Institute State University and the United States Navy Nuclear Power Program. He has a Masters in Bio Chemistry and a Doctorate in Philosophy and Religion. He spent 10 years participating and training in the nuclear power program of the U.S. Navy and was decorated as "Sailor of the Year" in 1989. Nick was a nuclear instructor in the Navy for four years and graduated first in his class, completing over 26 specialty schools. While on tour, Nick was the Leading Chief of the Reactor Laboratory Division of the Dwight D Eisenhower (CVN69) and was responsible for all chemistries in both reactor plants.

Nick has worked in the industrial water industry and the oil industry developing cutting-edge chemistry and patented processes all over the world. He has owned one of the top industrial water treatment companies in the Southwest, caring for companies such as Pepsi Cola, Coca Cola, United Dairymen and APS power plants. He currently owns several businesses ranging from business mentoring to down hole oil well chemistry.

HCD and NC2 are international oil enhancement and environmentally-friendly chemical companies working with oil wells in China, Syria and the Middle East and throughout the U.S. and Canada (www.nc2.biz). Nick is well known in both industries for his expert chemical and application knowledge as well as problem-solving capabilities and holds two Oil Well Chemistry Patents and one soil remediation Patent.

He is presently the director of the Business Mentorship International. This program started in 2001 and is still going very strong as it has educated over 1100 businesses in the Arizona area and has just expanded to four other states. This program was designed to empower businesses and individuals to release their power, focus their vision and embrace their destiny of success and wealth. Nick and his board of directors have developed a program that brings practical business. An overview of the program can be seen on his website at www.businessmentorshipintl.com. Nick has been instrumental in assisting over 400 business start-ups and guiding these businesses with sound business advice and wisdom.

Nick speaks throughout the U.S. and Canada, and in various international sites in South America, and is the author of *Awaken the Sleeper*. To learn more or contact him, visit his websites at www.awakenthesleeperbook.com or www.businessmentorshipintl.com.

CHAPTER SIXTY

APOSTOLIC CREATIVITY

CANDACE LONG

INTRODUCTION

Not long ago, I read a timely statement from German Chancellor, Angela Merkel, according to Reuters. Regarding the economic challenges in Europe, she is quoted as saying, "I'm convinced that this crisis, if a great crisis of the Western world is to be avoided, cannot be fought with a 'carry on' attitude. We need a fundamental rethink."

A fundamental rethink! Yes, exactly!

Not long thereafter, an issue of *Forbes Magazine* had as its cover story, "The 100 Most Powerful Women." My spiritual antennas tell me that women appear to be rising into key positions of leadership, moreso than usual. For example, the woman featured on the cover, Christine Lagarde, rose to power as head of the International Monetary Fund when her predecessor, Dominique Strauss-Kahn, resigned in May, 2011 over allegations of sexual assault. I see this story as somewhat portentous, for all too many male leaders are being felled by lapses in sexual and moral conduct. As a result, more women are rising into senior leadership.

I have been in the Arts & Entertainment sector for over 40 years, as a writer and developer of entertainment projects.

As a result, I've had the privilege of serving on the board of Women in Film and Television International with a dynamic group of industry women from all over the world. At our first International Summit in London in 2000, Paul Howarth, the British Council Director of Film, addressed our delegates and said, "I believe you, as women, have a particularly important role to play in bringing a sense of moral responsibility to the entertainment industry."

Why is this significant? I want to submit the proposition that more women than men are right-brain thinkers...and that is exactly what the world needs now! We need the giftedness inherent in women to come forth in leadership as never before, to bring a sense of moral responsibility to every sector in our culture. If there was ever a time we need to address the world's problems using both hemispheres of the brain, it is now!

WOMEN SEE THINGS DIFFERENTLY

In 2008, I graduated from a very demanding, challenging Executive MBA program at Kennesaw State University's Coles College of Business. When the Dean offered me a seat in the class – before I had even formally applied – he remarked, "We have never had anyone from the Arts & Entertainment sector in our program before. You will definitely be the most creative person we've ever had." Admittedly, I puffed up a little with "pride," as if I had arrived at a place others had not. Little did I know the humbling experience that awaited me.

Many a night, as I was working on the supply and demand principles of economics, capital budgeting, or regression analysis to determine a project's valuation, I would lie down on my studio floor and cry out for the ability to understand these things! My brain actually "hurt!" Frankly, there was a point I did not think I could complete the program. To make matters worse, many of our graded assignments were ones we had to complete with our "team," which meant that I no longer had the luxury of working by myself. I HAD to fit in with others who were brilliantly gifted...but totally different from me! They were left-brained, and approached every assignment from that vantage point. Being a right-brained thinker, I soon experienced the anxiety and self-recrimination that often come when searching for a middle ground between two completely different learning styles.

One of the more insightful class experiences revolved around the brain, and how its various compartments function. As you can see in this graphic below, there really IS a right-brained thinking person and a left-brained one.

Neither is right or wrong...merely different.*

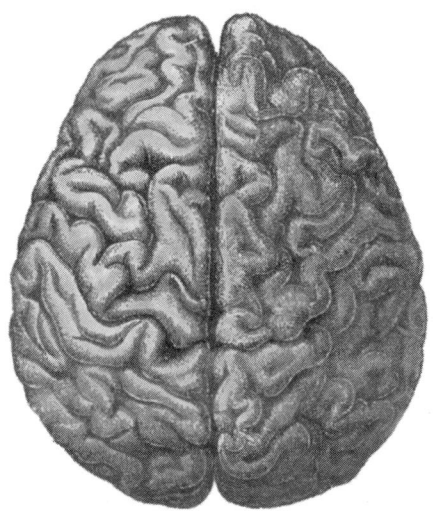

*Figure 3. Cerebral Lobes. Source: Wikipedia (a derivative work of Gutenberg Encyclopedia). Author unknown.
Image licensed by Creative Commons for public use.
http://commons.wikimedia.org/wiki/File:Cerebral_lobes.png.*

It would be incorrect to label all men as left-brained and all women as right-brained, for we are uniquely a combination of each hemisphere. However, I would like to point out a couple of things. Many women have strong right-brain components. Even more to the point, the ability to tap into the realm of inspiration lies mostly in the right-brain, an area of strength in many women. The right-brain involves another spiritual component. It is that part of the brain that is able to see the "big picture." The Old Testament prophet Isaiah wrote, *"God sees the end from the beginning."* This is the visionary gifting evidenced in many CEOs and entrepreneurs. They are able to see what others in the corporation do not. The challenge in communicating with those of a different thinking style is seen in the following scenario:

- **Right-Brained Woman**

  I want to borrow money to start a new venture. I'm going to quit my job and open up a store selling widgets.

- **Left-Brained Investor**

  Where is your data to prove that your plan will work and be profitable?

- **Right-Brained Woman**

  Data? Who cares about data! I just "know" that I'm supposed to do this!

- **Left-Brained Investor**

  You're asking for money based on a "feeling?" Forget it ... next?

I could not be any more serious in writing the above interaction. My observation, after years of study as to the uniqueness of what I call "creatives," tells me that right-brained people "know" inherently what we are destined to do...but we have serious problems communicating the vision to left-brained people who typically control the money. The ingenious way each of us is wired brings certain strengths to the table and we would be wise to acknowledge our differences and learn from each other. To deny the input of another side of the brain would be to deny a perspective that has the potential for turning a situation around.

Let me illustrate.

Two left-brained men sat in front of me in the EMBA program. They did not "get" me and I did not "get" them. In fact, there arose an "adversarial" sort of relationship between us...especially with Jack (not his real name). One day, our class had a breakout team assignment to analyze a *Harvard Business Review* case involving a company that designed and manufactured microwaves, and yet was losing money. Unfortunately, Jack and I were on the same "team." He took the lead in our analysis and proposed ways the company could lower the cost of manufacturing these microwaves. His total focus was how to cut expenses and improve the bottom line. I took my typical "observer" posture and waited for ideas to kick in.

Suddenly, I raised my hand to speak. Jack responded with a look that said, "Now what could YOU possibly have to add to this discussion?" I said, "I believe one key problem this company has is that the engineers have not had the benefit of findings from women's focus groups." He shot back, "What do women have to do with this?!" With everything in me, I remained calm and answered, "Women are the ones who buy microwaves. Engineers need to know what they're looking for. For example, one thing that would really appeal to women today is a microwave that will cook meals in a hurry, yet maintain the nutritional value of the food."

Jack was quiet the rest of the meeting. He came up to me later and pensively remarked, "You know, you really brought something to the discussion I would never have thought of. The more I thought about it...my wife would buy that kind of microwave!'" By graduation, he and I had developed a mutual respect for each other's differences.

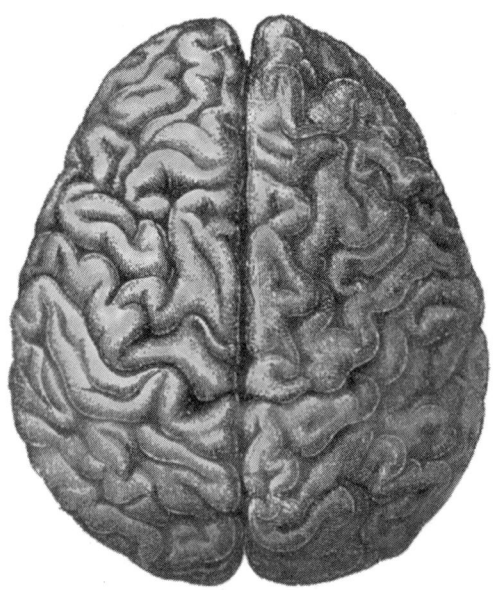

Looking at Figure 3 again, each person is distinct ... all are uniquely created. Jack falsely concluded that as a "creative," I had nothing to offer. My strengths lie primarily in the right-brain areas, whereas the majority in Corporate America operate in the left-brain areas.

The sad realities inherent within the corporate sector are:

- Right-brained people typically do not fit in a structured, left-brained world.

- Left-brained people are leading businesses without the benefit of the other half of the brain.

One of the mandates of Creativity Training Institute is to try to bridge this "cranial divide." I believe that women can be uniquely used in Corporate America to bring a much-needed sense of perspective and moral responsibility. My desire is to empower them to come to the table with their unique giftedness...and help them see that they have strengths that are desperately needed in this time in history. With the many challenges facing our world, we have to work together using ALL cylinders. The way women see things could make all the difference.

In case you are wondering...I am not a feminist. Far from it. Rather, I have simply struggled to make my way in this life as a right-brain thinker. You see, I am a "creative."

WHAT IS A CREATIVE?

Creatives are wired differently from others. We do not seem to fit in anywhere, certainly not in mainstream Corporate America. We go through life largely misunderstood and criticized... often referred to by family and friends as weirdos, dreamers, flakes, rebels, "out-there," non-conformists, and loners. A creative's journey is excruciatingly hard. My own has included heartache, divorce, widowhood, family rejection, confusion, brokenness, racial discrimination, and financial devastation. There is a price to pay in order to walk in the true creative gifting.

I remember the first workshop I held in 2004, on "Understanding The Creative Gifting." One attendee signed up after hearing a radio interview where I was discussing my book, *Wired For Creativity*. He said, "When I heard you talking about being a creative, I sat down on the floor and cried for an hour." Though I was floored by his vulnerability, his reaction has not proved uncommon. He added, "I had never heard anyone describe ME...all of a sudden I didn't feel like a freak anymore. I realized that I was made this way and there is a unique purpose for my life."

I define the word "creative" as someone who is "wired to hear" inspired ideas. Scientists describe this phenomenon as "bursts of neural activity." They can actually map these bursts of creativity taking place inside the brain...amazing! Creatives experience such "downloads" all the time. I have had them all my life, and assumed everybody else had them, too.

MY FIRST COMPANY WAS BIRTHED BY INSPIRED DOWNLOAD

In retrospect, I must say that the birth of an inspired idea is one of the greatest adrenaline rushes in life. After a five-year stint performing and speaking on the college circuit, and another five years in and out of Nashville working on my songwriting career, my husband and I moved to Georgia in 1980, and I began an advertising agency in order to support my songwriting pursuits. Creative Concepts Advertising began as a jingle writing/production company, but mushroomed after I implemented a creative strategy download I received to help local businesses in Northeast Georgia.

This idea, which challenged existing FCC broadcast regulations at the time, took months to develop. I created an entirely new paradigm of broadcast production that I termed M.A.G.I.C. Spots (Multi-Advertiser Group Image Campaigns). Through them, small-town businesses could be grouped together in a single, uniquely-produced commercial and share the cost of a major-market advertising campaign. Getting the okay from FM Program Directors and General Managers was no piece of cake. I produced demos of the new advertising format and made endless presentations to Atlanta radio execs. The entire process from conception to implementation took nine months. But once the spots aired, the success of these M.A.G.I.C. campaigns not only enabled these businesses to reach their target market and grow, but it grew my advertising agency into one of the most respected agencies in Northeast Georgia.

DOWNLOADS AS A WAY OF LIFE

Every time I would meet with a prospective client, I listened to their story and inevitably, would receive a download, either an idea for them or an entire business strategy. At first it startled me. In the early days, I used to share the ideas right away, without any monetary retainer or contractual relationship! This was not a great business move on my part...but I was so excited to receive a download for them, I couldn't wait to blurt it out. I think because my heart was in the right place, and they could sense my sincerity to help them, doing so always got me the job. Over the years I grew to trust that I would have a "download," because I knew they were given to help my clients accomplish what they were purposed to do.

Over the years the assignments became more challenging. One international conglomerate contracted me to develop new revenue streams for one of their companies. By then, I had earned an Executive MBA degree and knew better how to work with left-brain thinkers. The project took three months. I performed extensive research on their company as well as their competition, during which time I had my "ears" open for the inspired downloads as they came. They did. The thrill of helping companies in this way is tremendous. I ultimately presented them with a business proposal outlining three new revenue streams, maximizing their strengths and utilizing already existing assets. These new initiatives required very little upfront costs, and were projected to net over $300,000 a year.

Creativity = Creating something now where nothing existed before

Are you wired differently?

Y N	Do you have emotional highs and lows?
Y N	Have you felt you were created for a purpose, but you don't know what it is?
Y N	Have you experienced unusual or "supernatural" revelation of ideas?
Y N	Do you often feel different from others, like you don't fit in?
Y N	Can you easily "sense" things about other people or situations?
Y N	Have you had vivid dreams or visions?
Y N	Have you had ideas in the past that have now become the latest craze?
Y N	Is your mind often churning with so many ideas you don't know what to do first?
Y N	Have you experienced blocks, setbacks, and disappointments when trying to pursue your passion?
Y N	Are you drawn to spiritual things?

This non-scientific test is designed to see how genetically wired for creativity you are. There are no right or wrong answers ... just circle Yes or No.

If you answered NO to all 10 questions, would you please come to my program?

If you answered YES to all 10, you are genetically wired to receive inspired creativity, and are likely in the 1 to 5% of people with this gifting who have no clue what you were created to do. Plus, you have had a difficult time thus far in your career path.

If you answered YES to 5 or less, your creativity can be expanded.

If you answered YES to 6 or more, you are highly wired and probably struggling to understand the journey.

Figure 4. Non-scientific Creativity Aptitude Test

Imagine hearing a "voice from the heavens" that says, "Here is the answer to the problem you are struggling with!" That's how huge this revelation is! Such is the way of life for one who learns to unlock this gifting. As you can imagine, creatives therefore possess an internal wiring that can be of tremendous help to businesses and organizations that are flailing over the "no way out scenario" we find ourselves in. My heart's desire is to see left-brain and right-brain thinkers work together, to bring us through these turbulent waters.

Years ago, amidst the struggle to understand this gifting, I prayed for wisdom to help me "walk in the calling," for this is how I view it: a calling. By that I mean: how to remain faithful to the "downloads" without getting wiped out by others who try to steal or sabotage the whole thing. What I learned changed my life, but the price tag to learn it was great.

WISDOM IS OFTEN LEARNED IN CRISIS

Ten years ago, I headed into the biggest business venture of my life: re-staging the world premiere of my award-winning musical, *A Time To Dance*, and taking it on the road. It had been a 15-year journey thus far, and when the opportunity presented itself, it demanded 15 months of dedicated pre-production and raising capital from investors looking for diversification in the entertainment sector. With a gifted cast and crew, all systems were "go" until the morning dawned on our Atlanta premiere date: September 11, 2001 – the day when all hell flew into our country.

We postponed our premiere, naturally, but when we opened five days later, people were still afraid to get out of their homes, fearing Atlanta was next. Make no mistake:

our loss paled in comparison to the thousands who were killed that day...but the events surrounding 9-11 changed the trajectory of my life in a major way.

The bottom line: the production company was forced to close after only eight performances...and I ended up limping away from the experience financially, emotionally and spiritually devastated.

You ask, "What does your personal story have to do with the topic?" Everything. Remember, a "creative" is someone who is genetically "wired to hear" divine inspiration. The initial calling to write this musical took place in 1986, and was the strongest download I had experienced until that time. As music director of a theatrical production, I was conducting auditions. A young black woman came in. I looked down at the script...there were no parts for black actors. Nevertheless, she came anyway, sang a song *a cappella*...and blew me away. The "download" was so real it was palpable. I knew with everything in me that I was to write a vehicle to showcase undiscovered black talent. Mind you, this was in the deep south where we stayed out of each other's neighborhoods...black musicals were not big business as they are now...and Tyler Perry probably wasn't even born yet!

And here I was, this white woman who "heard" in 1986 that the entertainment industry needed inspirational, family-friendly musicals...and that African Americans needed to be brought to center stage. Within a couple of months, I received a grant from the Georgia Council for the Arts to write the musical, and a year later had completed it. Within a month or so, I was approached by a well-respected Atlanta producer who wanted to stage it.

A creative hears the inner "beacon" so loudly sometimes that nothing can stand in the way of completing such an assignment. In 1989, *A Time To Dance* first premiered in Atlanta to packed houses, half-black, half-white. I "saw" the vision of bringing the races together and telling the stories of life in the '80s for my brothers and sisters of color. After our run, I pulled out all the stops to market the musical further. That's when the doors of reverse racial discrimination slammed in my face. Although the music garnered 11 various songwriting awards, I could take it no further. The musical went on the shelf for 11 years...only to come back front and center in 2000 when Atlanta-based songstress Francine Reed asked to read it and said, "I want to star in your musical."

I had no clue how to be a theatrical producer, but I knew that producing it was part of my destiny. Thus, when the events of 9-11 and its aftermath caused the musical debut to be postponed, and then shortlived, it wasn't just a 15-month venture that died ... it was the better part of a 15-year calling.

There was no mistaking my premiere date either. You see, it had originally been planned for September 25th. However, Maya Angelou was scheduled to speak in Atlanta, and her PR people wanted my date. Being the nice, accommodating person that I am, I said, "Sure, you can have my date...and I will take yours: September 11th!" That day was my date with destiny.

Looking back on the experience, I know with certainty that 9-11 eventually brought me face to face with wisdom and insight I had been seeking for years...wisdom that I believe is critically needed today. What I learned in my three-year wilderness of seeking the Lord was over 60 biblical principles on how to unlock the creative DNA deposited into each of us, and walk out our personal, corporate and national destinies.

WHAT IS CREATIVITY?

Everyone is looking for the next "hot" idea. That is today's corporate mantra, yet research shows that it is not enough to just come up with an idea, because the failure rate for new "innovative" products companies come up with is 70%! That's because there is a world of difference between a good idea and an inspired one...and those who are wired to hear these inspired ideas are the ones with the creative edge.

The meaning of the word "creativity" is grossly misunderstood. It is not setting up an easel and painting a landscape or learning how to play the guitar. Rather, the word comes from the Hebrew word *bara'* [pronounced bawrah'] and is used always with the Creator as the subject. It is the divine act of bringing forth something that did not exist before.

True creativity can be found in every sector, not just in the Arts. As we become more and more free to operate in our creative heritage, we will become creativity-in-motion: coming up with strategies, formulas, income streams, business systems, innovations and product lines never before imagined.

HOW TO TELL A GOOD IDEA FROM AN INSPIRED IDEA

In the beginning, all ideas basically look alike. They mentally or emotionally intrigue you; they tantalize you for a brief moment, much like a horse that takes a look at a carrot dangling in front of his eyes. Throughout years of studying this subject, I have noted several key principles that help water the ground, so to speak, for the truly inspired ideas to more easily take root. They are:

PRINCIPLE #1:
REVERE THE GIVER OF IDEAS

Napoleon Hill authored the bestselling book *Think & Grow Rich*. Commissioned by the late Andrew Carnegie, Hill interviewed the most successful people in the country in the early 1900's in order to develop the science of success: people like John D. Rockefeller, Henry Ford, Thomas Edison, Franklin D. Roosevelt, Albert Einstein, and countless others over a 20-year span. He discovered that these successful idea people viewed the ideas they were given with awe and reverence, knowing they came from a divine source. He tells of the time he interviewed R. G. LeTourneau, builder of heavy earth-moving equipment.

LeTourneau had little formal education, but his engineering feats were legendary. Earlier in his career, he lost a fortune sub-contracting the Hoover Dam because he came across an unexpected strata of rock. The cost of drilling through the rock was more than he had budgeted for, and he went broke fulfilling his end of the contract. Hill writes, "Instead of brooding over his loss, LeTourneau turned to prayer, and thanked God for what he had left: a sound body, a strong pair of hands, and a brain that could think."

Over an 18-month period, Napoleon Hill spent time with LeTourneau, who had developed by then into a gifted, inspirational speaker traveling the country in his private plane. Hill writes that on one trip, LeTourneau went to sleep soon after his pilot took off. After about 30 minutes,

Hill saw him take a little notebook from his pocket and write several lines in it. When the plane landed, Hill asked him if he remembered writing something down. He did not. Immediately LeTourneau pulled the notebook from his pocket and looked at it. He said, "Here it is! I've been looking for this for several months! Here's the answer to a problem that has kept me from completing a machine we are working on!"[1]

PRINCIPLE #2: INSPIRED IDEAS OFTEN COME IN DREAMS OR VISIONS

This principle may shock Western pragmatists...but consider again the exhortation of German Chancellor Angela Merkel, "To get out of this crisis, we need a fundamental rethink!" Dreams and their interpretation belong to the right-brain hemisphere, and they are an Eastern style of communication. They are metaphorical in nature, to be more precise. Whereas in the West we prefer bottom-line, in-your-face bullet points, dreams are an indirect method of communication, leaving the responsibility of "getting it" to the listener rather than the speaker.

Consider these creatives who were "wired to hear" inspired ideas:

Albert Einstein developed the theory of relativity using only a pencil and a piece of paper, because he was inspired by a dream.

Elias Howe invented the sewing machine which he saw in a dream.

Niels Bohr was a physicist who conceived the atomic structure based on what he was shown in a dream.

Handel wrote the "Messiah" from music he heard in a dream.

Sarah Breedlove was given an entire business strategy. She had a dream that changed her life, and the lives of millions of African American women. This woman was born in 1867, and forged her way from slavery to become independent and industrious. She worked hard as a washerwoman, earning about $1.50 a day, but longed for a better life for herself and her daughter. She struggled with her self-image, and agonized over the fact that her hair had begun breaking off and falling out. Everything she tried failed. In her own words, Sarah wrote in her journal, "I was on the verge of becoming entirely bald, and prayed to the Lord for guidance. One night I had a dream, and in that dream a big black man appeared to me and told me what to mix for my hair. Some of the remedy was from Africa, but I sent for it, mixed it, put it on my scalp and in a few weeks my hair was coming in faster than it had ever fallen out. After seeing the same results on my daughter and neighbors, I made up my mind to begin selling it." She became known as Madam C.J. Walker, and her discovery – her inspired idea – resulted in a hairdressing formula that revolutionized the hair care industry for women of color. By 1919, the Madam C.J. Walker Manufacturing Company stretched an entire city block and provided employment for over 3,000 people.[2]

There is a Creator, and He has an unlimited supply of ideas. And yes, you may be shown one in a dream. Would you be able to hear it? Sadly, most Westerners dismiss this concept as nonsense. That's where the creative has his or her place in the global cry for innovation. You see, thinking as God intended is both left-brained (bottom-line, detail-oriented and purpose-driven) and right-brained (revelatory, visionary and metaphoric). Both hemispheres were made to work together to meet the challenges we are facing in our world.

PRINCIPLE #3: CREATIVITY GROWS WHEN YOU USE WHAT YOU HAVE

In a well-known parable, Jesus said: *"Take heed to what you hear."* In other words, pay attention to the ideas you receive. He continues, *"For the measure you give will be the measure you get and still more will be given you. For to him who has will more be given; and from him who has not, even what he has will be taken away."* This passage is saying: Whatever amount you have, use it...and more will be given. If you don't use it, whatever you have will be taken away and given to someone else.

PRINCIPLE #4: EVERY INSPIRED IDEA IS TESTED

I heard of an oncologist in England who has been working on a cure for cancer for several years...shown to him in stages over many months through dreams. He is now waiting to receive the final stage. You see, God will not drop a goldmine idea into someone's mind without testing him to see if he has been diligent to carry through with what little he initially was given.

When I "hear" what I believe is an inspired idea, I wait for additional confirmation and enlightenment, for I have learned that the life-changing ideas are ones that have had time to emotionally germinate inside of me, and morph from "just an idea" to an "internal vision." Only then does it have the power to impact other people. My rule of thumb is: the hot idea...the inspired idea...will NOT leave you alone. You find your mind going to it time and again, seeing more possibilities with it. When you do, write them down. When the idea gets too large for one sheet of paper in an ideas file, then create its own folder. Every time you have further insight about it, put those thoughts in there.

PRINCIPLE #5: SIT IN SILENCE FOR YOUR INSPIRED SOLUTION

Napoleon Hill tells the story of Dr. Elmer Gates, a great American teacher and scientist who developed hundreds of inventions in the various arts and sciences. When Hill first visited Dr. Gates at his Chevy Chase laboratory in the early 1900's, he only had a letter of introduction from Andrew Carnegie. When he arrived, Dr. Gates' secretary told him, "I'm sorry, but...I'm not permitted to disturb Dr. Gates at this time."

"How long do you think it will be before I can see him," Hill asked.

"I don't know, but it might take as long as three hours," she responded.

Puzzled, he asked, "Do you mind telling me why you are unable to disturb him?"

She hesitated and then said, "He is sitting for ideas."

When Dr. Gates finally came into the room, he read the letter of introduction and asked Hill, 'Would you be interested in seeing where I sit for ideas and how I go about it?' He led him to a small, soundproof room. The only furniture in the room consisted of a plain table and a chair. On the table were pads of paper, several pencils, and a push-button to turn the lights off and on. Dr. Gates explained that when he was unable to get an answer to a problem, he went into the room, closed the door, sat down, turned off the lights, and engaged in deep concentration. He asked for an answer to his specific problem, and took however long it would take to receive inspiration and write it down.[3]

Now really, how many of us would take time to do that? Dr. Gates revered the Giver of ideas, and paid keen attention to them. In fact, he went on to refine and develop over 200 patents that other inventors had started, but failed to complete. The truth is that the "measure" or amount of attention you give to your ideas will be equal to the number of ideas you'll be given in the future.

PRINCIPLE #6: PRACTICE MEDIA FASTS

This is a discipline I stumbled into quite by chance. Being an idea person ... a conceptual ... and a composer, my ears are always tuned to hear a download. It is my way of life, and probably would drive most people crazy. Many years ago I signed up for a study group that met once a week for eight weeks. We were studying Julia Cameron's excellent book, *The Artist's Way*. In our eight-member group were artists, writers, producers, directors, and a cartoonist. I found it a great support group to encourage each other on our creative journeys.

One week's assignment made me smile. The facilitator said, "This week is media deprivation week. For the next seven days, you can't read magazines or newspapers, turn on the TV or listen to radio." Internet wasn't really big then, but if it had been, we wouldn't have been able to go online, check our Facebook page, or Tweet. Nada...for one whole week. Everyone else in the group let out a collective groan. I smiled. I drove home that night thinking, "This is a cinch... this is the way I live!" Sure enough, that assignment was gravy for me...but what I wasn't expecting was the reaction I got when we got together the following week.

My teammates were incredulous when talking about the assignment: "I can't believe all the ideas that were coming to me!" Over and over, each one told the same story. The stopper was pulled out of their creative well. The same thing can happen for you.

FINAL THOUGHTS

If you are a creative, you are desperately needed, for you are genetically "wired to hear" the ideas the corporate sector needs.

If you are a business owner, I encourage you to share this chapter with your people and foster an environment in which creatives can be nurtured.

And finally, if you've never considered yourself particularly creative, you can grow in your potential as you become more attuned to the ideas you are given. We are wired...all of us... to hear and receive inspiration and ideas. It is part of the divine DNA given us by the Father.

There are answers to every challenge we are facing ... will you listen, or hire someone who will?

ENDNOTES

1. Napoleon Hill and W. Clement Stone, *Success Through A Positive Mental Attitude*, pp. 68-69. New York, NY: Pocket Books, a division of Simon & Schuster, Inc., 1960, 1977.

2. Dr. Elizabeth Hairston, *Apostolic Intervention*, pp. 88-89. Miami, FL: Xulon Press, 2004.

3. Napoleon Hill and W. Clement Stone, *Success Through A Positive Mental Attitude,* pp. 70-72.

ABOUT THE AUTHOR

Candace Long has been in the Arts & Entertainment sector since 1970 as a performer, writer, composer, theatrical producer, entertainment project developer, branding and marketing consultant, arts leader and marketplace minister. She understands the calling and the struggles of the creative journey...and is known as a biblical commentator on "inspired creativity." She is the Founder and CEO of Creativity Training Institute (Atlanta, Ga.), has an MBA degree, and is ordained and commissioned as a Marketplace Apostle. For more information or to contact her, visit her web sites at www.creativitytraininginstitute.com and www.candacelong.com.

CHAPTER SIXTY-ONE

MOSES: THE OTHER WORSHIP LEADER

DR. RAY HUGHES

When I was invited to be a contributor to this book, I experienced somewhat of a flurry of thoughts and emotions. I vacillated between honored, inadequate, and excited.

Yet once the flurry settled, I could not deny that inner knowing that I'd love to speak to the subject of Apostolic Worship. I was not quite sure what I was going to say. However, after 40 years of ministry and decades of study and research on the subject of biblical worship and musicology, I did what any respectable student of the Word would do: I Googled it.

I found everything from emotionally-charged Pentecostal YouTube videos to blogs written by whining musicians who have become musical hostages to church systems. Apparently, there are pastors and leaders out there who do not understand the true greatness that lies hidden in the hands of their drummers. Yes, drummers, they're the loud ones, the ones they usually keep in the glass cages on the stage. I also discovered wonderful and sincere people exploring worship music as a means of making their churches more relevant and effective against all of the negativity in their culture.

In contrast, one church leader stated that "music has two overriding purposes: to make the liturgy more beautiful and to emphasize its sacred character." He goes on to say, "Only music that is truly beautiful should have a place in the liturgy." He continues with many valid and wonderful points, many of which that I feel would not be fully embraced by most charismatic tambourine players that are more given to spontaneous expressions of joyful clatter. I'm also quite confident that he would not find an agreeable audience amongst the head-banging scream ("scream" is an actual music genre now, so "Screamo" worship is a music style) of worship bands that have decided to harness the sounds of brutality and unrefined rage as their unique contribution to the Kingdom.

Whether you are exploring the Chronicles and Psalms and discovering all the many facets of biblical praise and worship exemplified in the life of King David, or you are simply trying to understand why some modern worship music sounds like airplanes crashing on an earthquake, either way, there is no shortage of intriguing options when it comes to worship music these days. There are many voices, sounds, and musical styles being heard. As confusing as it can appear to a church culture that typically strives to create unity, oneness, and a sense of same-ness, I believe that creativity and diversity are major factors and part of the beauty of this new and wondrous age that we are in.

The Church seems to consistently function about 20 years behind the cutting edge of creativity. When something comes along that exemplifies cutting-edge creativity, the Church tends to criticize it for the first 10 years and then emulate it for the next 10 years, all the while confused as to why they are 20 years behind. But why should we act surprised at this? Musicians and "creative" have tendencies to live so much in the now moment of their creative flow that they are oblivious as to the full impact they are having on their culture or where it fits in the larger picture.

Pastors and church leaders, on the other hand, typically come from more of an administrative mindset. Their concerns are usually more theological and management-based and are more about function and efficiency. Now, I am not implying that there are no creative church leaders today; nothing could be further from the truth. To say that they are not creative simply because they may not be artistic is a misnomer. I am pointing out the distinctive difference between creative church leadership and the creatively artistic community of rising leaders that have become a powerful presence in modern Christianity.

I have a great appreciation for their individuality and unique giftings, but I will speak of them as a collective "they." They are quickly becoming a collective voice of a fresh movement and their impact is global. One of the reasons they are having such global impact is that they think globally without losing their intimate connection to local church and community. This is due in part to the age we live in.

THE INFORMATION AGE

It is no secret that we are living in a time of incredible technological advances. Information can be dispensed at alarming speeds to astounding numbers of people. Impossibilities are no longer impossible and the unreachable has become reachable. The unachievable is, well, you get the idea. What an amazing and wonderful time to be alive. To potentially speak to or sing to a whole generation of humanity from a handheld device is nothing short of phenomenal. And yes, there can be downsides and dangers o'plenty, for with all the wonderful potential comes the weight of responsibility. Man's belief systems and matters of life are so connected to language that they have proven over time to be inseparable. Never has there been a time in history that man has had this level of connectedness. People who live very small lives in silence and obscurity now have the ability to bring their ideas, their sound, their language, and their beliefs to the many cultures and subcultures around the globe.

We live in a world of forward-thinking genius that has created devices that have quickly created a new us, and continue to do so at an alarming rate. The technologies have certainly punctured our privacy and robbed us of our much-needed solitude, but they have also introduced us to unimaginable possibilities. It's the modern-day marketers' job to change non-customers into customers, right? They don't just market to a culture according to the needs of the culture. They first change the perception of the culture as to what they perceive to be their needs. If you change the people, you expand your market.

And for the last 30 years or more, marketers have successfully turned us into a people who are addicted to the new, so addicted that the huddled masses will line up on a sidewalk and sleep on frozen concrete and shiver to the glowing presence of the latest electronic gadget peering out through a veil of glass at the gadget store. It's becoming more and more important to learn how to turn off the technology and warm at the hearths of truth again. But, in the meantime, we live our lives from upgrade to upgrade. (Feel free to tweet the last two sentences to your friends and followers.)

The cultural implications here are enormously significant. We now live in a world with more people more willing to change more often than at any time in history. And that means that we are a restless, willing-to-change generation that rejects same-ness more and more. What a wonderful and extremely volatile time to be alive. We want the new and we want it now, for new and now is how we define our social and global significance as a culture. The new and the now has become an obsession that insatiably cries out for the next new and now. It is an ever-present and perfect climactic condition for numerous perfect storms. These have-to-have, can't-live-without technological gadgets are one thing, but how they have impacted our daily lives are another.

There is a "now language," a "new sound" arising, and never have so many voices had so much access to so many hearers. The YouTube phenomena is only one example of what I'm talking about and the numbers there are astounding and revealing. Here are some of them:

- Over 800 million unique users visit YouTube each month
- Over 4 billion hours of video are watched each month on YouTube
- 72 hours of video are uploaded to YouTube every minute
- 70% of YouTube traffic comes from outside the U.S.
- YouTube is localized in 43 countries and across 60 languages

- In 2011, YouTube had more than 1 trillion views or around 140 views for every person on Earth

- Millions of subscriptions happen each day. Subscriptions allow you to connect with someone you're interested in or desire to "follow"

- 500 years of YouTube video are watched every day on Facebook, and over 700 YouTube videos are shared on Twitter each minute

Throughout history, many significant contributors to society arose from obscurity to become voices to their generation. Notoriety and awareness, good or bad, that used to take decades can happen now at any and in every minute. Now, granted, we don't have to look far into the "worship industry" to find some who are building their platforms of fan-based Christianity, and the potential downsides to that are obvious. But, we also don't have to look far to find some wondrously creative, globally-minded, pure–hearted, worshipping creatives who just live to worship. They are wonderful examples of a complex innocence that God will use mightily in days to come.

There is no shortage of examples in history of creative, cutting-edge thinkers who simply did what they did artistically and had no idea that their creative expression would change cultures and impact nations. From Beethoven to the Beatles and from King David to King Elvis and all across the cultures and genres and generations, there were those who did not and could not have fully known what they were doing to their world and/or for their world, for the greater purposes of what they were doing carried a timeless awe that was silently hidden in tones and rhymes that not even they could have understood. Their long-term impact proved that what they did was beyond just a "hit." Many of them died in poverty and went cluelessly to their early graves. Sadly, some of them were the misunderstood sent-ones ever longing for the new and unfound frontiers.

The lives of Luther and Wesley and Knox and Williams and Watts and Carey and Moody and Sankey—the list goes on and on—carried a global and multi-generational impact. These were the songwriters of centuries ago who taught us who God is through their tones and rhymes. They also changed nations, changed man's theology, rocked religious systems, impacted economic structures, and introduced new technologies. I know, it's hard to think of them in this way when you look at the picture of them in their black robes, their stoic expressions somberly glaring at you. But, those pictures were painted in their later years after they had become institutions. Most of them started with incredible encounters and demonstrations of God's power and creativity in their twenties. I believe that there are young, cutting-edge, creative-seer geniuses with prophetic sensibilities today that are sent to point us toward new horizons.

A NEW BREED

There is a breed of hidden-ones today with such profound creativity coursing through their veins that they will cause the Church to see and know God in new and glorious ways. There is a grace on them to see God and know Him in ways that man's dreary liturgies and creeds could never explain. In days past when God was singing through frail instruments of flesh, many times the Church was too religious to listen. Many of the sent-ones were sent away into the hills of obscurity because they were dressed in

Egyptian clothes with Hebrew hearts. Well, thankfully, that unfortunate reality is being broken in dramatic fashion today. This is not a time to shrink back into complacent and predictable same-ness.

Now, I know that the number one rule among writers is to never assume that your reader knows anything about your subject. Please allow me the liberty to break that number one rule and assume that you have heard the story of Moses and the children of Israel marching out of Egypt and crossing the Red Sea. If you have not, I encourage you to read this fascinating story in the book of Exodus. Also, allow me to present numerous ideas and concepts around that amazing event without presenting pages and pages of details and elaboration. In other words, I want to give you the short and sweet version.

Moses, to me, epitomizes many of the qualities that are found among the apostles of the New Testament. His story also speaks to the present phenomenon that is happening in the body of Christ that is being called a new apostolic movement or apostolic age. Like all new or unusual movements, it has its extremes and abuses, I'm sure. I'll be careful not to further complicate those issues with my opinion. Fixing things is above my pay grade.

Now back to the short and sweet: The Greek word for apostle in the New Testament is the word *apóstolos*. It means, "A delegate; an ambassador of the Gospel (good news); officially a commissioner of Christ ("apostle") (with miraculous powers):-- apostle, messenger, he that is sent, a delegate, messenger, one sent forth with orders."

Moses was sent—sent into the world, sent down the river, sent to the wilderness, sent by God to Pharaoh, sent to the mountain of his encounter with God. From the first mention of Moses until his last, he was in a state of movement, journeying, or being sent. Even during times of anchorage in Egypt or the 40 years in the desert wilderness, there was always a sense of forward motion and a journeying implied. The nature of the apostle is always one of being sent or sending, even when they are stationary. They are typically natural born—mobilizers. They have an innate desire for movement; same-ness is a problem for them. They sometimes find it difficult to move the masses and determine that it's easier and more beneficial to move God. And, they do move God as pure compassionate intercessors of the highest order.

Moses was also divinely protected at birth to carry seeds of destiny for others in his generation. He was exposed to and sensitive to the conditions of humanity and was passionately moved by the injustices in his day. He did not spend his life cocooned away in a sterilized Egyptian aristocratic environment. True liberators with apostolic mandates find it difficult to sequester themselves away in religious, inauthentic, and irrelevant Church atmospheres. Deep in their being is a heart that is moved by a profound love for others and a compassion for humanity and the human condition.

Many times, they carry a connectedness to creation and a sense of awareness of the big picture that many don't see. Sometimes their passion and compassion can cause them to have wrong timing issues accompanied by massive blunders. These blunders can send them into seasons of unhealthy isolation or healthy seasons of renewing and refocusing. They are many times clumsy with one-on-one relationships, as they carry a weightiness in knowing that they are called to impact the masses. At times, they are the ones whom God uses to change economic systems and to shift and alter political and governmental systems in societies that are running amuck by opposing basic biblical principles.

Their experiences give them a broad view of life, for many times their journey is one of extremes. Moses experienced the best that man could provide in Pharaoh's palace. He was educated by the world's highest standards of academia. He knew firsthand the loneliness of the desert, for he spent many years in obscurity and isolation.

GOD USES THE UNLIKELY LEADER

Sometimes God delights to demonstrate His great abilities through the unlikeliest of characters. I know that there are inconsistencies in the way that many apostolic leaders present themselves today. Sometimes ambition and arrogance can expose unhealthy aspects of their personalities. Some are repulsed by idolatry while others try to become idols. It is what it is. Regardless of our preferences, opinions, and questions about the whole thing, these people don't just show up; they are sent. They are sent with purpose, commission, and authority, and stabilizing the status quo and maintaining same-ness is not on their agenda. Some have been sent and re-sent and sent again. They are mobilizers hell-bent on getting themselves and the people of God into their new day. And, like Moses, their feats will be remembered in such a way as to create an understanding of the nature of God for future generations—because that's what sent ones do.

Moses had many amazing incidents throughout his life that were obviously God-ordained hints of his destiny. They involved everything from a divinely-protected birth to a basket in the bulrushes to becoming a murderer and a fugitive. He spent 40 years on the backside of the desert in the valley of same-ness. Then a profound encounter with God changed everything for him. And, like most people who have encounters with God, it's never just about them. God told Moses to go and tell Pharaoh to let His people go.

He did not say to Moses to go and "ask;" He said go and "tell Pharaoh" to let His people go that they may come away and worship, which is what they were created for. So, we see that Moses was called and sent to be a part of a God-ordained process that was to ultimately take God's people into their destiny as a worshipping people.

Mark Twain once said, "The two most important days in your life are the day you were born, and the day that you found out why." Well, Moses was born or sent to carry a word. And not just any word, but a powerful and strategic word of liberation from the bondage and same-ness that had been the morbid and mundane existence for God's people for some 400 years. Water-dirt-straw-mud-bricks; water-dirt-straw-mud-bricks—day after day, year after year, century after century. Same-ness. Mashing out mud between their toes to make bricks and bricks and more bricks. Same-ness. The moans and groans of same-ness had become the sound that God's people were born to and died to. Same-ness. I wonder how many years had passed since they had lost even the thought in their collective understanding that they were God's chosen people.

But wait, Moses was carrying a word, for he had had an encounter with God. God's people were about to walk in places they had never walked and see things that they had never seen. They were about to look back over their shoulders at same-ness for one last time. But, the process of change always has its challenges, for soon you find the children of Israel standing at the Red Sea looking back at the pursuing Egyptian army and believing that death was inevitable.

Now, that Moses who was standing at the Red Sea, was not yet the great leader that everyone would later name their kids after. At that point, he was the one being complained to and griped at. His motives were being questioned, his position was being questioned, and his calling was being questioned. He had not yet become Moses Heston, the great movie star; he was still just Moses, and he was still suspect.

While everyone else was acting out of fear and suspicion, Moses responded out of that nature that God had developed in him. He was once again hearing God's new and present word of instruction for the next step. Apostles seem to always have a next step, focus, and anointing. And a glorious and fearful next step it was. Moses obediently raised his staff and a mighty wind blew in and parted the waters and held them in suspension for hours while some two million people began to walk in miracles. They no longer walked in water-dirt-straw-and mud of Egypt, for now they – every one of them – walked in the supernatural. God not only divided the sea, He also divided or dried the mud, for they walked across on dry land. It astounds me to think of the impact that must have had on their hearts and minds. To begin to experience and walk in the impossible causes an explosion of possibilities to come into your view.

God freed Israel from Egypt as they walked through the process of Moses' obedient responses to God's actions and words. Moses' obedience and responses are clear in the fact that he was not asked to part the sea. It was not necessary for him to have sea-parting faith. But, it was necessary that he have stick-raising obedience when God told him to do so.

I'm not implying that the Church has been in such a season of darkness or bondage that a modern exodus is needed. I am proposing that this new era that we are all attempting to step into is a significant crossing, and at times a clumsy one with very real changes and challenges. It will require both supernatural faith and supernatural obedience in leaders as they raise up their staffs for the purpose of ushering in an era of miracles, signs, and wonders that alerts the whole world to the fact that God is in the midst of His people, and they in fact are walking into a new day.

SPONTANEOUS CREATIVITY HAS A BIBLICAL PRECEDENT

I'm sure it must have been confusing for God's people, Israel, at the Red Sea crossing when Miriam grabbed an Egyptian instrument (a spoil of an idolatrous nation) and began singing and expressing herself in song and dance with sounds completely foreign to Israel, for they had not sung or danced or even had reason to rejoice for 400 years. You might say that God's people were about 400 years behind in the realm of cutting-edge creativity and, for them, worship did not exist. Yet, no one had to tell Miriam what to do, what to sing, or how to dance.

No one coached her on musical styles or platform etiquette or how to get your song heard by the masses, though I'm sure if she had had the opportunity to attend a songwriting clinic, she would have enjoyed it. All of those topics can be important to those who wish to lead God's people into their musical new day, but Miriam's experience was that of one who is exploding with joy and emotion through a spontaneous expression of praise to God for one of the most outrageously creative demonstrations of His power in history.

One of the most pivotal moments in the history of Israel was clearly marked as a new day by a new sound, a new song and a new language from the heart of God's people. Every person in that massive exodus out of Egypt saw what God did, but Miriam evidently considered this to be a very personal encounter with God, for when she saw what God had done, her thankfulness of heart overtook her. It was not about being the sister of Moses or leading a group of maidens in a dance. It was not about position or prestige. It was not the time for contemplative musings wrapped in lofty rhetoric. It was about the God that she had just encountered. She sang unto the Lord a melody of the purest well of her gratitude and it became a river of song that carried all of Israel into their new day. And, in that glorious moment, a group of maidens with the same heart went out after her and fully experienced a brand new thing.

From that day until this, every significant move of God in the Earth has had a new and significant sound and song connected to it. It is a stretch for some of my musical friends when they realize that Israel's first worship leader was a woman, and if that's not enough, a woman with a tambourine. It's also a stretch for some religious people when questions arise about her using an Egyptian instrument. For the first time in 400 years, God's people had encountered the goodness of God and the song and dance was an inevitable response.

I believe that the Church has now come to another of those defining moments in history and we are at a crossing even now, a crossroads, if you will. Miriam did not need to know how to lead congregational worship anymore than Moses needed to know how to muster up enough faith to part the sea. God freed Israel from Egypt as they walked through the process of obedient responses to His actions and words.

It's important to note some of the things that changed about the people after the crossing. They became worshipers, songwriters, and singers. They became a nation of people, complete with wonderful and unique characteristics in their culture. No one can realistically look at the Jewish people and deny their global impact. Their contributions in Business, Government, Media, Arts and Entertainment, Education, Family and Religion are astounding. They have been entrepreneurs, leaders in governments of many nations, as well as actors, movie directors, script writers, composers, entertainers, world-renowned medical doctors, research scientists, physicists, chemists, attorneys, inventors, professors and teachers, doing what they were sent to do. They truly are a gift that has been sent to teach all nations. It is no wonder that they are still looking back and rejoicing. They are still celebrating the time that a sent-one named Moses led them to a place of worship where same-ness was shattered by a song.

CROSSROADS

Throughout history, the Church has been defined and redefined by the choices that were made at many crossroads. Crossroads are points and seasons of decision that have shaped peoples' and nations' understandings of God. History tells us that God placed many unique individuals like Moses and Miriam, who had had fresh encounters with Him, at many crossroads. Because they had had revelatory encounters, they were willing to stand

and direct the masses when they came to those points of decision. It's easy to see in history the way that God sent some to preach His Word with supernatural results in the face of much resistance. It's as if they were created for conflict and controversy, and they boldly pointed the new way. They were and are known as reformers. Some called them revolutionists; others considered them to be radical rebels and enemies to the cause of Christ. Some were branded mystics and heretics and were written out of the history books as quickly as possible.

Then there are those who were celebrated. But, the statements that they made with their very lives then have become so familiar to us that we often consider the truths that they brought to be so fundamental that we treat them as elementary concepts. The fact is, however, that their ideas were so profoundly radical in their day that they challenged the foundational beliefs of all of Christendom. Martin Luther, John Knox, John Calvin, George Whitefield, John and Charles Wesley were some, and the list goes on; like Moses, they rose up at critical times and not only influenced their generation, but they profoundly impacted the generations that would follow. I think that we should be reminded that before they became "institutions," they were simply young men full of questions, and they asked the hard ones. Systems and institutions that are not willing to hear the questions are usually not willing to embrace the answers when they come.

Many religious institutions have missed very real and valid visitations by closing their doors to anything that challenges their former experience. We as Christians are also known to resist any experience or theology that was not initiated within the ranks of our own movement. It is also true that many of our past experiences serve to keep us from embracing what God desires to do in our future. Basically, we become so full of what God said that we can't hear what God is saying. And, we feel that we have an obligation to God to resist anything that challenges the sanctity of what we have built for Him, based upon our present theology. This is a very subtle yet debilitating form of same-ness.

What if a holy and pure-hearted generation full of passion and hunger for a fresh revelation of God surfaced today? I wonder what that would look like. I believe it would look like gatherings standing at crossroads, willing to ask questions that many do not want to face. They know in their heart of hearts that God is far more wondrous and wonderful than He is depicted in modern society and in the church. They believe that He is so awesome and infinitely multi-dimensional that many aspects of His true nature have never been realized in generations past. They believe that unimaginable facets of His nature and unknown expressions of His presence are possible when they worship Him. They are the bold ones who are willing to stand at the crossroads and contend for God.

They accept nothing less than real signs and wonders, immeasurable miracles, and un-precedented outpourings. They are looking for culture-shaping, society-shaking demonstrations of God's love. They are willing to stand as long as it takes at the point of decision and ask the questions until the answer comes. They are the ones who find honest, authentic joy even in the days of contending, for they know that contenders eventually become inheritors. They are willing to look past the present and into the throne room of eternity and embrace a fresh revelation of God. They are willing to question, for they know that their generation is not only defined by the statements that they make, but also by the questions that they ask.

Well, they have surfaced and they have been sent. They are raising up their staffs in every sphere of society as new winds are blowing and old seas are parting. They understand that they will never change culture by becoming like it. They also understand that they will never change the church by becoming like it. They have no interest in worship songs that simply create an atmosphere that constrains the imagination and protects the politeness of the church service and prevents worship. They wholeheartedly give themselves to worship songs that flow out of their worship experience and carry a liberating language of life that introduces God's people to new options and possibilities. Right now, Heaven is resonating with boundless grace and unlimited creativity. Our generation is about to be invaded with songs and sounds that not only acknowledge this, but actually demonstrate this with amazing manifestations of the creativity of Holy Spirit.

AN UNPRECEDENTED MOVEMENT

The more we understand and embrace God as the infinite Creator of music, sounds, drama, fashion, culinary arts, film innovations, inventions, scientific discovery, medical breakthroughs, and more, the more we will be able to impact and influence the world around us. I see a collective Moses, a "sent generation," stepping forward, and the nations are being prepared for an unprecedented movement.

No longer will the nations look at the people of God in scorn. The nations will begin to look to those who are truly the "sent" ones. The "sent" are those who are determined to embrace the God who sends them to their generation with a very clear message of hope. Man's governmental systems will yield and seas will part for these passionate, worshiping, obedient stick-raisers. They are sent to show those who are in bondage and enslaved to same-ness that God is a God of boundless grace and unlimited creativity. They believe that their Creator created them to be creative and worship is about creativity; it's about endless options. It's about the wonder, the beauty, the power, the mercy, the grace, the presence, the infinite, incomprehensible, glorious person of God—God who has sent them to tell the world to let His people go, that they might worship Him as they were created to do.

ABOUT THE AUTHOR

Ray Hughes, founder of Selah Ministries, has been in full-time ministry for 40 years. He received his Doctorate of Divinity in 1996. He travels in the U.S. and internationally as a speaker, author, storyteller, singer/songwriter, and musicologist. In addition to his research and teaching expertise, Ray is recognized internationally as a clear prophetic voice.

Ray is passionate about training musicians, releasing creative people into their destinies, and launching them with purpose into the world and church. He is a prophetic historian who re-digs the wells of biblical, world, and recent history for the purpose of releasing the fresh word of God for the kingdom today. To learn more or contact Ray, visit his website at www.selahministries.com.

VOLUME ONE

ALIGNING WITH THE APOSTOLIC
A FIVE VOLUME ANTHOLOGY OF
APOSTLESHIP & THE APOSTOLIC MOVEMENT
DR. BRUCE COOK, GENERAL EDITOR

Foreword by C. Peter Wagner
Foreword by Kent Humphreys

Volume One contains the Introduction and Overview to this historic work by 70 authors, written by General Editor, Dr. Bruce Cook. This volume contains an explanation of the research methodology used in compilation of the anthology and an extensive glossary of 80 apostolic terms.

VOLUME ONE

SECTION 1:
Introduction & Overview—
- Coming Into Apostolic Alignment
- What an Apostle Is, and Is Not
- Levels of Maturity and Types of Apostles
- Apostolic Authority: A Two-Edged Sword
- Origins of the Patriarchs & Judaism Are Found in the Marketplace
- Origins of the Church and Christianity Are Found in the Marketplace
- Apostolic Reformers in the Marketplace

w w w . K i n g d o m H o u s e . n e t

KINGDOM HOUSE
P U B L I S H I N G

VOLUME TWO

ALIGNING WITH THE APOSTOLIC
A FIVE VOLUME ANTHOLOGY OF
APOSTLESHIP & THE APOSTOLIC MOVEMENT
DR. BRUCE COOK, GENERAL EDITOR

Foreword by Dr. Lance Wallnau
Foreword by Dr. Paula A. Price

VOLUME TWO

SECTION 2:
Apostolic Government

SECTION 3:
Apostolic Foundations

www.KingdomHouse.net

KINGDOM HOUSE
PUBLISHING

VOLUME THREE

ALIGNING WITH THE APOSTOLIC
A FIVE VOLUME ANTHOLOGY OF
APOSTLESHIP & THE APOSTOLIC MOVEMENT
DR. BRUCE COOK, GENERAL EDITOR

Foreword by Dr. Gordon Bradshaw
Foreword by Dr. Bill Hamon

VOLUME THREE

SECTION 4:
Apostolic Intercession

SECTION 5:
Apostolic Character & Maturity

SECTION 6:
Apostolic Education

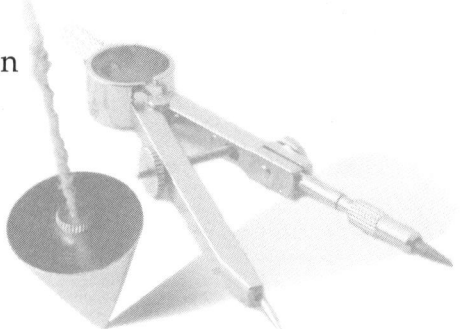

www.KingdomHouse.net

KINGDOM HOUSE
P U B L I S H I N G

VOLUME FIVE

ALIGNING WITH THE APOSTOLIC
A FIVE VOLUME ANTHOLOGY OF
APOSTLESHIP & THE APOSTOLIC MOVEMENT
DR. BRUCE COOK, GENERAL EDITOR

Foreword by Lynn Wilford Scarborough
Foreword by Dr. John Louis Muratori

VOLUME FIVE

SECTION 10:
Apostolic Multiplication & Wealth

SECTION 11:
Apostolic Culture

SECTION 12:
Summary & Conclusion

www.KingdomHouse.net

KINGDOM HOUSE
PUBLISHING

ALSO BY DR. BRUCE COOK

Finally, the one book on the prophetic that I can use both in my graduate level course on 5-Fold Ministry at Regent University, as well as in the equipping ministries in the churches that I oversee. In a time of traveling light, this is the one book on the prophetic that will give you focus and passion for its full restoration.

Dr. Joseph Umidi |
Professor, Overseer, CEO

Partnering with the Prophetic is a resource that every student or minister of the prophetic should have in their library. Bruce skillfully teaches, instructs, and imparts faith for activation in this timely book. I have witnessed the operation of Bruce Cook's prophetic gift and received prophetic blessing and encouragement from God through him. Both Bruce and his gift are authentic—true gifts to the Body of Christ.

Patricia King | Co-Founder of XPmedia

Prophets are not the only ones who need to understand the prophetic. The whole body needs to understand the prophetic and allow the Holy Spirit to move in that way. *Partnering with the Prophetic* will bring clarity and unity to the church. It will give us ... a release, a great understanding to our native people that believe in the prophetic, which they call THE DREAMER.

Dr. Negiel Bigpond | *Morning Star Church of All Nations Co-founder Two Rivers Native American Training Center*

www.KingdomHouse.net

THE TECHNOLOGY OF APOSTOLIC SUCCESSION
TRANSFERRING THE PURPOSES OF GOD TO THE
NEXT GENERATION OF KINGDOM CITIZENS
DR. GORDON BRADSHAW

"God is assembling something in our day that is so silent and massive that it can only be discerned by those who have felt the shaping of God's chisel in the quarry. Gordon Bradshaw has given us a work that reflects years of shaping and consecrated thought, measuring and carefully layering line upon line until a great architectural blueprint is drawn."

Dr. Lance Wallnau
Founder & President, The Lance Learning Group

www.KingdomHouse.net

AUTHORITY FOR ASSIGNMENT
RELEASING THE MANTLE OF GOD'S
GOVERNMENT IN THE MARKETPLACE
DR. GORDON BRADSHAW

How will "God's Government" affect the marketplace today?

It will come through the restoration of one of God's greatest supernatural technologies … "The Mantle of Misrah!" Misrah is a Hebrew word that means "government and prevailing power." Inside this powerful mantle we've been given a supernatural problem-solving dynamic that restores the marketplace to its highest level of function for the Kingdom of God!

www.KingdomHouse.net

NOT FOR PRICE OR REWARD
MOTIVES OF THE HEART REGARDING
RICHES, WEALTH, AND STEWARDSHIP
DR. BRUCE COOK

If the complexities of economics are not enough, add to the equation the attitudes, motivation, and behaviors of men. The rise and fall of currencies parallels the rise and fall of nations, since money is a creation of man and its use is controlled by men.

Our motives matter to God, and character counts. *Not for Price or Reward* targets the personal level—focusing on motives of the heart related to money, and the subtle ways that Mammon lies to and seduces us. Watch for news of this book's release!

w w w . K i n g d o m H o u s e . n e t

KINGDOM HOUSE
P U B L I S H I N G